AF669337

THE PHILOSOPHICAL CONCEPT OF SAṂSKĀRA

THE PHILOSOPHICAL CONCEPT OF SAṂSKĀRA

LAKSHMI KAPANI

MOTILAL BANARSIDASS PUBLISHERS
PRIVATE LIMITED • DELHI

First Edition : Delhi, 2013

© Lakshmi Kapani
All Rights Reserved

ISBN : 978-81-208-3612-9

MOTILAL BANARSIDASS
41 U.A. Bungalow Road, Jawahar Nagar, Delhi 110 007
8 Mahalaxmi Chamber, 22 Bhulabhai Desai Road, Mumbai 400 026
203 Royapettah High Road, Mylapore, Chennai 600 004
236, 9th Main III Block, Jayanagar, Bangalore 560 011
Sanas Plaza, 1302 Baji Rao Road, Pune 411 002
8 Camac Street, Kolkata 700 017
Ashok Rajpath, Patna 800 004
Chowk, Varanasi 221 001

Cover Illustration :
Viṣṇu reclining on the serpent Śeṣa (Ananta)
on a side panel of the Viṣṇu temple of 5th century,
Daśāvatāra Temple, Deogarh, India.

Printed in India

By RP Jain at NAB Printing Unit,
A-44, Naraina, Phase-I, New Delhi 110 028
and Published by JP Jain for
Motilal Banarsidass Publishers (P) Ltd, 40-41 U.A.
Bungalow Road, Jawahar Nagar, Delhi 110 007

To my beloved parents,
my family,
and friends

FOREWORD

Lakshmi Kapani's *The Philosophical Concept of Saṃskāra* is the finest book of its kind on this fundamental notion emphasizing the interrelatedness of its ritual, psychological and philosophical aspects.

The aim of this work has been to present the originality of the concept of *saṃskāra*. The work is, in fact, a comprehensive survey of this concept based on all textual references, starting right from the *Veda* to end up with the classical *darśanas*, especially in *Vaiśeṣika*, *Vedānta*, *Sāṃkhya-Yoga*. Passing through the *Gṛhyasūtras* and *Dharmaśāstra* was not less important because of the impact of rituals on the psychological level of the human mind. The topics taken up are indeed an indepth study of each problem she has chosen. She has been successful in highlighting the differences between the Buddhist attitude and the Brahmanical attitude towards *saṃskāra*. All the conclusions of the author are authenticated by quoting relevant texts from the respective commentaries. This has enhanced the authenticity of this work.

Moreover Lakshmi Kapani has included valuable comparisons with Western Philosophy and Psychoanalysis. No other work known to me gives so complete a critical appreciation of the similarities and dissimilarities between Psychoanalysis and *Yoga*. She has particularly shown how the yogin can overcome the propensity of the subconscious impressions by creating true yogic *saṃskāra* which lead to deconditioning of the mind till mental formations simply get burnt up in the fire of *Yoga*.

First published in French, this original and irreplaceable book has unfortunately been not widely circulated in the anglophone world including India and an English translation was therefore urgently needed.

Pr François CHENET
25th July 2012 University of Paris-Sorbonne

CONTENTS

PREFACE

The philosophical quest about the concept of *saṃskāra* arose in my mind while listening to my mother. In everyday talk, especially while looking for a future suitor for one of her daughters, the first question that she used to put to people of her circle was, "do you know something about the *saṃskāras* of this person?" This set phrase, a current cliché was easily understood by everybody and called for no further explanation.

Yet, after serious reflection, the meaning and scope of this word appeared to me to be so rich and complex, clear and obscure, that I undertook a study of this concept based on Brahmanical and Buddhist texts. The object of my enquiry is to understand as to what extent the word *saṃskāra* is univocal or equivocal, multivocal and overdetermined.

Indeed, on the one hand, the question about the young man had obviously a psychological meaning—what are his tendencies, habits, traits of character, bent of mind? What sort of behaviour can be expected from his side? In this sense, it was a question that anybody could put in any other family, culture, country.

On the other hand, and at the same time, it was full of other implications that could only be understood in the context of Indian culture and civilization (*bhāratīya saṃskṛti*), precisely, in relation with ones socio-religious duties during a particular stage of life (*varṇāśrama dharma*). Speaking about an eventual partner, this meant—what is his socio-religious status and family background? To which community, group or tradition does he belong to? What sort of education has he received? What are his personal qualifications and qualities? These two intimately linked personal and social dimensions can be summarized in the following manner— what sort of man is he? This question is all the more pertinent when one knows that *saṃskāra* covers both conscious and unconscious tendencies of our psyche: past, present and future.

The extreme amplitude and diversity of the concept obliged me to leave aside the *Tantra* and the *Āgama* literature, as well as the Jaina texts. I have mentioned, in the last part of Chapter II, five *Vaiṣnava-saṃskāra,* necessary for "initiation"; ten *saṃskāras* confered to a *mantra (Śāradātilaka Tantra);* and the *ātma-saṃskāra* of the *Śaiva* tradition (*Soma Śambhu Paddhati*), necessary for *nirvāṇa-dīkṣā;* so very different from the *śarīra-saṃskāras* of *Gṛhya-* and *Dharmasūtras.*

To my knowledge, the concept of *saṃskāra,* in its ritual, psycho-moral, or epistemological dimensions, has not received an independant explanation or elaboration in early Jaina literature. It was rather treated under the head of other major pan-Indian concepts such as *karman* ("act", "deeds"), *vāsanā* ("latent desire", "impregnation", "residual impressions" of acts and experiences), *leśyā:* "colouration", material and spiritual, (*dravya-* and *bhāva-leśyā*), *kaṣāya* ("passion"), etc. In any case, the subject requires a supplementary study.

Three broad areas of my survey are—1. Brahmanical and Hindu ritualistic texts (Chs. I-II). 2. Buddhist texts (Ch. III). 3. Philosophical systems or *darśanas* (lit. "views", Points of view on the reality), Chs. IV-VIII, followed by Conclusion. Hence, my enquiry into the concept of *saṃskāra* reveals a threefold interest—relative to cultural and religious anthropology, psychology and ethics, epistemology and philosophy. The whole work is a testimony of the cultural heritage of India in its opening towards Western thought.

My investigation goes back first to the use of *saṃskṛ-, abhisaṃskṛ-* in the *Brāhmaṇas,* where they are closely related to sacrificial activity (*yajña, karman*). From a historical and philosophical point of view, it should be reminded that the noun *saṃskāra* is not attested in the *Śruti*. In its psycho-moral, philosophical and epistemological acceptations, the noun appears for the first time in the Buddhist Pāli Canon (*saṃkhāra. abhisaṃkhāra*). As to the adjectives *saṃskṛta, asaṃskṛta* (Pāli *saṃkhata, asaṃkhata*), they are found since the *Ṛg Veda*, and throughout the history of Brahmanical, Buddhist and Hindu literature.

Explanations and justifications are furnished as to why one and the same translation for *saṃskṛ-, abhisaṃskṛ-, saṃskāra, abhi-saṃskāra, saṃskṛta, abhisaṃskṛta* cannot always be maintained in Brahmanical, Buddhist, and *darśana* contexts.

The present book offers the quintessence of my previous major publication in French *La notion de saṃskāra dans l'Inde brahmanique et bouddhique,* fascicule 59^1-59^2, Collège de France / Institut de Civilisation Indienne, Paris, Édition-Diffusion De Boccard, 1992–93, 600 pages. I am grateful to Professor Gérard Fussman, Collège de France, who gave me his kind permission for the publication of this English version, as I am to Shri Narendra Prakash Jain, Motilal Banarsidass Publishers, Delhi, India, who warmly greeted the same.

ABBREVIATIONS

AB	Aitareya Brāhmaṇa
ABORI	Annals of the Bhandarkar Research Institute
AK	Abhidharma-Kośa
AN	Aṅguttara-Nikāya
Āpas.-gṛ-sū	Āpastamba Gṛhya Sūtra
ASS	Ānandāśrama Sanskrit Series
Āśv.-gṛ-sū	Āśvalāyana Gṛhya Sūtra
AV	Atharva Veda
BĀU	Bṛhadāraṇyaka Upaniṣad
BĀUBH	Bṛhadāraṇyaka Upaniṣad Bhāṣya
Baudh.-dh.sū	Baudhāyana dharma sūtra
Bh.-gītā	Bhagavad Gītā
BHGBH	Bhagavad Gītā Bhāṣya
BS	Brahma Sūtra
BSBH	Brahma Sūtra Bhāṣya
CHU	Chāndogya Upaniṣad
CHUBH	Chāndogya Upaniṣad Bhāṣya
CSS	Chowkhamba Sanskrit Series
Dhp	Dhammapada
DN	Dīgha Nikāya
Gaut.-dh-sū	Gautama Dharma Sūtra
GB	Gopatha Brāhmaṇa
Hir.-gṛ.-sū	Hiraṇyakeśin Gṛhya Sūtra
HOS	Harvard Oriental Series
ICI	Institute de Civilisation Indienne
It	Itivuttaka
KSS	Kashmir Sanskrit Series
MK	Madhyamaka Kārikā
MS	Manu Smṛti

MUBH	Māṇḍūkya Upaniṣad Bhāṣya
NK	Nyāya Kośa
Pāras.gṛ.-sū	Pāraskara Gṛhya Sūtra
POS	Poona Oriental Series
Pr	Prasannapadā
PTS	Pali Text Society
RV	Ṛg Veda
ŚB	Śatapatha Brāhmaṇa
SBE	Sacred Books of the East
Sk	Sanskrit
SK	Sāṃkhya Kārikā
SKBH	Ṣāṃkhya Kārikā Bhāṣya
SN	Saṃyutta Nikāya
Sn	Sutta Nipāta
TK	Tattva Kaumudī
TS	Tarka Saṃgraha
TV	Tattva Vaiśāradī
Ud	Udāna
Vaikh.-s.-s.	Vaikhānasa Smārta Sūtra (-Dharma and Gṛhya Sūtra)
Vin	Vinaya
Vis	Visuddhimagga
VS	Vaiśeṣika Sūtra
YBH	Yoga Bhāṣya
Yāj.-smṛti	Yājñavalkya Smṛti
YD	Yukti Dīpikā
YS	Yoga Sūtra
Y.-Vārt	Yoga Vārttika

CHAPTER I

The Philosophy of Sacrificial Act

1. The verb *saṃskṛ-* in the *Brāhamaṇa*: mythical, ritual, and symbolic dimensions

The Vedic ritual of fire altar (*agnicayana*),[1] specially its symbolism, offers a privileged occasion of illustrating the range of *saṃskṛ-* attested not less than 95 times.

The substantive *saṃskāra* is not attested in the *Śruti*. The adjective *saṃskṛta* is found as early as in the *Ṛgveda*.[2] So we should first assess the richness of the verbal form *saṃskṛ-*. From *kṛ-* to do, to act or perform (with the insertion of "s") and prefix *sam-* (together, completely), *saṃskṛ-* signifies literally, "to make or assemble together (into a perfect whole)", "to make ready", to prepare or construct, to make perfect (through embellishment and purification).

1.1 The *agnicayana* and its symbolism

In the *agnicayana* context, I have often rendered *saṃskṛ-* to reconstruct, reconstitute, recompose, restore, etc., though fully aware of the fact that *sam-* does not contain any idea of reiteration. It rather indicates the act of synthesization and co-ordination, aiming perfect organization and (re)integration. Structural unity and perfection go together. The prefix *abhi-* "towards" only strengthens this very idea in

---

[1] See *Śatapatha Brāhmana* (=ŚB) ed. A. WEBER, Berlin-London, 1855 Mādhyaṃdina recension, translated by J. EGGELING, S.B.E., Vols. XLI–XLII, Part III–IV, Books VI–X, Delhi, Motilal Banarsidass, 1963.

[2] See *Ṛg Veda Saṃhitā*, V, 76 ; VIII, 33, 9 ; X, 82, 4 (ed. Th. Aufrecht, 3 vol., 2e edition, Bonn, 1877).

all its intensity and refers to "fullness", completeness, criteria of excellence. Whole is wholesome.

Rites are justified by myths, specially cosmogonical ones. World creation preceded by desire (*kāma*), ardour (*tapas*) and effort (*śrama*), is likened to "emission" expressed through *sṛj-*, *vi-sṛj-*. This results in total exhaustion of Prajāpati, who falls asunder (*śraṃs-*, vi-*śraṃs*). Thus beginning implies rupture, scattering, dispersal, death. This inherent evil, different from Christian idea of original sin, lies in the very fact that things have had a beginning in time. So the figures of evil, malady, death, disorder (*pāpa, mṛtyu, nirṛti, anṛta*), etc., are to be eliminated and perfectly harmonious order (*ṛta*) is to be instituted.

1.2 The passage from the One to the multiple

Whereas the procreative process or the passage from One (*eka*) to scattered multiple (*aneka, nānā, bhūyas*) is indicated by *vi-*, the ritual effort (corporal, vocal, mental) of bringing together the multiple towards One is expressed through verbs like *saṃskṛ-* (reuniting the scattered parts into one homogenous whole), *sam-tan-*(to tend or weave together to articulate) *sam-dhā-* (to put together, gather, compose perfectly).

On a supra-human level, in reference to the mythico-ritualistic aspect of sacrifice (*yajña*), the activity expressed by *saṃskṛ-* and *abhi-saṃskṛ-* is that of gods (*deva*) and seers (*ṛṣi*). In the sacrificial area, the officiating priest (*ṛtvij*) is supposed to continue the work of gods. Finally, it qualifies the conduct of human sacrificer (*yajamāna*). His symbolic abandonment (*tyāga*) of his own self is the core of the sacrificial activity (*yajña*).

1.3 The passage from the multiple to the ordained

Now, the very aim of *agnicayana* is to reunite the disintegrated body of Prajāpati = Sacrifice = first sacrificer = sacrificial victim (human sacrificer). He is identified with the universe—space and time. Because Prajāpati, the Year (*saṃvatsara*) felt asunder and had no foundation whatsoever, *saṃskṛ-* in *agnicayana* refers mainly to a perfect construction and organization of space and time restoring the foundation (*pratiṣṭhām saṃskṛ-*)[3] and the year (*saṃvatsaram saṃskaroti*).[4] Piling up of bricks for the fire altar should be carried on during the length of a whole year so that days and nights, months and seasons, continuity (*saṃtāna, saṃtati*), exempt of intervals (*antarāya*) can be established. This spatio-temporal unity is not a mere sum-total of parts, but a surplus. Therefore goes the famous refrain—"He makes Prajāpati, perfectly whole and integral" (*sarvaṃ kṛstnaṃ prajāpatiṃ saṃskaroti*).[5] Surmounting the void or that which was emptied over (*riricāna, rikta*), *saṃskṛ-* aims at plenum (*pūrṇa*), the integral whole (*sarva*).

It is easy to pass from the ritual construction of Prajāpati's body to that of sacrificer's own self (*ātman*), once the identity of *Puruṣa*, Prajāpati, *yajña* and *yajamāna* is established.[6] The space covered by fire altar is measured by the size of the sacrificer's body. This Vedic rule still applies to the construction of a temple in Hinduism. The *vāstupuruṣa-maṇḍala* represents the *yajamāna* himself.

2. The ritual making of the sacrificer's Self

The main idea underlying the ritual construction of the sacrificer's self (*ātmānaṃ saṃskṛ-*) is to effectuate a spiritual transformation, through a biological scheme of gestation. The consecratory ceremony (*dīkṣā*), considered as his new or second birth, makes him fit to enter in relation with deities. Several factors intervene here—

---

[3] ŚB VII, 2, I, 5–6; *Pañcaviṃśa Brāhmaṇa* XV, 3, 28–29 (ed. Chinnaswami Shastri, Benares, 1935, translation by W. Caland, Calcutta, 1931 (*Bibliotheca Indica* 255).

[4] ŚB X, 4, 1, 12.

[5] ŚB VI, 2, 2, 11; VI, S, 3, 7; VII, 3, 1, 42.

[6] See for example *Taittirīya Brāhmaṇa* III, 2, 7, 4 (ed. V.G. Apte, 3 vol., Poona, 1934–38 (Ānandāśrama Sanskrit Series 37).

2.1 By means of the sacrificial fire(s)

Fire placed on the sacrificial ground or Agni himself.[7]

2.2 By means of the Vedic speech or *mantras*

Through Vedic speech or recitation of *mantras* the sacrificer's total person is made ready (*saṃskṛ-*).[8] The *Aitareya Brāhmaṇa* II.40 explains well the ritual making of the senses and bodily functions of the sacrificer through vedic speech, "He repeats the hymn, ...". Thus the *Hotṛ* produces the vital breath (for the sacrificer), and makes it ready (for use)—*prāṇaṃ saṃskurute.* He repeats [....]. Thus he produces the mind (of the sacrificer), and makes it ready (for use)—*manaḥ saṃskurute* [....]. By repeating this verse the *Hotṛ* produces speech (in the sacrificer) and makes it ready (for use)—*vācaṃ saṃskurute* [....]. By repeating this verse he produces the sense of hearing (in...) and makes it ready (for use)—*śrotraṃ saṃskurute.* By [....], he produces the down-going breath [....] and makes it ready (for use)—*apānaṃ saṃskurute.* By [....] he produces the eye (...) and makes it ready (for use)—*caksus saṃskurute.* By [....], he thus produces the soul as the aggregate man and makes it ready (for use)—*ātmānaṃ samastam saṃskurute.*

2.2.1 *Hymns called "work of art"*

The recitation of the hymns called *śilpa* ("work of art", hymns for producing wonderful pieces of art) also helps to reconstruct a new body for the sacrificer—a body made of meteres.

> They repeat the *śilpas* [....]. There are such wonder-works of the gods, and the arts in this world are to be understood as an imitation [*anukṛti*] there of [....]. The *śilpas* make ready the soul [*ātmā saṃskṛti*],

[7] See *Aitareya Brāhmaṇa* (=AB) II, 14, Ed. V. G. Apte, 2 vol., Poona, 1930, (Ānandāśrama Sanskrit Series 32). Translation by A. B. KEITH, Rigveda Brâhmaṇas. *The Aitareya and Kauṣītaki Brâhmaṇas,* Cambrige / Mass., 1920, Harvard Oriental series 25, pp. 107–343. (Re-ed. Motilal Banarsidass, Delhi, 1977). *The Aitareya Brahmanam of the Rigveda,* 2 vols., Martin HAUG, Bharatiya Publishing House, Bombay, 1853 (first edition); Delhi 1976–77 (second ed.).

[8] See for ex. AB, VI, 29–31; 39.

> and imbue it with the knowledge of the sacred hymns. By means of them the Hotṛ-priest prepares the soul of the sacrificer [*ātmānaṃ saṃskurute*].
>
> He repeats a *Yājyā mantra*. The *Yājyā* is a gift, meritorious and fortunate. By repeating it, he makes him (the sacrificer) a pure (goddess) of fortune (Lakṣmī) and prepares her for assisting him.[9]

Other passages convey the same idea. When, for example, the priest recites twenty-one or twenty-five *mantras* corresponding to the same number of limbs or senses of the *Puruṣa* or of the human sacrificer, he thus makes ready his *ātman* as a whole and as a surplus.[10]

2.3 By means of ritual acts

Sacrificial activity (*yajña, karman*) is by itself source of perfection. As to the perfection and success (*samṛddhi*) of the sacrificial activity (*yajña*), confidence (*śraddhā*), truth and exactitude (*satya*) are necessary. Since the first moment of firm resolution (*saṃkalpa*) till final lustration (*avabhṛtha*), prescribed rules are to be followed, without omission or inversion of any kind. As says the ŚB XII.8.1.17 by performing the *agnicayana* rite, the sacrificer makes ready (*saṃskṛ-*) his own self for the other world. The immortal sacrificial body of the *yajamāna* is made of strophes (*ṛc*), prose formulas (*yajus*) and chants (*sāman*). He who sacrifices to the self (*ātmayājin*) is better than he who sacrifices to Gods (*devayājin*). An *ātmayājin* knows that by this (sacrificial act or by the recitation of this or that portion of *Veda*), this particular part of his body is purified or made perfect.[11]

The officiating priests contribute fully in this normative and perfective activity (expressed by *saṃskṛ-*). They make the sacrificer ready by means of "deliberate sacrificial proceedings" (*yajña-kratu*).[12] The intervention of the Vedas is absolutely necessary in this enterprise.

---

[9] See AB VI, 27. Also GB II, 6, 7.

[10] See AB I, 19 : *ātmānam ekaviṃśaṃ saṃskurute;* variant in the *Aitareya Āraṇyaka,* I, 1, 2, 8 : *ātmānam pañcaviṃśaṃ saṃskurute*

[11] See ŚB XI, 2, 16, 13–14.

[12] See AB VI, 31.

The priest *Hotṛ* is related with the *Ṛgveda* (or the *Veda* made of strophes). The *Adhvaryu* with the *Yajurveda* (or the Veda made of prose formulas). The *Udgātṛ* with the *Sāmaveda* (made of chants, a melody). The *Brahman* is the quintessence of the triple science (*trayī vidyā*) and the priest *Brāhmaṇa* is related to this totality. He surveys, in silence (*tūṣṇīm*) the unrolling of sacrificial operations.

2.3.1 *Body, speech, and thought*

Body (*śarīra, kāya, tanu*), speech (*vāc*) and thought (*manas*) intervene conjointly in the sacrificial acts. Thought and speech are compared to two paths of sacrifice.[13] The three priests—*Hotṛ, Adhvaryu* and *Udgātṛ* make ready (*saṃskṛ-*) one of these two paths by means of speech (*vāc*); the priest *Brāhmaṇa* makes ready the other path, by means of thought (*manas*); that is why he sits in silence (*tūṣṇīm*).[14]

2.4 By means of the "ritual fees"

Another significant factor is the "ritual fees" (*dakṣiṇā*). By making ready (*saṃskṛ-*) plentiful gifts, the sacrificer constructs [....] a "bridge" (*setu*) which will allow him to reach the heaven.[15] The *Śatapatha Brāhmaṇa* equally justifies the neccessity of *dakṣiṇā* for the *Ṛtvijs,* who make ready [....] another sacrificial body for the sacrificer. By recalling – it is they who have given birth to me – the sacrificer offers *dakṣiṇā* to priests.[16] This enables him to buy back his mortal body (*ātmānaṃ niṣkrī-*), kept engaged during the sacrificial ceremony, and also the ritual construction of his new perfected body (*ātmānaṃ saṃskṛ-*). Herein lies the inherent

---

[13] AB V, 33; *Gopatha Brāhmaṇa* (=GB) I, 3, 2; *Jaiminīya Upaniṣad Brāhmaṇa,* III. 2, 2–3 (ed. Bellikoth Rāmachandra Sharma, Tripati, 1967, Kendriya Sanskrit Series 5–6). English translation by H. ORTEL, JAOS, 1894.

[14] See *Kauṣītaki Brāh.,* VI, 11; *Chāndogya Upaniṣad,* IV, 16, 2–4.

[15] GB II, 3, 17.

[16] ŚB IV, 3, 4, 4–5; AB VI, 34. "Debt" (*ṛṇa*), "consecration" (*dīkṣā*) and "ritual fees" (*dakṣiṇā*) are interrelated themes.

dialectics of the human condition the desire of conquering immortality and, at the same time, keeping one's finitude.

The doctrine of sacrifice contains important considerations on debt (*ṛṇa*) towards gods, seers, manes. They can be paid off through permanent and daily sacrifices called *mahāyajñas.*[17] These obligatory duties of a "twice-born" (*dvija*) can only be accomplished after "initiation" (*upanayana*) and "marriage" (*vivāha*)—two fundamental "purificatory and perfective rites of the human body" (*śarīra-saṃskāra*). This relation between *saṃskāra* and *adhikāra* (right, ability, eligibility) is examined in the second chapter.

[17] See ŚB I, 7, 2, 1–6; XI, S, 6, 1–3.

CHAPTER II

Representation of Hindu Life-cycle

1. Introduction

A religion is lived through performance of rites which leave their imprints on an individual psyche. This is particularly true of the rites performed for a "twice-born" (*dvija*), which mark all singular occasions of his life. Since remote past this practice has remained alive, at least in orthodox brahmanical families.

1.1 Translation problems for the word *saṃskāra*

In the context of *Gṛhya-* and *Dharma Sūtras,* the noun *saṃskāra* is generally rendered by "sacrament".[1] This translation does not seem to apply to all Hindu *saṃskāras,* but only, and in a certain measure, to three of them—initiation (*upanayana*), marriage (*vivāha*), cremation (*antyeṣṭi,* lit. "last offering"). In Christian theology, "sacrament" is defined as that which enables man to participate in the divine life.

The generic designation given to rites for a "twice-born" is *śarīra-saṃskāra* ("purificatory and perfective rite for the human body").[2] Though grammatically a singular (*ekavacana*) the compound *śarīra-saṃskāra* refers to the totality of purificatory and perfective rites for the human

[1] P.V. Kane (1930–62); R.B. Pandey (1969). Also by some French translators, for example, L. Renou, Jean Varenne, A. Loiseleur-Deslongchamps, etc.

[2] See *Mānava Dharma Śāstra* or *Manu Smṛti* (= MS) II. 26. Ed. Mandlik, (1855), by G. Bühler, (1866); (SBE) XXV (1967); *Vaikhānasa Smārta Sūtra* I. 1. (1927).

body.[3] They belong to the category of "domestic" (*gṛhya*) and "occasional" rites (*naimittika*). Unlike solemn ritual they need the domestic fire only. Except three fundamental *saṃskāras* mentioned above, all others can be confered by the householder himself to his wife and children.

1.2 Number of *śarīra-saṃskāras* listed in the *Dharma Śāstras*

The number (ten, sixteen, eighteen, or forty) and the way of enumerating these *saṃskāras* varies from one text to another. Considered as an unauspicious event (*amaṅgala*), authors generally omit the description of the last *saṃskāra*—*antyeṣṭi* or the "last offering". The *Gautama Dharma Sūtra*[4] or the *Vaikhānasa Smārta Sūtra*[5] do not even mention this last *saṃskāra*. The *Gṛhya Sūtras,* except the *Hiraṇyakeśī Gṛhya Sūtra*[6], start with the marriage ceremony and continue with the conception rite till the bath (*snāna*) and the return of the Vedic student in his family (*samāvartana*), without even mentioning the last perfective rite. Only the *Āśvālāyana Gṛhya Sūtra,* mentions the *antyeṣṭi* while describing the solemn funeral ceremonies confered to an *āhitāgni* (one who has laid his ritual or sacrificial fires).[7]

The *Gautama Dharma Sūtra* VIII.4–21 enumerates forty *saṃskāras* and eight qualities of the soul (*ātma-guṇa* VIII. 22–25), to which great importance is attached. This list includes along with fourteen *saṃskāras* five *mahāyajñas,* seven *pākayajñas,* seven *haviryajñas* and seven *somayajñas* (see also *Vaikhānasa Smārta Sūtras* IX.1 *sq.*). Vertus like compassion for all creatures (*dayā*), patience or forbearance (*kṣānti*), freedom from anger and jealousy (*anasūya*), purity (*śauca*),

[3] See *Medhātithi* on MS II, 26.

[4] Umesh Chandra Pandey 1966; tr. by G. BÜHLER, Press, 1879, SBE II, pp. 175–310, cf. p. 221.

[5] *Vaikhānasa Dharma-* and *Gṛhya Sūtra,* critical edition by W. CALAND, Calcutta, 1927 (*Bibliotheca Indica* 242), tr. by W. CALAND, Calcutta 1929 (BI 251).

[6] J. Kirste, Vienna, 1889, tr. by H. OLDENBERG, 1892, SBE XXX, Pt. II, 1964. pp.136–246.

[7] A.F. Stenzler, Leipzig, 1864 (Abh. DMG III. 4); tr. by H. OLDENBERG, 1886, SBE XXIX, pp. 159–259.

"quietism" or non-agitation (*anāyāsa*), auspiciousness (*maṅgala*), freedom from avarice (*akārpaṇya*), and freedom from covetousness (*aspṛha*) are called the eight good qualities of the soul (*ātma-guṇa*). Here is the list of *saṃskāras* found in the *Gautama Dharma Sūtra,* VIII.14–16—the ceremony to cause conception (*garbhādhāna*), the ceremony to cause the birth of a male child (*puṃsavana*), the arranging or parting of the pregnant wife's hair (*sīmantonnayana*), the ceremony on the birth of the child (*jātakarman*), the ceremony of naming the child (*nāmakaraṇa*), the first feeding (*annaprāśana*), tonsure of the head of the child (*caula* or *cūḍākaraṇa*), the initiation (*upanayana*), followed by the four vows undertaken for the study of the *Veda* (*catvāri veda-vratāni*), the bath (on completion of the studentship *snāna,* cf. *samāvartana*), the taking of a help-mate for fulfilment of the religious duties (*sahadharmacāriṇīsaṁyoga* = *vivāha*), the performance of five "great" sacrifices (*mahāyajña*) to gods, manes, men, goblins, and *Brahman.*

The *Hārita Dharma Sūtra* XI.1–5 classifies "sacraments" under two heads—"relative to *brahman*" (*brahma-saṃskāra* = *smārta-saṃskāra*), "rite for depositing an embryo" (*garbhādhāna*) or conception rite onwards "relative to Gods" (*daiva-saṃskāra*) which comprehend sacrifices.

2. Human life-cycle rites

For better clarity, these life-cycle rites can be subdivided under four sections—

I. Prenatal *saṃskāras* such as "conception" (*garbhādhāna)* "rite for quickening a male" (*puṃsavana*), "parting of the hair (of a woman) upwards" (*sīmāntonnayana*).

II. Birth-rite (*jātakarman*) until *cūḍākarman* (*caula*) "the first cutting of the hair on the child's head, keeping a lock or tuft of hair", and *vidyārambha* "commencement of learning the alphabet."

III. *Saṃskāras* marking entry in adolescent and in adult life—*upanayana, keśānta or godāna. samāvartana, vivāha.*

IV. *Antyeṣṭi* (followed by *śrāddhas,* mainly *sapiṇḍīkaraṇa*).

2.1 Seven major purposes of *śarīra-saṃskāras*

Instead of describing purely and simply the content of each *śarīra-ṣaṃskāra,* here have been listed seven major purposes or functions of Hindu *saṃskāras.* They are—

1. Purification, perfection.
2. Protection (through invocation and propitiation of Deities, as well as by other means).
3. Fortification of the delicate transitional passages of the human life-cycle.
4. Institution and sacralization of relations, between parents-children, master-disciple, husband-wife, between the living and the dead, men and *ṛṣis,* men and gods.
5. Qualification and transformation of status. Better integration in the group or community of those who are alive and those who are dead (i.e., the ancestors).
6. Continuity of generatious. Transmission and conservation of *Veda.* Perpetuation of *Dharma.*
7. Imposition of norms in order to bring out the best of perfection. Psycho-somatic, moral and intellectual dressage.

	Saṃskāras	Purposes of *śarīra-saṃskāras*				
I.	*Garbhādhāna*	1	2		4	6
	Puṃsavana		2		4	6
	Sīmantonnayana		2			
II.	*Jātakarman*	1	2	3	4	
	Nāmakaraṇa	1			4	
	Niṣkramaṇa			3		
	Annaprāśana			3		
	Cūḍākaraṇa	1	2	3		

III. *Upanayana*	1	2	3	4	5	6	7
Keśānta	1	2					
Samāvartana			3				7
Vivāha	1	2	3	4	5	6	7
IV. *Antyeṣṭi*	1	2	3	4	5	6	
Śrāddha, sapiṇḍīkaraṇa							

These ritual, educational and cultural purposes are obviously interrelated and found in a more or less in each *śarīra-saṃskāra*. As shown in the Table (which can be consulted in both horizontal and vertical order), all of them are present in *upanayana* and *vivāha*.

2.2 Purification leading to perfection

Purification is the common function of all the *śarīra-saṃskāras,* so says the *Manu Smṛti* II.26–27

> With holy rites prescribed by the *Veda,* must the ceremony on conception and other sacraments be performed for twice-born men, which sanctify the body and purify (from sin) in this (life) and after death. By burnt oblations during (the mother's) pregnancy, by the *Gātakarman* (the ceremony after birth), the *Kauda* (tonsure), and the *Mauṅgībandhana* (the tying of the sacred girdle of *Muñga* grass) is the taint, derived from both parents, removed from twice-born men.[8]

Yājñavalkya shares the same opinion (*Yājñavalkya Smṛti* 1.13).[9] Medhātithi as well as Vijñāneśvara comment the word *enas* "taint" by *pāpa*—"sin", "blemish", "fault", "demerit", "impurity". This taint is related to semen and blood[10] as well to the transmission of hereditary diseases. The "stain" (*enas*)

---

[8] Tr. by G. Bühler, SBE, pp. 33–34.

vaidikaiḥ karmabhiḥ puṇyair niṣekādir dvijanmanām /
kāryaḥ śarīrasaṃskāraḥ pāvanaḥ pretya ceha ca //
garbhair homair jātakarmacauḍamauñjinibandhanaiḥ /
baijikaṃ gārbhikaṃ caino dvijānām apamṛjyate //

[9] *Yājñavalkya Smṛti* with the *Mitākṣarā,* Commentary by Vijñāneśvara, ed., Narayan Ram Acharya, 1949.

[10] Manu V.135 counts them amongst twelve impure substances of the body.

or the "evil" related to blood and semen is the "invisible" (*adṛṣṭa*) evil, cause of suffering (*duḥkha kāraṇam*) explains Medhātithi on *Manu* II.27. The pre-natal *saṃskāras* (such as the *garbhādhāna, puṃsavana, sīmantonnayana*) are also called "perfective rites of the soil" (*kṣetra-saṃskāras,* the matrix is considered to be the soil receiving the semen or *bīja).*[11] These are supposed to have some positive action in the removal of the biological and hereditary impurity including hereditary diseases (*kṣetriya-* or *saṃcārī-roga*).[12] Although they are inefficacious in removing the psycho-moral kārmic heritage which is one's own personal acquisition accumulated during the past lives.

The *Gṛhya Sūtras* furnish a detailed description about the *saṃskāras* of the human life-cycle. The treatises on the sacred laws of the Āryas (*Dharma Sūtras*) abound in rules and regulations, the prescriptions to be followed, etc. But as social and religious anthropology cannot be put aside from a philosophical enquiry, specially in the Indian context, I had made it a point to go through these texts systematically and quote them whenever necessary. Let us see the importance of this first function or purpose in some of the major *saṃskāras.* Apart from the objects or ingredients such as the sacred herbs – *kuṣa, darbha, muñja,* a new cloth (in *upanayana, vivāha, antyeṣṭi*) – the main purifying elements

---

[11] The expression *kṣetra-saṃskāra* figures in the *Mitākṣarā and Yājñavalkya-Smṛti* I, 13. For the comparison between matrix = soil and semen = *bīja* "seed" or "grain", see *Manu Smṛti* IX. 33, 36–38.

[12] For *kṣetriya* diseases (called *saṃcārī-roga* in *Yājñavalkya-Smṛti* I.54), see *Atharva Veda* II.10.1–2; 4–5; II.8.1; (tr. by W.D. WHITNEY, 2 vols., Harvard Oriental Series 7–8, 1904, Reprint, Delhi, 1962). The commentator Sāyaṇa (*ad* AV II.8.1) explains that a *kṣetriya* disease such as phthisis or consumption (*kṣaya*), leprosy (*kuṣṭha*), epilepsy (*apasmara*: loss of memory), etc., is an illness which has or needs to be cured in the body of the son, the grand son, etc., (*kṣetre parakṣetre putrapautrādiśarīre cikitsyaḥ...*). For the *mantra* used by the father during the *garbhādhāna* and *jātakarman* in order to eliminate the possibility of such diseases for the child, see for example *Hiraṇyakeśi Gṛhya Sūtra* II.1.3.10; I.7.25.1. The wife or the future mother must be a person exempt from diseases (*aroginī, Yājñavalkya Smṛti,* I.53).

intervening during each *saṃskāra* are the Vedic *mantras* and the Vedic fires (*agni*) duly laid down after the marriage ceremony and water for aspersions, ritual bath, etc. All *saṃskāras* for a male are celebrated along with the recitation of *mantras*— Vedic prayers, chants or formulas. For a female, these purifying and perfective rites are performed in silence (*tūṣṇīm*), except during the marriage ceremony (*vivāha, pāṇigrahaṇa,* equivalent to a sort of "initiation" for her) in which wonderful Vedic *mantras* are recited.

2.3 Impurity due to birth and death

In the Indian context (specially in Brahmanism, Hinduism), the two events of life, birth and death, situated at two borderlines or edges are by themselves cause of impurity, because they mark a rupture. The impurity due to birth (*jananāśauca, sūtikāśauca*) for ten nights (or days) touches not only the mother and the new-born, but also the father and all the *sapiṇḍas* (close relatives, "those who share a common ball of rice, having common body particles", *piṇḍa*).[13] The birth, or the mere fact of having a beginning in time, is tainted with evil. Even the birth of ritual fire (*agni*) produced through friction, evil which gods had to remove by means of ritual oblations. On a different plane, the *Śvetāśvatara Upaniṣad* (Commentary on I.5) counts birth amongst one of the five sorrows (*pañca-duḥkha*) of human existence, the other four being the embryo stage, old age, illness and death. The Buddhist influence is quite evident here as in the *Maitrāyaṇa Upaniṣad* III.4. The *Upaniṣad* of the embryo (*Garbhopaniṣad*)[14] says long on the discredit

[13] See *Manu Smṛti* V.62; *Baudhayāna Dharma Sūtra* I.5.11.19.*sq.* For the ritual impurity due to death (*maraṇāśauca*) in the family, see *Āśvalāyana Gṛhya Sūtra* IV.4.17–18; *Viṣṇu Smṛti* XXII.1–4.

[14] See *One hundred and eight Upanishads (Īshâ and others) with various readings,* edited by Pansikar, 1921; Paul Deussen, *Sixty Upaniṣads of the Veda,* tr. from German by V.M. Bedekar and G.B. Palsule, Pt. 2, pp. 639–44; L. Kapani, *Garbhopaniṣad,* 1976, pp. 1–19. "Upaniṣad of the Embryo, Note on the Garbha-Upaniṣad", in *Fragments for a History of the Human Body,* Part Three, ZONE, ed. by Michel Feher, 1989, pp. 177–96.

thrown on the mere fact of being born. The good resolutions made by the foetus during his sojourn in the womb are instantly forgotten (due to a violent pressure of the *vaiṣṇava vāyu,* "wind of Viṣṇu") as soon as the baby comes out of the womb.

Moreover, according to the *Veda,* the simple fact of being born supposes that one is indebted[15] to the God of Death, Yama. By sacrificing one purchases back one's person from the jaws of death. Only a *dvija,* who has duly received the fundamental *saṃskāras, upanayana* and *vivāha,* is capable of paying back his debts (*ṛṇa*).

After the birth the child has a physical form (*rūpa*), but not yet a name (*nāma*). Till one does not have a name, one is as if concerned with evil (*pāpa*), says the *Śatapatha Brāhmaṇa* VI.1.3.9. relating the case of Prajāpati's son Kumāra with Uśas. All that had received a name and a form when created, should carry on to be like this. Except in the perspective of the *Advaita Vedānta* philosophy, (also in Buddhism), where *nāma-rūpa* is considered to be a mere designation of empirical individuality. So a secret name, derived from the name of a constellation (*nakṣatra*), is first given by the parents to the new-born. Later a name with which he will introduce himself and salute others (*abhivādanīya-nāma*).[16] Name giving rite is important because this is the first thing about which his master in *Veda* (*ācārya*) will question him before the *upanayana.* "What is your name?[17]" which means "Who are you?" "From which *gotra-ṛṣi* you descend?" The name indicates the *gotra* to which the male belongs—that of a *Brāhmaṇa* ends or finishes with the particule *Śarman,* of a *Kṣatriya* with *Varman,* of a *Vaiśya* with *Gupta.*[18] It should also be noted that a *piṇḍa* (rice ball)

[15] On the theory of three (or five) debts (*ṛṇa*) according to the Veda: debt to Gods (*deva*), to Seers (*ṛṣis*), and to Manes (*pitṛ*), see for example *Śatapatha Brāhmaṇa* III. 6.2.16.

[16] See *Āśvalāyana Gṛhya Sūtra,* I.15.8; Caraka, *Śārīra Sthāna,* VIII.50.

[17] *Śāṅkhyāyana Gṛhya Sūtra,* II.2.4–7.

[18] *Pāraskara-Gṛhya.-Sūtra,* I.17.4; Caraka, *Śarīra Sthāna,* VIII.50.

offered to the dead is never anonymous, the personal name and the *gotra* of the dead (*preta*) must be mentioned.[19]

2.4 The second birth, ritual and symbolic

The initiation rite (*upanayana*) is particularly purifying in as much as it is likened to a second birth, ritual and symbolical.[20] It is a new sacred birth to the *Veda*, to the *Brahman*[21] through the Vedic *mantras*. After *upanayana*, the male enters in the *brahmacaryāśrama* and during this period (twelve years) he circulates in the *Brahman* or the *Veda* in complete chastity, learning it by heart, and bringing greater purity and perfection in his life.

For the young girl the marriage sacrament (*vivāha, pāṇigrahaṇa*) is equivalent to the initiatory ceremony.[22] Purificatory for her (and for the father too who donates his girl, *kanyādāna*) because after marriage only she can come in contact with the ritual fires, the sacrificial rites and the *Veda*, in company of his master (*svāmin, pati*), more or less directly or indirectly. Marriage inaugurates the *gṛhasthāśrama* (the stage of master of the house) in which both husband and wife can fully accomplish all their sacred duties (*dharma*).

In the cremation (*antyeṣṭi, saṃskāra* par excellence) the purificatory elements are water (the dead body is duly washed, all the cavities cleaned and filled up with sacrificial ingredients), part of a new cloth never worn before with which the body is wrapped, the *mantras* recited during the funeral ceremony, (most of them are from the *Ṛgveda*),[23]

---

19 *Vaikhānasa Smārta Sūtra*, V.13.

20 See *Manu Smṛti* II. 147–48; *Viṣṇu Smṛti* XXVIII. 37; *Yājñavalkya Smṛti*, I, 39. For a description of *upanayana*. See, for example, *Hir.-gr. sū.*, I.1.1.1 to I.2.8.1–16; *Gobhila Gṛhya Sūtra* II.10.1 to III.3.36; *Āpastamba-gṛ.-sū.*, 4.10.1–4; 11; 16, etc. For the *Gṛhya Sūtras* (Rules of Vedic Domestic Ceremonies) see SBE, vol. XXIX–XXX, Part I–II, tr. by H. Oldenberg and F. Max Müller, 1964 sq.

21 Medhātithi *ad* Manu, II.46.

22 *Manu Smṛti* II.67.

23 For a good description of the last rite see *Āśvalāyana Gṛhya Sūtra*, IV.1, 16–18; IV.2–IV.6.

and above all the ritual fire (*agni*) in which the body of the defunct is offered as a last sacrificial oblation or offering (*antya-iṣṭi*). This offering to the God Agni promises a new or a third ritual and symbolic birth[24] to the *yajamāna*. After the purificatory and perfecting ceremony at the cremation ground (*śmaśāna*), and all that follows—collection of the bones (*asthisañcayana*), etc., the process of purification continues with the help of post-mortem rites aiming the transformation of the dead (*preta*) into an ancestor (*pitṛ*) through rites called *śrāddha* and *sapiṇḍīkaraṇa*.

3. Invocation and propitiation of divinities

A second function of the *śarīra-saṃskāras* is to protect from all sorts of malefic or invisible influences. The *mantras* pronounced during the accomplishment of these perfective rites of a "twice born" are quite often quoted from the *Atharvaveda*[25] and present a great affinity with magical charms or incantations. These magico-ritualistic and symbolical gestures provide man with a sentiment of security against visible and invisible dangers. Hence these domestic rites include all sorts of practices to conjure the evil and give an auspicious or favorable turn to all important events of life. Are these practices mere superstitions?—Who knows? May be.

3.1 Divinities invoked during each *saṃskāra*

For protection purpose different divinities[26] are invoked before conferring each and every *saṃskāra*. The astral and

---

[24] See *Śatapatha Brāhmaṇa* XI.2.1.1.

[25] AV I.1; 11; 35; II.10;13;15; 28–29; III.8, 23; IV.30; V.25; VI.11; 68; 10; VIII.1; 2; 6; XIX.68; 69.

[26] *Garbhādhāna*: Prajāpati, Viṣṇu, Dhātṛ, Sinīvālī, Gandharva, Tvāṣṭṛ. *Puṃsavana*: Mitra and Varuṇa. *Sīmāntonnayana*: Dhātṛ, Viṣṇu, Rāka. *Jātakarman*: Savitṛ, Sarasvatī, Agni, Viṣṇu, Soma, Aditi, during the first solid food intake or *annaprāśana*. Savitṛ, Aditi, Soma, Varuṇa, Dhātṛ, Bṛhaspati during the first cutting of the hair (*keśānta*, *cūḍākarman*). Deities evoked during *upanayana*: Savitṛ, Bṛhaspati, Aśvin, Pūṣan, Bhaga, Aryaman, Agni, Viśvedevās, Mitra, Varuṇa, Dhātṛ. In the marriage ceremony or *vivāha*:

astrological moments or conjuctions are properly chosen. Attention is given to the choice of direction, north and east being auspicious, south inauspicious. The way of wearing the sacrificial cordon or girdle, the sense of circumambulation, *pradakṣiṇā* for auspicious rites, *apasavya* for inauspicious rites (for the dead), the use of the right or the left hand (or any other side or part of the body, right is considered to be auspicious, left inauspicious), etc., should be taken care of. All sorts of ingredients are used to assure the protection against evil spell. Many of these practices, real or symbolical, seem to reflect an archaic mentality—the preparation of the delivery room (*sūtikā-gṛha*), the parting of the hair in the middle with the porcupine, prefiguring a happy delivery exempt of danger for the future mother (and the child), burying (to hide) the first cut hair after *caula* or *keśānta* in a dig, hair being the symbol of virility and power, etc.

3.2 Symbolical practices

Without looking for a psychoanalytical interpretation, we should rather put forward the magico-ritual symbolism. For instance, during the *puṃsavana* rite, given the importance of having a male child, the *Gṛhya Sūtras* enjoin several practices accompanied with sacred formulas.[27] Even doctors like Caraka[28] advise to accomplish the *puṃsavana saṃskāra* according to Vedic prescriptions in order to obtain the "change" (*vivartana*) of sex. For instance, the husband makes his wife drink some curd and milk by adding two beans and a grain of barley each time, asking her, "what are you

Agni, Soma, Viṣṇu, Prajāpati, Aryaman, Varuṇa, Puṣan, Indra, Indrāṇī, Bhaga, Tvāṣṭṛ, Agni-Gārhapatya, Gandharva, etc. And obviously Agni and Yama in *antyeṣṭi*.

[27] See *Āśvalāyana Gṛhya Sūtra* I.13.2–3, SBE, vol. XXIX, Pt. I., pp.179–80.

[28] Caraka, *Śārīra Sthāna* VIII.19. Agniveśa's *Caraka Saṃhitā* (Text with English translation and critical exposition based on Cakrapaṇidatta's *Āyurveda Dīpikā*) by Ram Karan SHARMA and Vaidya Bhagawan DASH, Vol. I: *Sūtrasthāna*, Varanasi, 1976 (Chowkhamba Sanskrit Series XCIV). Vol II: *Nidānasthāna, Vimānasthāna, Śārīrasthāna*, 1977.

drinking"? The symbolism of the grain of barley and the two beans (testicles) is clear.

Other symbolical practices such as *āśmārohana* ("treading on a stone"), by putting the right foot first, which take place in *upanayana* and *vivāha*, showing or gazing at the polestar (*dhruva-darśana*), reflect the desire to inculcate good and strong psycho-moral qualities such as stability and self-determination.[29]

The last rite includes many interesting practices to protect the defunct from the burning fire, "eater of the raw" (*agni kravyāda*), ready to consume the body, and at the same time to carry this last oblation to God Agni[30] and to heaven. After the cremation rite (*antyeṣṭi*)[31] several ritual ceremonies intervene to protect the living against the dead and the errant spirits.[32]

4. Fortifying the delicate "passages"

All these Hindu *saṃskāras* are equivalent to *rites de passage* because they institute a harmonious transition from one state or stage of life to another. A passage supposes a rupture or discontinuity and as such some danger. By fortifying these important articulations of the human life through rituals, the person who receives them is prepared or made ready to accept the changes coming in and insert them well on the psychosomatique, moral and intellectual level. Amongst these moments of rupture there is birth at one end, death on the other. As the *Vaikhānasa Smārta Sūtra* VIII.1 puts it—

> There are two sorts of sacraments—the sacrament accomplished at the birth and the sacrament accomplished at the death (*jāta-* and *mṛta-saṃskāra*). By the first one gains this world, by the second, one gains the other world.

By birth, one passes from the non-manifested state to a manifested state. The cutting of the umbilical cord

---

[29] See *Āśvalayana Gṛhya Sūtra,* I.8.22; *Śāṅkhyāyana-Gṛhya-Sūtra,* I.17.3–4; *Pāraskara-Gṛhya-Sūtra.,* I.8.19–20; *Hir.-gr.- sū.,* I.1.4.1.

[30] See *Ṛg Veda,* X, 16, 4; 7.

[31] See *Āśvalayana Gṛhya Sūtra,* IV.4.6; 9; IV.6.4; 10.

[32] See *Āśvalayana Gṛhya Sūtra,* IV.6.10 and 4.

(equivalent to an ontological scission) is a decisive moment and that's why the *jātakarman saṃskāra* contains so many ritual practices with recitation of chants or formulas.[33]

The first outing or stepping out of the house of the child (*niṣkramaṇa*), when the father makes him look at the sun (*āditya-darśana*), the first feeding with solid food (*annaprāśana*), etc., all these events are duly ritualized.

4.1 Rupture, discontinuity, separation

The separation of the adolescent from his parents at the age of eight, ten or twelve (for the son of a *Brāhmaṇa, Kṣatriya* or *Vaiśya* caste respectively), when he is conducted to his master's (*ācārya*) house for his initiation to the *Veda* (or *upanayana*) marks a real transition. As such this is object of elaborate ritual ceremonies and prayers. The child enters in the world regulated by *dharma* or socio-religious norms and there is no place in his life for desire or eros (*kāma*) during the *brahmacarya* period.

Same sort of separation takes place in the marriage sacrament (*vivāha*), when the young nubile girl, who must be a virgin, is taken away by the husband from her parental house to his new unknown house where she will live under his authority with his family. Moreover, there is a similarity between the condition of the *brahmacārin*, who has to live under the authority of his master, and the bride who has to live under the authority of her husband, her Lord(*pati, svāmin*). But with the difference that in the married life there will be ample place for *kāma* or *rati* (amorous desire, sexual love), although the main objective will be procreation *prajā*, above all that of a male. The married life stage (*gṛhasthāśrama*) is the occasion to fulfil all socio-religious duties, which can be assured through the means of *dharma* and *artha*. For the bride who passes her life in the kitchen, cooking and being cooked, sacrificing herself on all occasions, the married life reveals an aspect of her *tapas*. No

---

[33] See *Khādira-Gṛhya-Sūtra.*, II.2.32; *Pāraskara-Gṛhya-Sūtra*, I.16.1–3; 6.

need for her to renounce, because her whole life is made of dedication and renunciation.

As to the last *saṃskāra* (*antyeṣṭi,* followed by *śrāddhas*), it assures the transition from this world to another. These rites transform the dead from the state of a *preta* to that of an ancestor (*pitṛ*). Interesting descriptions about the rebuilding or reconstruction of a new body through rituals are found in the *Piṇḍopaniṣad,* and specially in the *Garuḍa Purāṇa, Pretakāṇḍa.*

5. Instituting and sacralizing human relations

As we have seen in the Chapter I, *saṃskṛ-* denotes the act of bringing together or reuniting the parts into a whole. As an activity of liaison, it aims at strengthening the ties. The Hindu *saṃskāras* tend to sacralize relations between persons in a selective manner. In the hierarchical Brahmanical milieu there is no possibilty however to establish relations haphazardly.

5.1 Between parents and children

The object of the prenatal *saṃskāra, garbhādhāna,* followed by *puṃsavana, jātakarman,* etc., is to sacralize, strengthen and make perfect the mother-child and the father-son relations. The womb (*garbha, yoni*) is the first world where we sojourn before entering in the social world. Hence the prenatal sacraments take care of the intra-uterine life. All physical or psycho-moral dispositions of the future mother are supposed to affect the foetus. In Caraka's opinion, there is a surprising homology between the desires, thoughts or behaviour of the mother and the sex of the child (to be born).[34] Her imagination can have an impact on the physical features or traits of the child. During the third month of gestation, a sort of dyad or symbiosis, a bi-cardique unity establishes between them, reason why the pregnant women is called *dvaihṛdaya.*[35]

[34] See Caraka, *Śārīra Sthāna,* II.24–25.

[35] *Ib.* IV.15, see also IV.16–19.

5.2 The father *is* the son

The rite for quickening a male (*puṃsavana*) contains interesting descriptions which shows that it is the father who is (re)born once again in his son and that's why his wife is called *jāyā,* one who engenders.[36] The *mantras* pronounced during the *jātakarman* bring out the deep symbolism of this intimate relation. The son is a reduplication of the father. The father *is* the son. After the death of the father, the son becomes the father of his father because he makes him to be born to his new condition that of a *pitṛ.*

5.3 Parallels between master-disciple and husband-wife relation

Obviously, this function of putting in perfect relationship comes out mainly in the major *saṃskāras* like *upanayana* (between the master and the disciple), *vivāha* (between the husband and the wife), and *antyeṣṭi* (between the living and the dead, once the latter is transformed into a mane or ancestor). Some parallels can be drawn between *upanayana* and *vivāha* as to the nature of the relation instituted by these *saṃskāras.* The disciple leaves his parental house and stays for a couple of years at his master's house (under his authority and that of his wife) where he learns to recite the *Veda* by heart in perfect chastity.

Similarly the young girl (who must be a virgin) leaves the house of her parents to live under his husband's authority and that of his in-laws to whom she owes due respect. Both the disciple and the young married girl owe complete obedience and fidelity to their masters, *ācārya* and *svāmin* (or *pati*) respectively. There is of course a mutual dependency and it is not a "one way" relation. The master in *Veda,* always a Brāhmaṇa, depends on the services rendered by his disciple (and *vice versa*), so does the husband on his wife (and *vice versa*). True, in the first, it is a *vidyā-saṃbandha,* because the teacher imparts the *Veda.* In the

[36] *Manu Smṛti* IX. 8; Cf. *Yājñavalkya-Smṛti* I.56; III.19.

second it is above all a relation for procreation purposes, *prajā*, to ensure one's descendance. The husband is for the wife, her teacher from whom she learns the *Veda* and the Vedic rites. From the point of view of the theory of human goals (*puruṣārtha*), in the master-disciple relation the consideration for the *dharma* intervens above all. In the husband-wife relation, it is the desire to procreate and enjoy life (*kāma, rati*) which occupies the main place, hand in hand obviously with the consideration of the other two objectives—*dharma* and *artha*. The married life is the occasion to fulfil the aspirations and values contained in the *trivarga*.

6. *Saṃskāra* and *adhikāra*

This fifth function or purpose of Hindu *saṃskāras* is one of the most important ones. The ritual qualification (*adhikāra*) confered by a *saṃskāra*, for example, by *upanayana*, produces a transformation in the status of one who receives it, making him capable, eligible, competent (*yogya, yogyatā*). This takes place by addition of new qualities or by substraction of defects or imperfections.[37] Rites produce an invisible power called *apūrva* ("without precedent", invisible fruits of rites), either after the death of the sacrificer (supposed to obtain a sojourn in the heaven or *svarga*), or in this world, here itself, in the person of one who is thus sacralised, in shape of "acquired dispositions" (*saṃskāra*).

6.1 Becoming a "twice-born"

All the *saṃskāras*, from the conception rite till the cremation rite, are supposed to confer a specific ritual qualification or capacitation (*adhikāra*) as says the *Manu Smṛti* II.16 and the *Vaikhānasa Smārta Sūtra* VIII.1–4. Nevertheless, it is

[37] See *Tantravārttika*, p. 1078; The rites which confer a capacity are called *saṃskāras*. See Śabara ad Jaimini, *Pūrva Mīmāṃsā Sūtra* III.1.3. A *saṃskāra* is that by which an object becomes capable of attaining its goal. Śaṅkara *ad Brahma Sūtra* (= *Brahma Sūtra Bhāṣya*), I.1.4 gives the same precision: sacralization takes place by the addition of a quality (*guṇa*) or by the substraction of a defect (*doṣa*).

upanayana, an obligatory *saṃskāra*, followed by *vivāha* in due time which really gives access to all sacrificial activities, solemn or domestic, making the person fit for accomplishing all his socio-religious duties.[38] One is not born a "twice-born" (*dvija, dvijāti*) but becomes one only after having been initiated to the *Veda* by the master (who must be a *Brāhmaṇa* himself). Only a male, belonging to three "pure" higher classes or castes (*varṇa*), *Brāhmaṇa*, *Kṣatriya*, *Vaiśya*, have the prequalification or the privilege to receive *upanayana* (inaugurating the *brahmacaryāśrama*). Rights depend on rites. The son of a *Śūdra* remains a "once born" (*eka-jāti*)[39] throughout his life, having no access to this fundamental *saṃskāra*. So being born from high caste parents is a factor which counts a lot and works like a "prequalification". But it is only after the initiation rite, by becoming a *dvija* oneself, independently on one's own account, that the person obtains the required qualification (*adhikāra*) or ability, capacity, competence, right, authority. Without having learnt the *Veda* by heart through daily recitation (*svādhyāya*), and all that the *Veda* teaches and prescribes, the son of a *dvija* remains a simple, once born, having a biological birth only.[40] The part played by pre-qualification plus by real qualification taken together, obtained by the *upanyana-saṃskāra*, is well mentioned in *Manusmṛti*.[41]

---

[38] On the components of ritual qualification (*adhikāra*), see Jaimini, *Pūrva Mīmāṃsā Sūtra* VI.1.1, *sq.* (*adhikāranyāya*) with the Commentary of Śabara.

[39] Contrary to *dvijāti* or *dvija* ("twice born"), a *śūdra* is devoid of the ritual qualification: *adhikārahīna*. See *Manu Smṛti* X, 4; *Gautama Dharma Sūtra*, X.50; *Yājñavalkya-Smṛti* III.262.

[40] See *Atri Smṛti* 141–142 quoted by P.V. Kane, vol. II, Pt. I, p. 189, note 444. R.B. Pandey, *Hindu Saṃskāras*, p. 30, n. 27. The *Yoga Vārttika* III.7 (Vijñānabhikṣu's Commentary on the *Yoga Sūtra* of Patañjali) quotes a text similar to the *Atri Smṛti* with some variants.

[41] See *Manu Smṛti* X.69 and X.59; Medhātithi *ad* Manu, I.28; *Parāśāra Smṛti* VIII.19.

6.2 Caste and *karman*

It is however a different question, although quite important from the philosophical angle, as to why one is born in a high or a low caste, why sane or insane, why healthy or sick, with physical or mental deformations? The link between caste and *karman* (deliberate or intentional act—corporal, vocal, mental—acts with their good and bad consequences, remaining as latent impressions deposited in the subtle psyche) is well established in ancient Indian texts. Where do rituals meet the psyche or leave their impact on it?—This is the issue. In contemporary India, the belief in the relationship between *karman* and caste is still very much alive although ritualistic part of the Hindu *saṃskāras* has almost fallen in oblivion.

This also means that although *saṃskāras*, understood in their psychological meaning can be somehow transferred from parents to children, in shape of natural dispositions (*bhāva, svabhāva*), the ritual qualification (*adhikāra*) cannot be so transferred. That is why if a male does not receive himself the *upanayana-saṃskāra*, latest by the age of eight, ten, or twelve (age limit for a son of *Brāhmaṇa, Kṣatriya*, and *Vaiśya* respectively), he falls from his condition and becomes a *patita-sāvitrīka*.[42] Vedic "transmission" rite (*saṃpratti*)[43] describes how the father when he is about to depart, transfers his holy knowledge, his sacrifices, his speech, breath, eye, ear [....], deeds (*karman*), etc., to his son, a transfer of *adhikāra* from father to son remains impossible.

An interesting question comes to mind in the light of the *Bhagavad Gītā*, XVIII.41–48 to other fundamental

[42] One who has fallen from his socio-religious rank because of not having been initiated by the Vedic *mantra*, the *sāvitrī*, pronounced by the *ācārya* during the ceremony. See *Manu Smṛti* II.38–40; *Vas.-Dharma-Sūtra*, XI.74; *Baudhāyana-Dharma-Sūtra*, II.1.1.16; *Gautama-Dharma-Sūtra*, XXI.11.

The *Sāvitrī (Ṛg Veda Saṃhitā* III.62.10) is the verse dedicated to Savitṛ, "Incitator", or the Sun worshipped as God.

[43] See (BĀU) = *Bṛhad Āraṇyaka Upaniṣad* V.1.17; and specially *Kauṣītaki Upaniṣad* II.15.

concepts such as *karman, svakarman, svadharma, svabhāva, guṇa,* etc. —Can a *saṃskāra* (ritually conferred to a person) be considered to be a sort of "graft" or "transplant" on one's raw intrinsic nature (*svabhāva*) with which one comes to the world? Or, is there an inherent predisposition to be so? To answer these questions we have to consider certain factors —the biological plus the kārmic heredity of a person, the inculcated cultural acquisitions through *saṃskāras*—marked and consecrated by these ceremonies jointly.

Only a *dvija* has the *adhikāra* of receiving the last sacrament (*antyeṣṭi*) with recitation of Vedic *mantras.*[44] The *post-mortem* rituals can be performed only after this ceremony. Through *śrāddhas,* and *sapiṇḍīkaraṇa* the staute of the dead changes because the *preta* becomes a *pitṛ.* This integration in the group of manes has such an importance that an orthodox Hindu even gets his *jīvatśrāddha* performed while he is still alive. During the cremation ceremony, preference is given to the eldest son. All *dvijas* and their legal wives (*dharma-patnī*) and children, whose *nāmakaraṇa* and *cūḍākaraṇa* were accomplished, can have their last rites done. Small age children are buried. Burial (and not incineration) is also the rule for ascetics or renouncers (*saṃnyāsin, yati*) also. Although there is an exception in the case of Siddhārtha Gautama, the Buddha, great ascetic, for whom a royal cremation was accomplished as described in the *Mahāparinibbāna Sutta.* The renouncers are purified by the inner fire of *tapas* and by the fire of knowledge (*jñāna-agni*).

7. Continuity of generations

An important function of the Hindu *saṃskāras* is continuity of generations. This is perpetuated through *garbhādhāna, puṃsavana, upanayana, vivāha* and *antyeṣṭi* (followed by *śrāddhas*). The birth of a male after marriage, once that the son (*putra*)[45] has duly received the *upanayana,* permits the

[44] See *Manu Smṛti* V.167–68.

[45] On the importance of a male, see *Manu Smṛti* IX.137–38; *Bṛhadāraṇyaka Upaniṣad,* I.5.16.

transmission of the *Veda* appertaining to one's own lineage or family ("branch", *svaśākhā*) and to keep it alive.[46] It is one and the same thing to beget a wife, to engender a son, and to perpetuate oneself as shows the classification of human "desires" (*eṣaṇā*)[47] equated with *vāsanā* in Śaṅkara's Commentary to the *Bṛhadāraṇyaka Upaniṣad* III. 5.1; IV.4.22.

7.1 Perpetuation of *dharma*

The master and the disciple belong to the same *Vedic-gotra*, have a same *gotra-ṛṣi* in common.[48] The daily and personal recitation of the Vedic text by the student (as well as the householder) consolidates the *vidyā-vaṃśa*.[49] The funeral rites hold good for the transmission of ancestral lineage and cultural heritage till the seventh generation. Texts insist that the manes (*pitṛ*) are supposed to confer a male descendant the continuation of generations.[50] This may be suggested that it is the ancestor who comes back or is "reborn" in the shape of a son. The treatise on laws (*Dharma Śāstra*) recommend that one who desires to beget a son should make his wife eat the rice ball (*piṇḍa*), which is offered to sacrifiant grand-father.[51] Here we can see the rapport of the two verb roots *sam-tān-* (to tend, to extend) and *saṃskṛ*. The modern

[46] The Veda is kept alive through the ceremony of *upanayana* and all that follows. If not one becomes a "killer of Veda" (*Āpas-Dharma-Sūtra*, I.1.1.32. On the contrary, if the Veda was kept well alive throughout the generations through the *Veda-vratas*, one can even draw a benefit out of this heritage: for instance the duration of the *vrata* relative to *mahānamni* verses can thus be reduced to one year (instead of twelve, nine, six or three years). See *Gobhila-Gṛhya.-Sūtra*, III.2.1–6.

[47] The "desire to preserve one's vital breaths" (*prāṇa-eṣaṇā*), the "desire to beget a son" (*putra-eṣaṇā*) and the "desire to beget a wife" (*dāra-eṣaṇā*) are strictly identical according to Caraka. See *Caraka Saṃhitā* XI.3; XXIX.7. See L. KAPANI: "Remarques sur la notion de *vāsanā*" in *Bulletin d'Études Indiennes*, n° 3, 1985, p. 79–102; 201–02.

[48] *Manu Smṛti* II.205; *Viṣṇu Smṛti* XXIV.9; *Āpas-Dharma-Sūtra*, I.2.7.12.

[49] *Āpas.-Dharma-Sūtra*, I.2.7.12.

[50] See *Gobhila-Gṛhya-Sūtra*, III.5.32; *Hir.-Gṛhya-Sūtra*, II.4.10; *Vai.-Smārta-Sūtra*, IV.6; *Viṣṇu Smṛti* LXII, 21; *Khādira-Gṛhya-Sūtra*, II.5.32.

[51] See *Manu Smṛti* III.262.

Hindi word for designating "children" (*samtāna*), those who prolong and transmit the tradition later on, receives all its meaning. They can do so because they themselves have received the cultural heritage through the eternal sacred chain of master-disciple *paraṃparā*, which keeps alive *sanatāna-dharma.*

8. *Saṃskāra* and *dharma*

In *Dharma Śāstra* literature these Hindu rites or *saṃskāras* are dealt with in the context of *varṇāśramadharma* (rights and duties of a male belonging to this or that caste while he is in this or that stage of his life). Norm is introduced in the life of an adolescent just after *upanayana* (till the *samāvartana*). After this during *brahmacaryāśrama*, the chaste Vedic student helps his master and his legal wife (*dharmapatnī*) for twelve (or more) years to accomplish their sacred duties (*dharma*) properly. His relation to the *dharma* is further established through daily *svādhyāya of* the *Veda*, which is equal to *Brahaman* and *Oṃ.*[52] The *Bhagavad Gītā* advises "continence (*brahmacarya*) and "non-violence" (*ahiṃsā*) during Vedic studies. "Worshipping the gods, the twice-born, teachers and wise men—purity, straight forwardness, continence, and abstinence from injury are termed the bodily austerity (*śārīram tapas*)".[53] His personal and active contribution in the perpetuation of *dharma* starts only after marriage (*vivāha*) in the company of his legal wife after the ritual fires are laid. The *gṛhasthāśrama* is the perfect stage for the pursuit and fulfilment of the three human worldly aims or goals (*trivarga, puruṣārtha*)–*kāma, artha* and *dharma*. What about the final or supreme human goal (*parama-puruṣārtha*), i.e., deliverance (*mokṣa*)?—Is there any

[52] See AB VI.32. Vedic *mantras* are preceded by the sacred syllable *oṃ* = A U M = *Ṛg Veda, Yajur Veda, Sāma Veda,* represented by the three liturgique exclamations: *bhūr, bhuvar, svar.* See =ŚB VI.1.1.10.

[53] *Bhagavad Gītā* XVII.14. See *The Bhagavad-Gītâ with the commentary of Śrī Śaṅkarācārya,* translated into English by A. Mahādeva Śastri, Mysore, India, 1901.

possibilty of pursuing it while one is in the *brahmacaryāśrama* or in the *gṛhasthāśrama*?—Yes, but such cases are rare. We know the case of Śaṅkarācārya (philosopher and exegate of the Veda), who remained life long with his master in the Vedas as a *naiṣṭhika-brahmacārin*. A *gṛhastha* can orient himself towards liberation (*mukti, mokṣa*) through the practice of egoless and desireless actions, by dedicating them to Lord Kṛṣṇa.[54]

To confer *saṃskāras* to his offspring is one of the sacred duties (*dharma*) of a father, specially the sacrament of *upanayana* and *vivāha*. A *dvija* becomes a *vrātya*[55] if he forgets to confer these perfective rites to his children. The relation between *saṃskāra* and *dharma* iṣ so deep that the *Dharma Śāstras* teach and enjoin rules to prohibit such omissions.[56]

9. *Vaiṣṇava* and *Śaiva-saṃskāras*

To conclude, let me just mention a word about the role played.by *saṃskāras* in *Vaiṣṇava, Śaiva,* and *Tantra* literature. There are five "sacraments" in the *Vaiṣṇavite* initiation—a red mark through heated iron rod (*tāpa*) on the two shoulders of the adept with the image of the two emblems of the disc and the conch of Viṣṇu. The sectarian sign traced on the front (*puṇḍara*), gift of a (initiatic) name (*nāman*) and a *mantra,* with the recommendation of adoring Viṣṇu with the help of his image (*yāga*).[57] What they have in common with the *śarīra-saṃskāras* is the purification brought about through rituals and the visible signs producing invisible effects on the psycho-somatic level.

9.1 *Śarīra-saṃskāra* versus *ātma-saṃskāra*

As to the Śaiva "sacraments", instead of the appellation *śarīra-saṃskāra,* the *Somaśambhupaddhati* names them *ātma-*

[54] See *Bhagavad Gītā* II.47–51; 71; III.27;30; VI.1, etc.

[55] See Manu X.20; XI.59 and 62.

[56] See *Vaikh-Dharma-Sūtra,* VI.1.sq.; VII.1.sq.

[57] See J. GONDA, *Change and Continuity in Indian Religion,* La Haye, 1965, pp. 398–403.

saṃskāra and insists on the fact that these rites affect the spiritual part of an adept.[58] The Vedic rites are considered to be an obstacle in the path of purificaton by the *Śaiva* masters. Whereas the *śarīra-saṃskāras* (expression found in Manu II.26) aim at a better integration of man in the socio-religious world, the *ātma-saṃskāras* have in view the integration of the adept in the person of *Śiva.* They are oriented towards deliverance or liberation (*mukti*). Liberation is in effect, the final aim of the *saṃskāra-dīkṣā* which precedes the final liberation or *nirvāṇa-dīkṣā.* The (individual) *ātman* is relieved from the hindrances or obstacles, specially of its inherent impurities (*mala*). Thus liberated (*mukta*), the *ātman* of the adept becomes a part and parcel of *Śiva* himself (*Śivāṇu*).

In the Tantric perspective, not only the adept but also the fire and the formulas are consecrated in order to render them efficient. Here are, for instance, the ten "sacraments" confered to a *mantra* according to the *Śāradātilaka Tantra*[59]—procreation (*janana*), vivification (*jīvana*), smiting (*tāḍana*), awakening (*bodhana*), sprinkling (*abhiṣeka*), purification (*vimalīkaraṇa*), fattening (*āpyayana*), satisfying through libation (*tarpaṇa*), illumination (*dīpana*), and concealment (*gopana*).

---

[58] *Somaśambhupaddhati*, texte, traduction et notes par Héléne Brunner-Lachaux, Institut Français d'Indologie, Pondichery, 1977, Pts. II and XLI.

[59] Quoted in the *Sarva-darśana-saṃgraha* of Madhvācārya, tr. by E.B. Cowell and A.E. Gough, Kegan Paul, 1st edn. 1904, (Popular re-issue, 1914, pp. 258–60).

CHAPTER III

The Buddhist Attitude Towards *Saṃskāras*

1. Introduction

Shifting from Brahmanical and Hindu tradition towards Buddhist texts *Sutta-*, *Vinaya-*, *Abhidhamma Piṭaka,* and *Mahāyāna* literature, one seems to enter in an altogether different world as far as vocabulary is concerned.

1.1 Vocabulary features

Words belonging to the same linguistic family, verbs *saṃskṛ-*, *abhisaṃskṛ-*, adjective *saṃskṛta* (Pāli *saṃkharoti, abhisaṃkharoti, saṃkhata*), which used to carry a deep sacramental significance are now desacralized, devalorized. On the contrary, their opposites are praised to an utmost degree. Thus *visaṅkhāra, visaṅkhita,* (Sk. *visaṃskāra, visaṃskṛta*) are used in the famous passage of Dhammapada 154 to indicate the supreme deconstruction, explicitly identified with *nibbāna* (Sk. *nirvāṇa* "extinction" of desires, passions, and ego bound to suffer, tied in the transmigration).[1]

---

[1] Cf. (Ud.=) *Udāna,* 31.7, PTS, London; ed. J. Kashyap, translation by F. L. Woodward, *The Minor Anthologies of the Pāli Canon,* Part 2, *Udāna: Verses of Uplift and Ittivuttaka:* as it was said, Sacred Books of the Buddhist, 8, Oxford, 1935, reprint 1948.

While quoting from the Pāli Canon I have used Pāli words giving its Sanskrit (=Sk.) equivalent most of the time. But to unify, and for all practical purposes, the word *saṃskāra* is retained and replaces *saṃkhāra.*

The *Mahāyāna Sūtrālaṃkāra* gives a privileged place to these pairs of opposites—*abhisaṃskāra/anabhisaṃskāra; abhisaṃskṛta/anabhisaṃskṛta.* Whereas effort, intention, coordinating tension sustain a *bodhisattva* during first seven stages (*bhūmi*). From the eighth stage onwards, called immobile (*acala*), his spiritual carrier continues to gain maturity all by itself, without effort or intention, spontaneously. Thus the hierarchy is inversed, *anabhisaṃskṛ-* appears as the crowning achievement of *abhisaṃskṛ-*.

1.2 Anthropological remarks

Some anthropological remarks are necessary. They show a complete reversal of values. The attitude of a layman, householder, versus that of a monk or renouncer towards house, fire, fire-cult, family life, presence of women—specially the feeling of security and comfort attached to these —is obviously not the same. The difference between those who stay at home and those who take up the homeless life (*agāra/anāgāra*) is well-known in Buddhist texts. A Buddhist monk takes refuge in the Buddha, in his doctrine (*Dhamma,* Sk. *Dharma*), in his community (*saṃgha*). The Buddhist attitude towards *saṃskāras* has to be understood in this particular anthropological context. The famous *Dhammapada* 153-54:

> Looking for the maker of this tabernacle, I shall have to run through a course of many births, so long as I do not find (him), and painful is birth again and again. But now, maker of the tabernacle, thou hast been seen; thou shalt not make up this tabernacle again. All thy rafters are broken, thy ridge-pole is sundered; the mind, approaching the Eternal (*visaṅkhāra, nirvāṇa*) has attained to the extinction of desires (lit., "having ceased to assemble, the mind has attained cessation of desires")[2]. "All, O! monks is on fire!";[3] "All

[2] The *Dhammapada,* A collection of verses, translated from Pāli by F. Max MÜLLER, SBE, Vol. X, Pt. I, Oxford University Press, 1881; Motilal Banarsidass, Delhi, 1965 sq.

[3] (Vin.=) *Vinaya* I.34 (*sabbaṃ bhikkhave ādittaṃ*). Vinaya Piṭaka, ed. H. OLDENBERG, 5 vols., London, 1879–83; ed. KASHYAP, 5 vols., Pāli Publication Board, Nalanda, 1956–58. Translation: *Vinaya Texts,* by RHYS DAVIDS and H. OLDENBERG, SBE, vol. 13, 17, 20, Oxford, 1881–85, *The Book of Discipline*

psycho-physical compositions are on fire!" (*ādīptāḥ sarve saṃskārāḥ*)[4] and so many other Buddhist texts become clearer, when axiological criterion is taken into consideration.

In these quotations, the negative and destructive aspect of fire comes out clearly, *nibbāna* being extinction of threefold fire—passion, hatred, delusion, (*rāga, dosa* [*Sk. dveṣa*], *moha*).[5]

The contrast in the evaluation of the concept of *saṃskāra* comes out much more clearly in Buddhist phraseology. Well-known refrains describe "psycho-physical constructions as worst of sorrows" (*saṅkhārā paramā dukkhā*), "Extinction as topmost happiness" (*nibbānaṃ paramaṃ sukhaṃ*)[6]; "transitory, in fact, are the constructions, their nature is to appear and disappear (...)". Verse pronounced by Indra-Sakka just before the Final Extinction (*parinibbāna*) of Gautama, the Buddha[7]; "transitory are all constructions, painful, deprived of self...)" (*aniccā sabbe saikhārā dukkhā anattā...*),[8] reveal the Buddhist attitude towards them. Going deeper into this analysis, one finds, in the very beginning of the Discourse on Dependent Origination— "conditioned by ignorance are the psycho-physical constructions" (*avijjā-paccayāsaṅkhāra*).[9] Therefore, they are similar to a banana plant (*saṅkhārā kadalūpamā*),[10] compared to the fallacious trunk of plantain

(*Vinayapiṭaka*), L.B. Horner, Sacred Books of the Buddhists, vol. 10, 11, 13, Oxford, 1938–42.

[4] (Pr=) *Prasannapadā*, 296, 13. Candrakīrti's Commentary on the *Mūlamadhyamaka Kārikās* of Nāgārjuna.

[5] (SN=) *Saṃyutta Nikāya*, IV, p. 359. In Buddhist texts *nibbāna = asaṅkhāra*, (Sk. *nirvāṇa = asaṃskṛta*) are identified with *rāga, dosa* (Sk. *dveṣa*), *moha*. The cessation of passion (passional attachment), hatred (and anger), mental distraction, is equal to Extinction known as Un-composed (*asaṅkhata*). See also Pr., 563–3. In the Hindu context, the *Bhagavad Gītā* verses II.62–63 come to mind where the expressions are: *saṅga-kāma-krodha-saṃmoha*.

[6] (DhP=) *Dhammapada*, 203.

[7] See (DN=) *Dīgha Nikāya*, II, p. 157.

[8] *Parivāra* 3, 1, Vin., V, p. 86.

[9] Vin., I, p.1; (MN=) *Majjhima Nikāya*, I, p. 261; SN, II, p. 1; (AN=) *Aṅguttara Nikāya*, II, p. 177, etc.

[10] SN II, p. 142.

tree, frequent symbol of unsubstantiality, transitoriness, worthlessness.[11] A monk should be aware of this and try to realize their blessed appeasement—*saṃskāropaśamaṃ śivaṃ.*[12]

The great sage (*mahesi*) is he who is "skilled in the knowledge of suppression of constructions" (*saṅkhāra-nirodha-ñāna kusala*)[13] when confronted with Māra, God of death and desire. In the classical list of four Māras, Kkhandha-Māra is particularly related to *saṅkhāra,* taken in a broad sense. In the *Saṃyutta Nikāya* III. (p.95), the five aggregates of appropriation are identified with Māra. A later list adds Abhisaṅkhāra-Māra as fifth, personification of *kamma* (Sk. *karman*).[14] Thus, the concept of *saṅkhāra/saṃskāra* works rather in a negative context in Buddhist texts.

1.3 Translation problems

Two most difficult words to translate in Western languages are undoubtedly *saṅkhāra* and *dhamma* (Sk. *dharma*), there being no perfect equivalent. Though "confection" is an exact philological reproduction for *saṃskāra,* a minor inconvenience is its strange and unexpected use in a philosophical context. "Coefficients", "Co-operants", seem better.[15] The dynamic meaning of the root *kṛ-*, (to do,

[11] See (Vis.=) *Visuddhimagga,* p. 479 : *kadalīkkhando viya saṅkhārā,* Pr. 41, 10 : *saṃskārāḥ kadalīnibhāḥ*

[12] Pr. 42, 3.

[13] (Sn.=) *Suttanipāta* 371.

[14] See Commentary on *Udāna* p. 216, 11 and MALALASEKERA, *Dictionary of Pāli Proper Names,* pp. 611–13.

[15] Translations for *saṃskāra* proposed by some eminent Sanskritists : "coefficients" (Oltramare, Gnoli), "opérants" (S. Lévi, De Jong); "synergies" (Rhys Davids); "gestaltungen" (Oldenberg), karma-gestaltende Kräfte, Triebkräfte (Glasenapp); karmisches Gestalten (Nyāṇaponika Bhikkhu); "formations mentales", "dispositions aquises" (Madeleine Biardeau); "formations mentales","schèmes dynamiques" (Olivier Lacombe); "motivations" (A. Wayman);"énergies coordonnatrices intentionnelles", "tendances subconscientes", "complexes" (L. Silburn);"confections", "constructions psychiques" (J. Filliozat); "compositions", "composants" (A. Bareau); "composants, composés" (J. May).

perform, act) and hence the idea of "synergy" should be kept in mind. The prefix *sam-*, "together" renders the idea of assembling together or uniting. Translations by "compositions", "composants", "composed", can result in a good comprehension, only if the musical acceptation of the word "composition" to make a singular arrangement with the help of a plurality of notes or words is present. Moreover, in the majority of cases, the word *saṅkhāra/saṃskāra* figures as a plural and should be adequately translated, because it has an organic role to play in the Buddhist doctrine of *karman* and non-substantiality of soul. Philological problems have their philosophical consequences. When singular, *saṃskāra* or *abhisaṃskāra* mean "intention" directed towards its realization.

Another problem, particularly important from a philosophical point of view is that a shift of meaning takes place between *saṃskāra/saṃskṛta*. Thus *sarve saṃskārāḥ* (lit.,"all compositions", "all psycho-physical constructions") signifies "all that is constructed or conditioned", meaning "all that exists". Far from being a misuse of language, an arbitrary laxity, this sort of use and semantic sliding reveal the Buddhist way of looking at things—*saṃskāra* covers all that falls under experience, internal or external, that of an ordinary human being (*puthujjana/pṛthagjana*) or of a *yogin*. Equal to *dharma saṃskṛta,* it is the opposite of *asaṃskṛta, nirvāṇa.* The pair *saṃskṛta/asaṃskṛta* represent the whole kārmic potential under both its active and passive aspects. This use is directly derived from the Law of Dependent Origination (*paṭiccasamuppāda/pratītyasamutpāda*).

2. *Saṃskāra* as the fourth appropriational group and as the second "link"

In Hīnayāna and Mahāyāna literature[16] the concept of *saṃskāra* is accepted—1. *saṅkhāra-kkhandha/saṃskāra-*

[16] The use of the word *saṃskāra* as a synonym of *saṃskṛta* is quite typical to Buddhist literature. Except *asaṅkhata/asaṃskṛta =nibbāna/nirvāṇa,* everything else is in the world is *saṃskṛta.*

skandha, fourth amongst the five groups of appropriation (*pañca-upādāna-skandha*); 2. *saṅkhāra/saṃskāra* is counted as the second "link" or "factor of becoming" (*nidāna, bhavāṅga*), in the context of *pratītyasamutpāda.*

A static analysis of the composed human personality, made of – *rūpa-, vedanā-, saññā-* (*saṃjñā-*) – *saṃkhāra-* (*saṃskāra*), and *viññāna-* (*vijññna-*) *upādāna-kkhandha* (*skandha*), is in fact an inventory of I, me, mine. The significant word "appropriation" (*upādāna*) indicates the making of our personality through gestures and reflexes. In other words, there is primacy of *kamma* (*karman*) on *attā* (*ātman*). The latter, in its ontological acceptation, is rejected in Buddhist thought.

In a nut-shell, the group of matter-form accounts for the physical frame of the human body in relation with the outer world. That of sensations (pleasant, unpleasant, neutral) cover our total emotional life. The third group of appropriation comprehends notions, ideas, concepts, denomination, in short, our linguistic equipment, a sort of software that we carry with ourselves everywhere.

2.1 Group of volitions or psycho-physical constructions

The *saṃskāra-upādāna-skandha* (group of volitions or psycho-physical constructions) is a sort of "packet" made of will-to-live, will-to-experience and will-to-become. This corresponds to the intentional vectorial dimension of our personality, neither circumscribed like our past by the *fait accompli,* nor by our immediate present. As future oriented, it comprises

---

The Buddha spoke in Pāli, mass language derived from Māgadhī, and not in Sanskrit reserved to the Brahmanical circle whose doctrines and table of values he criticized. It is but natural not to find a laudatory review of the Sanskrit language (*saṃskṛta-bhāṣā*) in the Pāli Canon, *saṃskṛta* denoting: "perfect", "purified" and "embellished" by grammatical rules. The pan-Indian normal and positive use of the verbs: *saṃskṛ-, abhisaṃskṛ-, prati-saṃskṛ-* is however attested in Buddhist texts, but on the transactional and practical level only: *vyavahāra-* or *saṃvṛti-satya.* For example preparing or elaborating a question: *te pañham abhisaṃkharonti* (MN II, p. 122); "repairing" a *stūpa,* etc. (*Divyāvadāna,* 22.18).

simultaneously a tension of will (*āyuhāna,* cf., *conatus*), a display of imagination. The part of deception is not yet totally explicit in it, though the idea of horizon is fully present. Objectively, it appears as a field of possibilities, subjectively, as a field of tendencies, a potential of action and of mobilization. This passage to action is of course not a *first* beginning. Generally, behind a present initiative, a set of ideomotor reactions are hidden. Let's call it taking a stand in response to a given situation, in which our emotional and vital interests are deeply involved. The Buddhist theory of *saṃskāra* needs to be interpreted in this sense. Herein lies the ambiguity of human freedom—freedom of reacting, not so much of acting. This argument is based on the very fact that amongst various factors which constitute the *saṃskāra-skandha,* "contact" or "touch" (*phassa, sparśa*) is the first constituent; then follows "ideation" or "volition" (*cetanā*). Contact plays an important part in the doctrine of *pratītyasamutpāda* too.

Moreover *saṃskāra-skandha* represents a field of forces inherited from past actions, which enter once again into action, on occasion of fresh circumstances. One re-assumes this potential, sometimes in a deliberate, voluntary manner, sometimes unconsciously, without prior knowledge or deliberation, in shape of drives or urges. Ancient Buddhist texts, those of *Vinaya,* put emphasis on deliberate and conscious appropriation. Those of *Mahāyāna,* make a larger place for subconscious or unconscious aspects of the same. In both cases, *saṃskāra-skandha* is the point of incessant transition from potential force to actions and from actions to accumulated forces reserved for future actions. This results in good or bad personality. This constitutes our personal series (*saṃtati*), and as such, our temporality–projects, worries, promises, interviews, wishes–so many ways of prefiguring all that we long "to be" and become. In this manner, we carry ourselves before and beyond ourselves, although, identifying ourselves with what we are.

2.2 Relation between *saṃskāra-skandha* and the other *skandhas*

Without the appropriational group of consciousness (*vijñāna-upādāna-skandha*), the whole material made of *skandhas* will remain unconscious, if it was not "informed" by so many acts of selective punctual attention, a sort of focusing and tuning. These flashes of consciousness are not separated from objects thus enlightened. No thinking soul or consciousness as such (over and above visible, tangible or any other sensory data) is admitted in Buddhism. For a Buddhist, as it is the case with analytical philosophy, the cartesian *cogito* is a pure illusion. Mobile, *vijñāna* is compared to a monkey, jumping from branch to branch.

All these five personality making factors work together. To this functional, nominal and conventional unity, the Buddhist prefer to give the designation of *pudgala* or *nāma-rūpa* (name and form). The (false) belief in a substantial ontological kernel like *ātman* ("self", "soul") cannot but render renunciation, philosophical deconstruction, and final extinction all the more difficult. The "chariot" (*ratha*) simile,[17] the famous dialogue of nun Vajīrā with Māra, etc., reveal justly that a human being is nothing but an assemblage or network of *saṃskāras* (*suddha saṃkhārapuñjo*)[18], *dharma saṃskṛta.* Thus, in the compound *saṃskāra-skandha, saṃskāra* oversteps the fourth *skandha* and extends to all other personality making factors taken together.[19]

2.3 Relation between *saṃskāra-skandha* and *cetanā*

An internal inventory of the *saṃskāra-skandha* examines the relation between *saṃskāra* and *cetanā,* one of the chief constituents of the list. The number of mental activities (*cittasampayuttā-cetasikā dhammā*), good, bad and morally

---

[17] *Saṃyukta Āgama,* anonyme, Taishō Issaikyō, nº 99, p. 327b, French translation, A. BAREAU in *Bouddha,* Paris, Seghers, 1962, p. 115.

[18] *Saṃyutta,* I, p. 135.

[19] *Saṃyutta,* III, p. 87.

neutral, listed under *saṃkhāra-kkhandha* differs: fifty-two (*Abhidhamma Sangha*), fifty (*Dhamma-saṅgaṇi*), fifty-eight (*Sarvastivāda* tradition).

In the *Dhamma-saṅgaṇi cetanā*, in a large sense "understanding", "active thought", "intention", "deliberation" (including "reasoning" and "reflection", *vitakka, vicāra*) is said to be synonymous with *saṃkhāra-kkhandha*. In a narrower sense, *cetanā* is that which coordinates perceptive data, an automatic mental activity, making full use of acquired habits, etc.[20] Here its affinity with *saṃkhāra* understood as "psychological construction" (conscious, subconscious, unconscious) is more evident.

The meaning of the word *cetanā* seems to have evolved a lot in course of time. It signifies the mental act (*manas-karman*) of decision, which involves the moral or kārmic responsibility of the agent. In any case, it remains the "conductor" of the *saṃskāra-skandha*, explicitly equated with "six classes of volitions".[21] The *Abhidharma Kośa*[22] defines *cetanā* as that condition, which informs and models the thought (*cittābhisaṃskāra*). An example taken from the domain of cookery compares the five groups (*pañca-upādāna-skandha*) to the cooking-pot, ailment, condiment, cook and eater respectively,[23] putting accent on the fabricating aspect of *saṃskāras*. The *Aṅgutara Nikāya* III (p. 415) identifies "act" (*kamma*) with *cetanā* ("ideation", "will", "intention") and *cetayitvā* with bodily, vocal and mental acts. In fact, the fabricating or synthesizing activity of *saṃskāras* works in the very field of all that is already composed, i.e., subject to origin, duration, destruction. These three characteristics of the

[20] A. Bareau, *Dhammasaṅgani*, trad. annotée: Index-Glossaire, p. 31, art. *cetanā;* and p. 23; 32.

[21] SN III, 60.

[22] AK=*Abhidharma Kośa* II, 24. See *Abhidharmakośa and Bhāṣya of Ācārya Vasubandhu with Sphuṭārthā Commentary of Ācārya Yaśomitra*, critically ed. by Swami Dwarkidas Shastri, Bauddha Bharati, Varanasi, 1970, Part I, p. 186–87.

[23] *Ibid.*, I, 22, Pt. I, p. 66–67.

composed (*saṃskṛta-lakṣaṇa*) belong to the category of *citta-viprayukta-saṃskāra* ("compositions disassociated from conscious thought"). The three characteristics of the uncomposed (*asaṃskṛta, nirvāṇa*) are just the opposites of the former.[24]

3. *Saṃskāra* as the second "link"

The Four Noble Truths expounded in the Sermon of Banaras[25] and the Law of Dependent Origination (*paṭiccasamuppapāda, pratītyasamutpāda* = P) are two well-known starting points of Buddhist doctrine. The use of *saṅkhāra* in the compound *saṅkhāra-kkhandha* (attested in the S) is more ancient than its use as the second "link" or "factor of becoming" (*nidāna, bhavāṅga*) in the twelve-fold circular chain of origination in mutual dependence, where the concept of *saṅkhāra* furnishes a dynamic analysis of the human condition. These two problematics are also quite different, though not without relationship.

In the Four Noble Truths (*ariya-sacca, ārya-satya*), etiology of suffering (*dukkha*, Sk. *duḥkha*) is primarily ascribed to "thirst" (*taṇhā*, Sk. *tṛṣṇā*) or desire, whereas in P, the first "link" is "misknowledge" or ignorance (*avijjā*, Sk. *avidyā*). This should not be interpreted as the first cause, there being no place for such a belief in the Buddhist perspective. Thirst comes in the eighth position as a sort of far-off echo of *avidyā*.

In its abstract and nonvariable aspects, *paṭiccasamuppapāda* is expounded as the Law of Things, how they come and pass away. A second dimension of this Law is its application to

[24]See AN I, p. 152. See Sanskrit equivalents in *Saṃyukta Āgama*, XII.21; *Prasannapadā*, 145. 4–5.

[25] (= S). It is the first Sermon of Siddhārtha Gautama the Buddha after his Enlightenment (*bodhi*, equal to *nibbāna/nirvāṇa* in this very life): *Dhamma-cakka-pabbatana-sutta = Dharma-cakra-pravartana-sūtra, Vinayapiṭāka* (of the Theravādins), *Mahāvagga*, I.6.17–29, pp. 10–11; *Saṃyutta Nikāya, Sacca-saṃyutta*, II.11.1-15, pp. 420–23. For the Sanskrit, see É. SENART, *Le Mahāvastu*. Texte sanskrit publié pour la première fois et accompagné d'introduction et d'un commentaire, T. III, Paris, Imprimerie Nationale, 1897, pp. 330, 17-333.17.

the human condition. When expounded in a "descending" or *anuloma* order, *avijjā/avidyā—saṅkhāra/saṃskāra—viññāna/vijñāna—nāma-rūpa—saḷāyatana/ṣaḍāyatana—phassa/sparśa—vedanā—taṅhā/tṛṣṇā—upādāna—bhava—jāti—jarā-maraṇa,* it appears as a deepening of the second Truth. In the "ascending" or "inverse" order (*pratiloma,* from *jarā-maraṇa* to *avidyā,* this Law works like a detailed verification of the therapeutical prognostic, a sort of check-up applied to the third Truth. The *anuloma* and the *pratiloma* orders can be expressed through two images—"Wheel of becoming" (*bhava-cakka/-cakra*), "Wheel of Law" (*dhamma-cakka/-cakra*). Buddha's profound insight of this Law corresponds to the *pratiloma* order. For pedagogical purposes, the *anuloma* order was followed. What is important is the idea of a circular (not linear) and mutual interdependency of these *nidānas.* The image is a circle not a chain.

3.1 *Saṃskāra* as past *karman*

A second classification of these twelve links found in the commentaries (see for example, Buddhaghoṣa) is temporal. The first two factors (*avidyā* and *saṃskāra*) belong to the past (lives), the last two (*jāti, jarā-maraṇa*) to the future (lives), the ten in the middle represents this actual present life. In this psycho-cosmological and soteriological context of *pratītyasamutpāda, saṃskāra* is nothing but an aspect of *karman.* Ignorance (*avidyā*) is not the cause of *saṃskāras* which are there since long. Both are without a (first) discernible beginning in time (*anādi*). Without commencement (*anādi*), certainly, but thank god, not without end. One can put an end to ignorance, kārmic tendencies, etc., through a clear vision of the true nature of *Dharmas* which is the task allotted to Buddhist *yoga* practices. *Avidyā* works like a release mechanism only—*un facteur déclenchant.* It does not create *saṃskāras* all alone or all the way but just activates them. Hence, it will certainly be a grave error to be dupe of this temporal scheme by giving it a logico-rational value or to interpret it through the category of causality (*hetutva*). As indicates the word *paccaya/pratyaya* (*avijjā paccayā saṅkhārā...*, *saṅkhārā paccayā viññānam...*, etc.), it the idea of a mutual and circular conditionality which should be retained.

Pratītyasamutpāda provides us with the psycho-cosmological frame in which *saṃskāras* (predispositions, tendencies to act, unconscious motivations, residual impressions, urges, drives), grouped under *kleśa* (afflictions, defilements, passions), represent a particular aspect of *karman,* a non-stop going on of acts, which remain incomplete until "fruits" or consequences are produced. These in turn become new causes or motivations for new acts, modeling our destiny. From a temporal point of view, *avidyā* and *saṃskāra* represent the total kārmic capital of past lives; the last two "links", life to come (future births and deaths); the eight intermediary "links", actual present life. Nevertheless, it would be a grave mistake indeed if one is duped by this temporal arrangement, graver still if a logico-rational value is attached to it. This succession should not be interpreted in terms of causality category. Both *avidyā* and *saṃskāra* are without beginning (*anādi*). Moreover, *avidyā* does not fabricate *saṃskāras,* it works like a catalyst only and sets them in motion. The transition from potential force to acts takes place without our knowledge and also due to lack of knowledge. Thus *avidyā* is a retrospective notion.

3.2 *Saṃskāra* and *vijñāna*

The dynamic relation of mutual conditionality between *saṃskāra* and *vijñāna* (embryonic consciousness present at the moment of conception, "linking thought", *pratisaṃdhi-citta, maraṇa-citta,* "thought-at-the-moment-of death") is of special interest. Some light has been also shed on the intricate relation between *vijñāna* (3rd *nidāna*) and *vijñāna-upādāna-skandha*; between *vijñāna* and *nāma-rūpa* (4th *nidāna*). A study of the technical concept of *vijñāna-bīja*[26] results in a better comprehension of the interdependency

[26] See the famous *Śālistamba-sūtra.*

between *saṃskāra* and *vijñāna* in the general framework of the Law of *Karman* and its corollary, belief in *saṃsāra*.

On a comparative level, reference can be made to Plato, Leibniz and Samuel Butler for this particular theme. Curiously enough, Samuel Butler's novel entitled *Erewhon* contains the idea of a subtle malicious being, a sort of *gandhabba/gandharva*[27] teasing and exciting the amorous couple before their sexual union. The presence of this "perfume eater" or celestial being counts as a third factor, plus semen and blood so that conception takes place. In Greece, Plato also conceives a sort of mythical prehistory of living beings quite similar to what is found in the context of the Law of *Karman* with its corollary the belief in the transmigratory process (*saṃsāra*). The Myth of Er the Pamphylien in Plato's *Republic*[28] is particularly interesting from a comparative point of view. Souls choose their future destiny in conformity with their past habits forged in previous lives.

Leibniz[29] uses the theatrical analogy of coming back to the stage frequently attested in ancient Indian philosophical and religious literature. He however refuses the idea of metempsychosis or transmigration of souls. Leibniz rather treats the question of metamorphosis in the realm of animal beings. He explains in his *Monadology* §72 that generations are equal to development or growth and deaths to envelopment or diminuation. This coming and going (to and fro) between two theatrical stages, gross and subtle, is quite similar to Brahmanical and Buddhist ideas about a subtle body. In Leibniz's writings metempsychosis is replaced by metamorphosis:

---

[27] AN I, pp. 223–24, *Bhavasutta*; DN II, p. 63.

[28] *Republic*, 620a. "Er said, indeed, that the spectacle of the soul's choices of lives was remarquable to see; to witness it produced pity, laughter and wonder in him. They choose in most cases according to the habits formed in their previous existence." See Plato: *Republic 10,* with translation and commentary by S. Halliwell, England, Arts & Phillips, 1988, p. 101.

[29] See *Principles of Nature and Grace, Based on Reason,* §6. Also Leibniz's *Letter to Arnaud* (1687), §5.

> The ancients believed that living things come from putrefication, that is, from formless chaos; but recent researches have shown and reason confirms that this is wrong. Plants and animals (the only living things whose anatomy we know) come from pre-formed seeds, and therefore from the transformation of pre-existing living beings. The seeds of big animals contain little animals; through the process of conception these take on new clothing (so to speak) which they make their own, and which gives them the means to feed and grow, so as to pass onto a larger stage and propagate [= "be hatched or born as"] the larger animal. Human sperm are animals that are not rational and don't become so until conception settles a human nature on them. And just as no animals *completely come into existence* when they are conceived or generated, so none *go completely out of existence* in what we call their death; for it is only reasonable that what doesn't begin naturally should not end naturally either. What happens at death is that the animal throws off its mask or its tattered costume and returns to a similar stage, where it can still be just as sensible [French, meaning "capable of *sensing*" or "capable of *being sensed*"] and as orderly as it was on the larger one. And what I have just said about large animals applies also to the generation and death, of those spermatic animals themselves; that is to say, they have grown up out of other still smaller spermatic animals, in relation to which they would count as *large*! For everything in nature goes on to infinity, including the nested series of smaller animals. So it is only souls that can't be brought into existence or driven out of it. The same applies to animals, in their birth and death they are only *transformed*—unfolded and refolded, stripped bare, re-covered. A soul never leaves behind its whole body, passing to an entirely new one. So there is no metempsychosis [= "a mind's switching from one body to another"], but there is metamorphosis [="a body's changing its form"]. Animals do change, but only by gaining and loosing parts. In the process of nutrition this happens continually—little by little, by tiny, imperceptible steps. It happens all at once and very perceptibly in conception or in death, which makes the animal gain or loose a great deal all at once.[30]

It should however be borne in mind that the whole lot of interest that Buddhist texts seem to take in the concept of *saṃskāra* boils down to a deep psycho-soteriological attempt of getting rid of them once for all. In this world conceived as a vast kārmic exchanger, *saṃskāras* represent all that is caused and conditioned. They are cause of the whole mass

[30] *Principles of Nature and Grace, Based on Reason*, §6.

of suffering (*duḥkha*). In this circularity of causes and consequences, no "cessation" (*nirodha*) except *nirvāṇa* is conceivable, which puts an end to causality and temporality categories.

3.3 *Saṃskāras*: good, bad and neutral

Two classifications of *saṃskāra* (2nd link) are for this reason an exact copy of those of acts. Identified with "ancient" or past acts (*paurāṇaṃ karma*), from the maturation (*vipāka*) or retribution point of view, they are—1. good (*puṇya-, kuśala*); 2. bad (*a-puṇya-, a-kuśala*); 3. morally neutral, "invariable", "non-agitated" (*aneñjya, āniñjya, avyākṛta*). End should be put to all of them.

From the point of view of organs or senses, these are subdivided under three heads—bodily compositions or actions (*kāya-saṅkhāra/-saṃskāra* = *kāya-karman*), vocal compositions or actions (*vacī-saṅkhāra/ -saṃskāra* = *vāk-karman*) mental compositions or actions (*mano-* or *citta-saṅkhāra/-saṃskāra* = *manas-karman*).[31] The third one is equal to *cetanā* (intention, ideation, volition, deliberation) and *cetayitvā*. Volition is a mental act from which issue two other sorts of acts, corporal and vocal.[32]

For instance, *kāya-saṃskāra* (in Buddhist texts)[33] has nothing to do with *śarīra-saṃsakāra* (of the Hindu rituals). The mechanism underlying these three classes of *saṃskāra* are—1. inhalation and exhalation (*assāsa-passāsa*)[34] for bodily compositions; 2. reasoning and reflection (*vitakka-vicāra*) for vocal compositions; 3. sensations and notions (*vedanā-saññā*) for mental compositions.[35] The most particular feature in these compounds (*kāya-, vacī-, mano-*

[31] See *Saṃyutta Nikāya*, pp. 4, 43–44, 58.

[32] AK IV, 1, Pt. II, pp. 567–68. See also Nāgārjuna, MK 17, 2-3 and Pr., 305, 12-307.4.

[33] It is not easy to translate *kāya-saṃskāra*. Alex WAYMAN rendres by "motivation of the body" or "body motivation", PTS Dictionary gives "the activity of the body".

[34] See MN, *sutta* n° 44, I, p. 301.

[35] *Ibidem*. See MN.

saṅkhāra) is that the word *saṅkhāra* here is a singular whereas this can be also used in plural. The reason is that it is not their constituents (two by two) that are *saṃskāras* but the functioning of these pairs.

3.4 Bodily, vocal and mental *saṃskāras*

Bodily compositions (*kāya-saṃskāra*) are treated in relation to three yogic exercises—mindfulness while breathing in and out (*ānāpāna-sati*), fourth "meditation" (*jhāna, dhyāna*), and cessation concentration or equipoise (*nirodha-samāpatti*). Some Buddhist texts mention *citta-saṃskāra* in the context of *ānāpāna sati*,[36] but this exercise excludes totally "verbal compositions" (*vacī-saṃkhāra*). Indeed, the *yogin* does not cease to breathe, nor is he absolutely thoughtless. Still, he should keep the noble yogic silence. During *ānāpāna-satī* the adept becomes vigilant and conscious about this two-time aeolien motor or the respiratory mechanism underlying the will-to-live (*bhava-taṅhā*).

3.5 *Saṃskāras* in yogic exercises

In the first *jhāna/dhyāna*, the constituents of *vāk-saṃskāra* are still present, absent in the second *dhyāna*. Bodily compositions (*kāya-saṃskāra*) cease to function in the fourth *dhyāna*, characterised by equanimity (*upekkhā/upekṣā*). An extreme slowing down of the respiratory process can be witnessed in this state. As to *citta-* or *manaḥ-saṃskāras*, they cease in the fifth *samāpatti*, which is objectless, even beyond the immaterial sphere, a sort of avant-gout of *nibbāna/nirvāṇa* on earth. Emotional and intellectual life is no more nourished or cherished. Still, this quasi-cataleptic state is transitory, because the *yogin* is not dead. His "vital compositions" (*āyu-saṅkhāra/āyuḥ-saṃskāra*) are not yet exhausted, which maintain him alive.[37]

[36] On the *ānāpāna-sati*, amongst many other references, see the *Satipaṭṭhāna-sutta, sutta* n° 10, MN I, p. 56; *sutta* n° 118, III, p. 82–83; DN sutta n° 22, *Mahāsatipaṭṭhāna-sutta*.

[37] On *āyuḥ-* and *jīvita-saṃskāra*, see AK II, 10, Pt. II, pp. 149–54. Also DN II, 99; SN V, 152; AN IV, 311; *Udāna*, VI, 1; *Jātaka* IV, 215; *Divyāvadāna*, 203, etc.

Taking a distance from texts quoted above, these three kinds of *saṃskāras* can be considered as the triple will of a person in its broadest meaning—1. will of the body to remain alive; 2. will to express oneself; 3. will to experience all sorts of sensations or will to appropriate (*upa-ā-DĀ-*), opposite of loosening one's grip (*an-upa-LABH-*).

4. The dialectics between conditioning and de-conditioning

The dialectics between taking and abandoning, is already expressed in Buddhist Pāli Canon,[38] much more elaborated in Mahāyāna texts. A dialectics between conditioning and de-conditioning works in the carrier of an Arhant and of a *bodhisattva*, expressed through the verbal roots: *abhisaṃskṛ-/anabhisaṃskṛ-*; (*upalabh-/anupalabh-*; and the vocables *ābhoga/anābhoga*); *sasaṃkhāra/asaṃkhāra*, etc. It even tends to be systematized in the carrier of a *bodhisattva* throughout the ten "stages" (*bhūmi*), preceded by a "preparatory stage" (*saṃskāra-bhūmi*).[39] We should not in any case forget that the whole lot interest that a Buddhist seems to take in *saṃskāras* boils down to methods of getting rid of them. They cause suffering (*duḥkha*) because they nourish the kārmic series and hence the *saṃsāra*.

4.1 Hierarchy between the "stages" in Buddhist Yoga

Depending on the presence or absence of intentional effort, in this hierarchy of stages, the *bodhisattva* is called *sābhisaṃskara*, *abhisa ıskāracārin* or, on the contrary, *anabhisaṃskāra*, *anabhisaṃskāracārin*. The first case corresponds to first six *bhūmis*; the second to 8th, 9th and 10th *bhūmi*. Between these two, the 7th *bhūmi* constitutes a sort of border line, a turning point, in which he is called *animittacārin*, circulating in the sphere of "absence of characteristics." Of course, it is on the cost of an exercise of will that he maintains himself void of all distinctive "markers"

[38] See *Saṃkhāruppatti-sutta*, *Cula-* and *Mahasuññatā-sutta*.

[39] See *Mahāyāna Sūtrālaṃkāra* and *Mahāyāna Saṃgraha*.

or "indicators". The 7th *bhūmi* is thus the interlinking field of the sixth *bhūmi* in which he is *sābhisaṃskāra,* with the last three in which he is *anabhisaṃskāra.* It corresponds to the fine point of an auto-abolitive intentionality. The transitional point between the 7th and 8th *bhūmi* is thus a critical threshold in the carrier of a *bodhisattva.*

4.2 The *saṃskāra-bhūmi*

An agricultural comparison, found in texts, suggests that between the "preparatory stage" (*saṃskāra-bhumi*) and the first seven stages, a *bodhisattva* is like a cultivator who drains and purifies the soil. This "(mental) culture" (*bhāvanā*) ceases from the 8th *bhūmi* onwards. Maturation takes place "without intentional activity" (*vinā saṃskāram*).

Another comparison, which is not found in Buddhist texts, is that of a ballistic trajectory. This answers the question, in what measure there is a discontinuity or continuity during the transitional period lying in-between the 7th and the 8th *bhūmi.* In other words, between *abhisaṃskṛ-* and *anabhisaṃskṛ-* or, between presence and absence of intentionality. With reference to the *Vajracchedikā* and *Vimalakīrinirdeśa,* animated by a paradoxical logic, the carrier of a *bodhisattva* is similar to a parabola.

Taking a distance from textual materials, it can be said that the trajectory of ten *bhūmis* marks a progressive "revolution of the psychosomatic support" (*āśraya-parāvṛtti*) for a *bodhisattva.* From tendency to grip, he goes towards loosening of grip. According to Asaṅga, this signifies a total reversion of "store-consciousness" (*ālaya-vijñāna*), which represents the inmost depths of our mind, into "immaculate consciousness" (*amala-vijñāna*). This revolution or transformation takes place between the passage from 7th to 8th *bhūmi.* The first seven *bhūmis* are governed by temporality category.

4.3 The anagogical intention

The dialectics announced in terms of *abhisaṃskṛ-/ anabhisaṃskṛ-* raises the general problem of anagogical intention. Not only Buddhists, but Patañjali and Śaṅkara, in the West, Plotinus[40] and Eckhart[41] were confronted with the same. In a nut-shell, deliverance does not belong to the register of doing, and is not a happening. It may be "realized" either gradually or suddenly. Two sorts of non-returners (*anāgāmin*) are distinguished in Buddhist texts— "those who attain extinction with the help of psychological compositions" (*sasaṃkhāra-parinibbāyin*), and "those who attain extinction without the help of psychological compositions" (*asaṃkhāra-parinibbāyin*).

4.4 The composed and the non-composed

In the same web of thought, it should be added that in the final run the pair composed *(saṃskṛta)* and the non-composed, *(asaṃskṛta)* philologically a pair of opposites, is a false pair from a philosophical and soteriological point of view. The analysis is based on texts from Pāli Canon and from Mahāyāna literature. A transition took place in between. In the former, what is made with the assemblage of parts and conditions, presents three characteristics – appearing, disappearing, and alteration in duration – is called *saṅkhāta*. Inversely that which is not made by reuniting (*sam-*) parts and conditions (*a-saṅkhāta*) is exempt of these three characteristics of the composed. Moreover the composed or the conditioned (*saṅkhāta*) represents the three passions of human experience: lust (*rāga*), hatred (*dosa/dveṣa*), confusion or delusion (*moha*). The non-composed (*a-saṅkhāta/asaṃskṛta*) designates extinction (*nibbāna/nirvāṇa:*

[40] See *The Enneads,* translated by Stephen MacKenna, 4th ed., revised by B. S. Page, London, Faber and Faber Limited, 1969, pp. 587–95.

[41] See Meister Eckhart, Sermon no 5, *in Selected Treatises and Sermons,* translated from Latin & German with Introduction and Notes by James M. Clark & John V. Skinner, London, Fount Classics, 1994.

liberation from desire, suffering and transmigration).[42] It is a name for the Absolute in the Pāli Canon. Becoming a sort of entity and a subject of speculation the non-composed is now the strict opposite (*viruddha*) of the composed and becomes the second term of the pair. *Saṅkhāta* and *a-saṅkhāta* are a pair of opposites (*dvandva*). In conformity with the teachings of the Buddha this duality should be abolished.

5. *Saṃskāra, saṃskṛta, asaṃskṛta* in Nāgārjuna's *Madhyamaka Kārikās*

Coming to the Mahāyāna literature the arbitrage of the *Laṅkāvatāra Sūtra* is interesting because it shows that this dichotomy is also a product of dualistic imagination.[43] The duality in question is itself fabricated (*saṃskṛta*), it is a (false) point of view (*dṛṣṭi*) or prejudice.

Special attention should be given to the *Madhyamaka Kārikās* of Nāgārjuna,[44] where a rich dialectical treatment of *saṃskāra, saṃskṛta/asaṃskṛta* is found. The five appropriational aggregates (*upādāna-skandha*) into which the human personality is analyzed in the Buddhist tradition should be understood to exist only as a process of production, not in themselves. And the same applies to the *saṃskāra-skandha* (Ch. 4). But the production or arising (*utpāda*) itself does not exist as an entity. Nothing, in reality is ever produced. Nāgārjuna, in conformity with the Pāli Canon texts, affirms that the three characteristics of the composed are themselves composed. He declares that "the conditioned does not exist" (*nāsti saṃskṛtam*).[45] The chapter on *saṃskāra-parīkṣā* (Ch.13) is examination of (pre-) dispositions or compositions and treats in fact about action and agent. Insisting on the illusory aspect, Nāgārjuna denounces the

[42] See AN I, p. 152; SN III.37; IV, p. 359; DN III, p. 274.

[43] *Laṅkāvatāra Sūtra, Sagāthakam,* stanza 19.

[44] MK Chapters 4, 7, 13, 16, 19, 22–23, 25–26.

[45] MK 7, 33b.

saṃskāras as "fallacious" (*mṛṣā*, 13.1) and comes to the conception of "emptiness" (*śūnyatā*) in the concluding verse of the chapter (13.8). If one admits (the existence of) *saṃskāras,* it is just for practical purposes, in order to explain wherein lies the motor of *saṃsāra* or wandering life-process. This is their only epistemological and soteriological function. Excelling in his dialectical talents, Nāgārjuna shows the incompatibility between *saṃskāra* and *saṃsāra,* whether the former are considered to be permanent or impermanent. "If it is assumed that dispositions transmigrate, they would not transmigrate as impermanent entities. Neither do they transmigrate as impermanent entities. The method (of analysis) is applicable even in the case of a sentient being" (16.1). The Buddha spoke about the "pacification of dispositions" (*saṅkhāra-upasama*) in relation to a living person who has attained freedom or *nibbāna.* What Nāgārjuna would like that metaphysical views about the person, or about arising and ceasing should be abandoned. This is expressed in the following *Kārikā*—"The cessation of disposition is somehow not appropriate. The cessation even of a sentient being is also not appropriate in any way".[46]

Besides, time (*kāla*), which constitutes the frame-work of intentional activity expressed by the verbs *saṃskṛ-*, *abhisaṃskṛ-* does not exist (MK 19).

Questions regarding the existence (or non-existence) of the Tathāgata (after death and freedom) was often raised in Buddhist texts. How to solve the problem? Truly, if existence of a "person" is supposed, that of the five aggregates has also to be accepted. In the chapter 22 of *Madhyamaka Kārikā*, on *Tathāgata-parīkṣā*, Nāgārjuna rejects this possibility. The Tathāgata is not an "agent", nor he is a "self" (*ātman*). "The Tathāgata is neither the aggregate nor different from them. The aggregates are not in him; nor is he in the aggregates. He is not possessed of the aggregates.

[46] MK 16.1 and 4. Translation David J. KALUPAHANA, *Nāgārjuna. The Philosophy of the Middle Way*, State University of New York, 1986.

In such a context, who is Tathāgata ?" (22.1). It was not possible for the disciples to attribute five ordinary appropriational aggregates to the Buddha. So the Ābhidharmika thinkers had invented five extraordinary or super-mundane (*lokottara*) *skandhas* without "flow" or "torrent" (*anāśrava*). Amongst them, the *saṃskāra-skandha* is replaced by its opposite, liberation (*vimukti*), in conformity with the *Aṅguttara*- IV.203. Truly *saṃskāras* knit and bound, while *dharma* undoes the knots and liberates. Candrakīrti invents an ingenious solution to the problem. The idea is that in extinction without kārmic residua (*sopadhiśeṣa-nirvāṇa*), the five *skandhas* subsist, but in a separated state, without forming a bundle (or network). This generates the false belief in personal identity (*sat-kāya-dṛṣi*). This solution permits to account for the existence of Tathāgata in the lapse of time flowing between his enlightenment (*bodhi, nirvāṇa* while alive, *sopadhiśeṣa-nirvāṇa*) and his physical death equal to extinction without substrate or final extinction (*nirupādhiśeṣa-nirvāṇa, pariṅirvāṇa*). The content of *Madhyamaka Kārikā* (Ch. 22) can be stated in a nut-shell, that the Tathāgata is not "somebody", no body is a Tathāgata.

The three passions (*kleśa*) – lust (*rāga*), hatred (*dveṣa*), and delusion or confusion (*moha*) – constitute the psychological content of the "composed" or conditioned (*saṅkhata/saṃskṛta*). According to Nāgārjuna they do not exist really, but are only a product of our imaginative thought or *saṃkalpa*. In any case, all sorts of perversions, impulsions or representations come to an end with the end of ignorance (*avidyā*). And ignorance ends with the end of difilements or passions (*kleśa*). Is there a vicious circle (*cakraka*) in this manner of reasoning? Or, is it simply an indication of the mutual dependency (*parasparāpekṣikī siddhi*) between all that is? This is the case with *saṃskāras* as the second link (*nidāna, bhavāṅga*) in the Law of *Pratītyasamutpāda*. "Thus, with the cessation of perversions, ignorance ceases. When ignorance has ceased, the dispositions, etc., come to cease" (MK 23.23). This circular conditioning between *avidyā*, error (*viparyaya*) and *saṃskāra* is expressed in MK 26.11 ab—"When ignorance has ceased, there is no occurrence of dispositions. However, the cessation of that ignorance takes place as a result of the practice of that [non-occurrence of dispositions] through wisdom".[47] What is important is to eliminate the idea of "origination" or production (*utpāda*), which is the only way of eliminating the substantialistic idea of self-nature (*svabhāva*). In other words, a better substitute will be the idea of a circular or mutual conditioning. Let us not forget that the compositions are themselves composed—*saṃskāras* are *saṃskṛta*.

Extinction or freedom (*nirvāṇa*) can neither be conceived as existence (or being, *bhāva*) or as non-existence (or non-being, *abhāva*). Here again the "conditioned" (*saṃskṛta*) and the "unconditioned" (*asaṃskṛta*) are recalled, because *bhāva* and *saṃskṛta* go hand in hand, although it cannot be said that this is the case with *abhāva* and *asaṃskṛta*, because *abhāva* is still related to *bhāva*. In conformity with the teachings of the Buddha, Nāgārjuna here criticizes the point of view of the Sarvāstivādin who equates *saṃskṛta* and *pratītyasamutpāda*. "Moreover, if freedom were to be existent, then freedom would be conditioned. Yet, an existent that is unconditioned is not evident anywhere" (MK 26.5). Taking position against the Vaibhāṣika, who conceives *nirvāṇa* to be existent and non-existent at the same time, Nāgārjuna's words as follows. "How could freedom be both existence and non-existence, for freedom is unconditioned while existence and non-existence are conditioned?" (MK 26.13).

Chapter 26 of the *Madhyamaka Kārikā* is devoted to the examination of the twelve causal factors. The second factor or link (*bhavāṅga, nidāna*) is *saṃskāra*, which works like the

---

[47] MK 26.11. Kalupahana rightly remarks that "The mutual relationship between cessation of ignorance and the non-arising of dispositions is emphasized by Nāgārjuna, keeping in mind the distinction between appeasement of dispositions (*saṃskāropaśama*) in the present life and their waning (*saṃskāra-kṣaya*) at the time of death, thereby not providing another oppurtunity for rebirth" (p. 375).

compliment of object of the roots *abhisaṃskṛ-* or *saṃskṛ-* in the 1st and the 10th *Kārikā* respectively:

> A person enveloped by ignorance forms such dispositions in the threefold ways leading to re-becoming, and through such actions he moves on to his destiny (MK 26.1).

The nuance of these verbs as signify the act of preparation ready is quite evident here:

> Thus, the ignorant forms dispositions that constitute the source of the life process. Therefore, it is the ignorant who is the agent, not the wise one, because of his [the latter's] perception of truth (MK 26.10).[48]

Thus the *saṃskāras* are at the root of the life-process or the existential flux (*saṃsāra*). As such ignorance (*avidyā*) can be compared to a motor at rest, while *saṃskāra* to a motor in movement. In any case the judgement here is depreciative (*saṃskāra* considered to be at the root of *saṃsāra*), just at the antipode of the Hindu ritualist attitude towards *saṃskāras.* The Hindu *saṃnyāsins* differ of course and take the same distance from the forged world as did the Buddha.

To resume, MK 23.23 shows that there is a circle between *avidyā* and *viparyaya,* while MK 26.10 states that there is a circle between *saṃskāra* and *saṃsāra.* MK 26.11 reveals that there is a circle between *avidyā* and *saṃskāra.*

Understood as the fourth appropriational aggregate, the *saṃskāras* do not exist by themselves as an entity but are simply a process of appearance-disappearance (MK 4.7). Same thing happen when *saṃskāra* is the second link or *bhavāṅga* (MK 23.23). This applies to all acts (*karman*) as such in continuous changing process (MK 17.21.33). The *saṃskāras* understood as the components of a living being (*sattva, pudgala*) are, paradoxically, not compatible with the idea of *saṃsāra* (MK 16.1–3 and 5). They cannot be the object of the verb *saṃskṛ-*. True, we cannot even think about

---

[48] We sculpt our destiny. Nāgārjuna's expression: "Therefore, it is the ignorant who is the agent" reminds that of Śaṅkara: "Therefore, it is only the ignorant who is the debitor" (*avidyāvān hi ṛṇī,* BĀUBH I.4.10).

their extinction (16.4). In other words, there is no place for them in the idea of liberation or freedom (*mokṣa*). *Nirvāṇa* can neither be conceived as *bhāva,* nor as *abhāva,* or a mixture of both (as explained by *Candrakīrti* in the *Prasannapada,* 531.4–5 in his commentary on MK 25.11). In this *Kārikā, saṃskāra* covers both—second *nidāna* and *saṃskāra-skandha.* This is in conformity with what explains Nāgārjuna in MK 26.10 and 11—the *saṃskāras* are at the root of transmigration (*saṃsāra-mūlam*). There is a triple circular conditionment between *saṃskāra* and *saṃsāra* (MK 26.11) and between *avidyā* and *viparyaya* (23.23). This shows the nonsubstantiality of each of these terms. They can function only in mutual relationship, not independently. Thus *saṃskāras* have no independent self-nature and one cannot "realize" them. They are a dynamic relay, in the process of arising, between thurst and its object, between the agent (*kartṛ*) and the consumer (*bhoktṛ*). From an existential point of view, the latter is neither the same nor different (MK 17 and 28). From an epistemological point of view, the *saṃskāras* are linking factors accounting for the dialectical movement.

Saṃskṛta/asaṃskṛta, existence and non-existence, *bhāva* and *abhāva* always result from a concourse of causes and conditions, they are *saṃskṛta* (MK 25.13). We may provisonally agree with the Vaibhāṣika on the point that *nirvāṇa* is *asaṃskṛta* because this is in accordance with canonic texts.[49] But what about the incomparable? First that which is composed does not exist (*nāsti saṃskṛtam*), because the three characteristics of the composed–production, duration, destruction (*utpāda-sthiti-bhaṅga*)–could not be established (MK 7.33). Since then, because the existence of the composed could not be demonstrated, how to speak about the uncomposed? (33cd). At this point one can appreciate the *Laṅkāvatāra sūtra* quoted above (*Sagāthakam,* stanza 19), the text which evacuates simultaneously the set of opposites. Light was thrown on this point by André Bareau and Jacques

[49] *Itivuttaka* 43, p. 37; *Udāna* 8.3, p. 80.

May.[50] When the Absolute comes to be "realized" and thus devalued at the rank of a superlative or super-relative, the human mind is conducted, by a sort of overbidding, to invoke a super-transcendence. In this optic we shall say that, the couple *saṃskṛta/asaṃskṛta* is a false couple, its symmetry is deceitful. The veritable *asaṃskṛta* is not a part or member of the couple, but is its absence.

6. The unconscious (mind) in Buddhist texts

Finally, there is an old as well as a contemporary problem—does one find a treatment of the unconscious (mind) in Buddhist texts, similar to Western depth Psychological theories and Psychoanalysis? In what measure the dialectics of conscious and unconscious can be applied to Buddhism? Do we find a sort of prehistory of the unconscious in Buddhism?—Not exactly.

Contemporary interpretators[51] have tried some rapprochement between the antique Brahmanical/Hindu and Buddhist concept of *saṃskāra* and the concept of unconscious drive in Western Psychology and Psychoanalysis, concepts belonging to two different cultural areas. Let me outline with some more precision the affinities and the differences between these two approaches of the unconscious (mind). The knowledge of Indian texts presents a double interest for Western psychologists, anthropologists and philosophers. Firstly, this may help them to appreciate a sort of prehistory of the conscious-unconscious mind, discovered twenty centuries before the emergence of these themes in the West. Secondly, a double lecture–provided that the respective problematics are faithfully restituted in their particular cultural contexts–can offer a binocular vision or relief. One comes to know oneself better by coming in relation with others.

---

[50] A. BAREAU, *L'Absolu en philosophie bouddhique*, pp. 174, 251–52, 282–83. J. MAY, *Douze Chapitres* (...), pp. 140–42, notes 397 and 406.

[51] For example Jean FILLIOZAT, E. FROMM, C. J. JUNG, Padmasiri DE SILVA, Alan W. WATTS.

It is uncontestable that while Greco-European philosophy and rational psychology were much more clear ancient Brahmanical, Hindu, Jaina, and Buddhist texts also were utilising concepts as means of analyzing and explaining human behaviour, the hidden and obscure zones of mind.

6.1 The "unconscious" in Sanskrit vocabulary

Among psycho-soteriological concepts like *anuśaya, leśya, vāsanā, saṃskāra, bīja,* the first three contain a common idea of *rémanence,* remnant or remainder. In Jaina thought, *leśya* indicates the different colourations or hues, from dark to clear, which attach themselves to the personal substance or *jīva* after his deeds.[52] In the Hindu or Buddhist context (as well as in Jainism), *vāsanā* designates the perfume or the odor which continues to impregnate the recipient after it is emptied over (if *vāsanā* is derived from the verbal root *Vas-* 2). If derived from *Vas-* 1, we rejoin nearly the same idea of envelopment. The etymology is uncertain but the significance certain. To pursue the same comparison, *anuśaya* is a sort of thin layer which continues to adhere to the surface of the recipient. In Buddhist psychology it corresponds to the torments and passions (*kleśa*) when they are lying down (*śī-*) in a dormant state. In sum, *vāsanā* and *anuśaya* signify what remains when nothing is left over. But from their latest state they will manifest their germinative potentiality sooner or later— "germ", "grain" or "semen" (*bīja*) is the dynamic aspect of these remanences, their face turned towards the future. Thus *bīja* on the one hand, *vāsanā, anuśaya* on the other hand, are like the inside-outside of the same energetic transit.

As to *saṃskāra,* Jean Filliozat[53] interprets this as a complex architecture or systems, sort of "montages", or veritable

[52] See Nagin J. SHAH, *Jaina Philosophy and Religion.* [English translation of Jaina Darsana by Muni Shri NYAYAVIJAYAJI], BLJI Series N° 12, Motilal Banarsidass, Bhogilal Lehar Chand Institute of Indology, 1998, 2000, pp. 198–200, 212–14, 214n, 215–16.

[53] "Les théories psychologiques de l'Inde". *Bulletin de la Société Française de Philosophie,* juillet-septembre, 1972, mainly pp. 80–81, 88.

"psychological constructions." Hence their elaboration represent a "secondary formation." Besides, the organization or the regroupment of unconscious traces or *vāsanās* may either be governed by the will or by intelligence, i.e., by the consciousness, or, it can be automatic if the consciousness is negligent. The problem is complex. If we add to this that in Pāli and Sanskrit texts the distinction between *vāsanās*, atomic so to say, and *saṃskāras* molecular, we understand better why there has been such a lot of hesitation amongst Western interpretors concerning this subject. They have a tendency to put accent on the unconscious dimension or aspect of *saṃskāras* which permit stimulating rapprochements with problems treated in contemporary psychology in the West. It should be reminded, however, that the Buddhist monks who defend the orthodoxy of the *Theravāda* are of opposite opinion. For them, *saṃskāras* are rather voluntary psychological "compositions", including the efforts and disciplinary constraints destined to reform and remodel the psyche in view of liberation or *nirvāṇa.*

Let us make a methodological research for words in Pāli or Sanskrit to render "subconscious" and "unconscious", as used in the western vocabulary. The first indication is that very often a perfect philological reproduction of terms cannot be found in Sanskrit vocabulary. For instance, the word *a-cetana,* though a perfect philological reproduction for "unconscious" seems quite unsatisfactory from a psycho-soteriological point of view. Moreover, Indian thinkers do not represent the conscious and the unconscious as two airtight departments, nor do they talk about layers such as Ego, *Id,* Superego.

6.2 The "unconscious" in Buddhist Yoga

A series of terms functioning in five different places of origin have been recensed here. Firstly, in some yogic exercises where different modalities of consciousness can be observed—going from gross (*sthūla*) to subtle (*sūkṣma*), and from dispersed (*nānā-citta*) to unified thought (*eka-citta*).

In Buddhist *Yoga* the progression through four meditations (*dhyāna*), till five equipoises (*samāpatti*) ends in an extenuation of consciousness for the adept, which is a sort of extenuation of the *skandhas*. The third aggregate or the *saṃjñā-skandha* (*saṃjñā* is percept, pragmatic concept and denomination at the same time) is absent in the fourth *samāpatti*— "equipoises with a domain which is neither notional nor non-notional" (*naivāsmjñā-nāsaṃjñā-āyatana-samāpatti*). In this subtle yogic exercise there is an equilibrium between consciousness and unconsciousness, at the peak of existence (*bhāvagra*).

If the equilibrium is broken and the meditating person leans towards the absence of *saṃjñā*, he will be disconnected with the natural and social environment—without perception of surrounding objects, without any idea of their utility, without remembering their names, thoughtless, and so in a state of unconsciousness. Is it something quite similar to approaching *nirvāṇa*? No. The treatises denounce the *asaṃjñī-samāpatti* and make a serious difference between this equipoises and the *saṃjñā-vedita-nirodha-samāpatti*, equipoises in which the functioning of the senses and understanding is really interrupted. In this *samāpatti* not only the understanding, with all sorts of representations relative to practical life are suspended, but also the affective sensibility. In the *asaṃjñī-samāpattis* there remains a non-qualified feeling of easiness or being well, which means the presence of affectivity. So only profanes (*pṛthagjana*) and not the noble ones (*ārya*) let themselves seduce by these states. In the ninth and last *samāpatti*, there is a complete affective impassivity and a complete notional void. But, the meditant comes out of this state due to the impulsion of the fourth *upādāna-skandha*, because of *saṃskāras*, and singularly, by the force of "vital compositions" (*āyuḥ-saṃskāra*). These yogic exercises reveal that *saṃskāras* have both facets, conscious and unconscious.

6.3 *Saṃskāra* as volitional effort and as subconscious or unconscious tendency

In the context of actions and its motivations, ignorance (*avidyā*) of the true nature of things (or reality) forms the background of human life. And the true nature of things is that they are not *things*, neither are they "real", because there is only a flux of forces, which produce when associated and destroy when dissociated. Living beings (*sattva*) or creatures are a sort of meeting point amongst these forces. Plunged deep down in ignorance about their true nature (which is in fact absence of the idea of self-nature), they take themselves too seriously, making projects and acting, thinking that these decisions are final and definitive. Alas, there is nothing but a distant horizon, always slipping away! Deceptions push us towards new actions, so on and so forth. Thera Nyanatiloka[54] explains that the term *saṅkhāra*, often rendered by "subconscious tendencies", fails to bring out the volitional dimension of *saṅkhāra* in the context of the law of conditioned co-production (*paṭiccasamuppapāda*). As the second link, *saṅkhāra* is neither equal to subconscious nor to a tendency but means volition, fully conscious and active, a *kamma/karman*. He excludes the unconscious dimension of *saṅkhāra*.

His judgement is bit categoric, because an act fully volitional and conscious is impossible. Our conscious motivations hide too many subconscious and unconscious impulsions. Most of the time the springs of our actions escape us. Moreover, we can also observe a change in the nuance of the term *saṅkhāra/saṃskāra* while we pass from the Pāli Canon to Mahāyāna texts. Agreed that only deliberate volitional acts fructify for the responsible agent and that the maturation/retribution of the fruits of acts (*karma-phala-*

[54] *Vocabulaire bouddhique de termes et doctrines du Canon pali*, Paris, 1961, p. 219. On the contrary, PADMASIRI DE SILVA insists on the subconscious dimension of *saṅkhāras* and makes some parallels with Freud. *See Buddhist and Freudian Psychology*, Colombo, 1973, 2nd ed., 1978.

vipāka) determine his future destinies (*gati*). A simple clumsiness or a mechanical gesture do not count.

Our actions are nothing but reactions. They reflect a hidden presence of subconscious-unconscious drives or urges. In the chain of causes and conditions, *saṃskāras* are like moved motors, pushing when pushed.

In any case, reason and passions are intermingled in our actions and motivations. It is difficult to separate them. Otherwise, we will not have expressions like "passionate reasoning", "sentimental logic." Neither expressions like "false consciousness"[55] nor Jean-Paul Sartre's famous "mauvaise foi",[56] ("bad faith", which consists in lying to ourselves or self-deceit).

In the psychology of passions and conversion, the concept of *kleśa* is important in Buddhist morality and contains the idea of afflictions or torments, affections and infections. They adhere to the personality, sully us, and make us suffer. In period of crisis, when the crisis slows down, passing from virulent to latent state, a *kleśa* is then named *anuśaya*—that which continues to lie down in the mind—sticking to it. Inversely, when an *anuśaya* manifests itself once again it is named a *kleśa.* So it is the same thing upside-down, inverse or reverse, at the state of envelopment or development. The main idea is that a passionate crises deposits strong *habitus* constituting the character of the person concerned, who is not actually conscious about this deposit. A passionate crises does not arise in face of a given present situation but results from the latent dynamism deposited by precedent crises as a reaction.

[55] Specialists of Social Psychology explain the double meaning of alienation: psycho-pathologic and socio-politic. See Dr Joseph GABEL, *La fausse conscience,* Paris, éditions de Minuit, 1962; *Sociologie de l'aliénation,* Paris, P.U.F., 1970.

[56] On the "Bad Faith" (*mauvaise foi*), see J.P. SARTRE, *Being and Nothingness,* Translation and Introduction by E. HAZEL-BARNES, Washington Square Press, 1992, chapter II, pp. 86–116.

6.4 The concept of *anuśaya*

Amongst the stock of concepts, *anuśaya* seems to be the nearest term which renders the "unconscious" of Western Psychology and Psychoanalysis. This contains the idea of an automatic "compulsion of repetition" (*Wiederholungszwang*) of acts. The human personality understood as a "series" (*saṃtati*) of mental states in Buddhism, the *anuśayas* are renewed from instance to instance in this kārmic series. Each and every event or affective experience leaves a punctual deposit in the mind, followed by the remembrance, which makes us say, after the crisis is over, "I was wrong to be angry", "I should have believed her", "She was hiding her plans", etc. Jean Filliozat rightly compares *saṃskāras* to "montages." This unconscious regroupment is accrued at each moment by conscious phenomena. There is close intrication of conscious and unconscious elements in our conditioned reflexes. In the final run, the character of a "person" is a complex of *saṃskāra*(s), some affective, others more intellectual. In terms of neurophysiological sciences, one will say that the original character of a person resides less in the cortical or thalamic phenomena, more in the functioning of these cortico-thalamic circuits. The continuous communication between these two areas defines the particular charm of each individual personality and gives an idea of the statistical probability of his reaction in a given situation.

A particular case of psychological latency is furnished by some "non-informations" (*avijñāpti*).[57] The classical example is that of a murder through command or through interposed murderers. The Buddhist morality being a morality of intention, it offers a similarity with Western and Christian conceptions—the commanditor is as important as the one who executes, if not more. What interests us here is the

---

[57] The concept of *avijñāpti* have been a subject of complex controversy. Advanced by some Buddhists sects such as the Mahāsaṃghika and the Sarvāstivādin, it is recused by the Sautrāntika, the Mādhyamika, and the Vijñānavādin.

psychological status of the commanditor. When the murder takes place, it may happen that his attention is elsewhere, absorbed in other occupations, or that he has simply forgotten about his order given long time before. At this precise moment it is not only others who ignore that he is the instigator of the murder, but also he himself. Nevertheless, inspite of this psychological void or lapse (of memory), he *is* the murderer, despite this "non-knowing". Even if an unexpected obstacle intervenes in between and stops the person who is supposed to excecute the order, the commanditor remains a murderer because of his intention.

How to conciliate this "blank" on the psychological series level with the "black" or sullied trace on the moral quality level? This "non-information" can be understood only if the range of the psyche extends and passes beyond the field of consciousness. Moreover, consciousness is intermittent, always selective. It jumps from one object to another as a monkey jumps from branch to branch.[58] There is also another example of *avijñāpti,* the case of a butcherman, who does not even know that he is a murderer, because it is his job (to kill).

6.5 The part played by the unconscious in the mechanism of conversion

Fortunately, the unconsciousness can also function in an opposite direction, for example in the mechanism of conversion. There is a well-known case, that of the brigand Aṅgulīmāla, who used to cut the fingers of the travellers passing by the woods of Jālinī, exacting a ransom from them. He was even ready to kill his own mother says the legend so as to bring the number of fingers to hundred in order to finish his garland. Nothing showed even a glimpse of good tendency in him. Yet, the Buddha could see, with his divine eye, that Aṅgulīmāla has now reached to a point in his

[58] See SN II, p. 95 where the *manas* or the *vijñāna* is compared to a monkey.

personal series that he is mature to enter in the community (*saṃgha*). Having consumed the demeritorious fruits of his past criminal deeds, other results, those of meritorious deeds, are now in course of maturation-fruition. The hour of conversion is a passage from dormant forces to their conscious and voluntary manifestation.

Same sort of remark can be made for the monastic "state" or vow. Although there are no solemn and definitive vows for entering in the *saṃgha*, the monk or the none is tied by the religious "state" till he or she has not explicitly denounced. This does not mean that they are all the time thinking about it. It also happens that he (monk) transgresses the disciplinary rules (*vinaya*) for which he must confess to testify the *pāṭimokkha* practices. Confession is typical to Buddhist monachism and is absent in Brahmanical *saṃnyāsa*.

In the psychology of sensorial and mental knowledge, the expression "psychology of knowledge" may shock scholars, because since 17th century rational and idealistic explanations are based on the premises that ideas are innate or the *a priori* of categories. But that there are also the empiricist and positivistic theories of knowledge. Accordingly in the 20th century, events like genetic psychology, sociology of knowledge, etc., have started exploring new fields of research.

Let us see how the Buddhist epistemology tackles these problems. The key-term here is *bhavāṅga-sota, bhavāṅga-citta, bhavāṅga-mano* resulting from scholastic speculations. Found only once in the *Sutta Piṭaka* (AN II.79), then sometimes in the recent part of the *Abhidhamma Piṭaka*, these concepts appears mostly in non-canonical text—*Atthasālinī, Abhidhamma Saṃgaha, Nettipakaraṇa, Visuddhimagga*, etc.

6.6 The sub-conscious life-continuum

Bhavāṅga, "factor of becoming", presents two characteristics— it is a force which pushes us to move forward, only way of perduration in existence and a force which pushes us to continue to exist. In this sense, *bhavāṅga* is quite similar to *jīvitendriya* (life, vitality, physical and mental) or to "vital compositions" (*āyuḥ-saṃskāra*).[59] Thus *bhavāṅga* is similar to subconscious or unconscious phenomena. Or, to be prudent, let us say that the thought underlying this surge or *élan* is subtle and habitual.

As to "subconscious life-continuum" (*bhavāṅga-sota*), we find the dynamic aspect of being as becoming (*bhava*), as a "current" or a "flow", not as a substrate. So, in any case it cannot be equated with the "unconscious", same remark for *bhavāṅga-citta*, where *citta* designates intentional thought (and not as thought as something abstract and static). Even when *bhavāṅga-citta* is a fruit of meritorious acts (*kusala-kamma*), preparing a good destiny, it remains of a mundane order and fluent (*āsava*). Hence, there is real contrast between *bhavāṅga-citta* and *bodhi-citta*.

Is there any filiation between *bhavāṅga-citta* and "store consciousness" (*ālayavijñāna*)? The Vijñānavādin insist on the dynamic aspect of *ālayavijñāna* in order to distinguish it from the ontological and substantial *ātman* of Brahmanism. The *ālayavijñāna* is compared to a river. The Buddha did not explicitly enter in details about the store consciousness while addressing himself to the *śrāvakas*. Now, this store consciousness, full of seeds or grains (*bīja*), conserves the dynamic potentialities of our past experiences, forming a couple with consciousness in act (*pravṛtti-vijñāna*). But once reversed, it is a mine or deposit of omniscience. Going further, let us add that the *ālayavijñāna* and the immaculate consciousness (*amala-vijñāna*) are also not two, but one and the same "reality".

---

[59] Without being identical to "genetic program", the concept of *āyuḥ-saṃskāra* has the same explanatory function: to account for the life duration of living individual being. Texts compare them to the "speed" or "momentam" (*vega*) residing in an arrow distended from the bow, which permits to rejoin the connotation of *saṃskāra* (= *vega*) in the vocabulary of the Vaiśeṣika.

On the nuances between *jīvita-* and *āyuḥ-saṃskāra*, see AK II.10, Pt. II, pp. 149–154.

6.7 *Saṃskāras* which are neither material nor mental

One can be tempted to include in the list of concepts presenting some affinities with the subconscious or unconscious activities of the mind. The "compositions" which are neither material nor mental, both at the same time or the fourteen *rūpa-citta-viprayukta-saṃskāra(s)*. The nature and status of these *saṃskāras* may seem to be interesting in comparison with the modern idea of unconscious phenomena. However, many precautions should be taken in such enterprises. Vasubandhu puts it as follows—these *dharmas* are not associated with the thought; they are not of the nature of matter; they are included in the *saṃskāra-skandha,* that's why they are called *cittaviprayukta-saṃskāras.* They are disjointed from the thought, because, being immaterial, they ressemble the thought.[60] But can we compare them with the "unconscious" in Psychoanalysis? —not exactly. To be prudent, let us enumerate them. According to the list given by the Sarvāstivādin, they are—1. possession (*prāpti*) 2. non-possession (*aprāpti*) 3. community of gender (*sabhāgata*) 4–6. the forces stopping the functioning of the mind, in the case of "unconscious gods" and *yogins—āsaṃjñika, āsaṃjñikasamāpatti, nirodha-samāpatti* 7. the vital force (*jīvitendriya*) 8–11. the four characteristics of the composed (*saṃskṛta*)—impermanence (*anityatā*), birth (*jāti*), duration (*sthiti*), old age (*jarā*), 12–14. collection of words (*nāma-kāya*), of sentences and phonemes (*pada-kāya, vyañjana-kāya*), generating ideas and representations.[61] Interestingly enough, the non-concord or the "schism of the community" (*saṃgha-bheda*) is a *citta-viprayukta-saṃskāra.*[62] It is not a material thing, neither it is something that participates in the thought of the schismatic (*bhetṛ*).

---

[60] AK II.35–36, Pt. I, pp. 209–10.

[61] For this list, see AK II.47, Pt. I, pp. 270–76.

[62] AK IV.98, Pt. II, p. 726.

Let us conclude that amongst the five points of rapprochement between Buddhist Psychology and Western Psychology plus Psychoanalysis, the first two can be eliminated as being non-pertinent—refinement of consciousness in some yogic exercises; the debate on the *saṃskāras*, neither material, nor mental. Three seem to be pertinent with all nuances to be introduced in the rapprochement—(a) the *anuśayas*, sort of passionate unconscious thoughts, (b) the *bhavāṅga*, sort of vital and epistemological reservoir, prolonged by the (concept of) *ālayavijñāna*, (c) our inconsequences, because we do not have any clear idea about the *suivi* or "what follows" of our acts. The concept of *bhavāṅga-* can be retained because it contains the "programme" of our life duration span or "vital compositions" (*āyuḥ-saṃskāra*), lived unconsciously. It is also in close relationship with the blind will-to-live (*bhava-tṛṣṇā*, *abhiniveśa*).[63]

Concepts which clearly evoke an unconscious functioning of the mind are—*saṃskāra, vāsanā, bīja* ("seed"); *anuśaya* (kārmic residue) in relation with *kleśa* (afflictions, defilements, passions), *avijñāpti* (non-notification, non-information) those of *bhavāṅga-sota, citta-, mano-* (subconscious life-continuum) and *ālayavijñāna* are of course specially important for this topic.

The concept of *āyu-saṃkhāra/āyuḥ-saṃskāra* ("vital compositions or energy", factors of longevity or life-duration factors) should also be considered because it reveals that we

---

[63] In the West, for Schopenhauer too, the Will (*Wille*) is a blind force, unconscious and "without reason" (*grundlos*) operating in the Nature as in man. See Arthur Schopenhauer, *The World as Will and as Representation*, translated by E.F. G. Payne, New York, Dover Publications, 1967, specially Book II, § 20–21; 23; 26–27. A human being lives in the battle-ground of two opposite tendencies: Affirmation of the Will-to-live/Negation of the Will-to-live. I have dealt with the subject elsewhere. See L. Kapani: *Schopenhauer et la pensée indienne. Similitudes et différences*, Paris, Hermann, 2011, 270 pages. *Journal Asiatique*, tome 290, n° 1, Peeters Orientalist; Leuven, Belgique, 2002, pp. 163–292.

live our lifespan unconsciously. Only an *arhant* has a conscious hold on them.

Some exercises of Buddhist *Yoga* reveal a better evaluation of the conscious/unconscious problematic. For example, equipoise appertaining neither to notional nor to non-notional domain (*naivasaṃjñā-nāsaṃjñā-āyatana-samāpatti*); equipoise consisting in cessation of notions and sensitivity (*saṃjñā-veditā-nirodha-samāpatti*); unconscious equipoise (*asaṃjñi-samāpatti*).

CHAPTER IV

Saṃskāra in *Vaiśeṣika* Thought: Mechanics and Psychology

1. Three kinds of phenomena

The *Vaiśeṣika* doctrine offers a privileged occasion of focusing light on the semantic unity of the concept of *saṃskāra* through its various fields of application. They count under the heading of *saṃskāra* (24th category) three kinds of *phenomena—vega, bhāvanā* and *sthitisthāpaka.*[1] 1. *vega*—momentum, impetus, speed, residual impulsion; 2. *bhāvanā*—force of imagination, of rendering the past once again present, reproduction, representation; 3. *sthitisthāpaka*—elasticity. They seem quite different from each other. This is rather unexpected and instructive. So our aim is to find out their common denominator. The first and the third belong to physics, precisely to mechanics, the second to psychology. All of them are considered to be "qualities" (*guṇa*), not "substances" (*dravya*).

2. Mechanics of propulsion and impulsion

The problem posed in the *Vaiśeṣika Sūtra* (3rd Century AD), developed by Praśastapāda (5th-6th century AD) and later commentators, is to a certain extent, analogous to that which was raised in the West, until the Law of Inertia was discovered. From Aristotle to Descartes, passing by Philoponus, Ockham,

[1] See (TS=) *Tarka Saṃgraha* II.24.I: *saṃskāra trividho vego bhāvanā sthitisthāpakaś ca/ Tarkasaṃgraha* and autocommentary *Dīpikā* ed. And transl. by J.R. BALLANTYNE in his *Lectures on the Nyāya Philosophy,* Allahabad, 1849, 2nd ed., *Hindu Philosophy,* Allahabad, 1879. French translation by A. FOUCHER, *Compendium des Topiques*, p. 82.

Buridan, etc., the problem was to understand, on the simile of a catapult, as to how a mobile, once separated from its engine, continues nevertheless to move. Wanting to prove that the hypothesis of vacuum is unnecessary to account for movement, and that it renders movement impossible, Aristotle examines in his *Physics*[2] the case of natural and forced movements. At this occasion he refers to all sorts of explanations proposed before him, accounting for the transport of projectiles, for the reactional impulse (*antiperistasis*) in the environment due to which the pushed wind becomes that which pushes in its turn. Aristotle invokes another model, that of a magnet, which communicates the force of movement to that which moves.[3] There is also the example of whirlwind in the liquids.[4] This boils down to filling up the gap between the engine and the mobile, by representing to oneself a series of contiguous engines or motors transmitting to themselves a certain *dunamis*. Philoponus and Middle Age thinkers are of the opinion that the motor or engine transmits the impetus directly to the mobile (or to that which moves), opinion shared by Galileo, known as the concept of vis *impressa*.

2.1 The concept of *vega*

Much earlier than western thinkers, the *Vaiśeṣikas* elaborate the concept of *vega* in order to resolve problems like propulsion, fall of bodies, etc., and specially the nature of motion. *Vega* can be rendered as "speed", "momentum", "impetus" or "residual impulsion".

Being a variety of *saṃskāra*, hence, capacity of prolongation and reiteration of motion as well as action, generally preceded by volitional effort (*prayatna*), the field of *vega* extends not only to tangible corporal substances (*mūrta-dravya*), but surprisingly enough, to the mental organ or mind (*manas*) also, sort of messenger or link between

[2] *Physics* IV.8.215a.

[3] *Ibidem* VIII.266b.27, 267a. 20.

[4] *Ibidem* IV.7.214.

the senses (*indriya*) and the "self" (*ātman*), the knowing subject. Inclusion of *manas* in consideration relating to mechanics, in the context of *vega*, is made plausible by the fact that in Indian systems of thought it is conceived on the model of a machine (*yantra*) whose functioning is by itself unconscious. Another reason for this inclusion is its instability, mind is always moving (*manaś calam*). In this sense, the idea of *vega* applies to this intangible mobile substance as it applies to four other tangible mobile substances.

2.2 *Vega:* a "quality", not a "substance"

It should be noted that *vega* although applying to substances (*dravya*) is not itself a substance but a "quality" or attribute (*guṇa*) belonging to the nature. Classified under the 24th category, *vega* is one of the three modes of the process of potentialisation and reiteration known as *saṃskāra.* As such it can qualify and modify substances without being a part of these substances or *mūrta-dravya.* For example, in the case of an arrow (*iṣu*), the arrow is the "consubstantial cause" (*samavāyī-kāraṇa*) inherent in the cause. It is the seat, the material support. Voluntary effort (*prayatna*), which commands the tension and then the release from the bow-string, as well as the gravitation (*gurutva*) are the "efficient causes" (*nimitta-kāraṇa*), exteriour to the effect. Finally, there is a third type of cause, intermediary between the two, it is interior to the effect, but not inherent or consubstantial (*asamavāyī-kāraṇa*). This is what precisely *vega* is, this residual impulsion gets attached to the material support of movement just for the time being, qualifies and models it, without having any identity relation (*tādātmya*) with it. This is the paradox of the concept of *vega* or impetus for Indian and Western physicists.

The combination of different forces, initial impulse, residual impulse, gravitation, etc., which intervene when an arrow is released from the bow-string is explained in the following way in the *Vaiśeṣika Sūtra* and by Śaṅkara Miśra in his commentary (the *Upaskāra*):

> The first movement of the arrow comes from the initial impulse (*nodana*). The next movement comes from the residual impulse (*saṃskāra*) produced by the first one, and hence onwards. When this residual energy is no more, the fall takes place due to gravitation.[5]

Śaṅkara Miśra further comments—

> When somebody, after bending the bow, through voluntary effort, releases the bow and the arrow goes away, the process develops itself in two times. There is a first movement, born from the impulsion. The arrow is its seat or the inherent cause (*samavāyī-kāraṇa*). Voluntary effort (*prayatna*) on the one hand, gravitation (*gurutva*) on the other, are the efficient causes (*nimitta-kāraṇa*).

And he adds—

> This first movement gives rise to or produces a residual energy called *vega* which acts in the same way.

2.3 *Vega* as cause and effect of motion

Residual energy develops a movement in the arrow. It constitutes non-inherent, non-consubstantial cause of this movement. The arrow continues to be the inherent cause whereas the efficient cause is a particular kind of intensive impulse (*nodana*). And so on and so forth till the fall of the arrow, due to gravitation, once the residual energy gets exhausted. Praśastapāda offers a more complete and rigorous variant of this analysis by adding the third factor—elasticity to the two forces mentioned above, *vega* and *gurutva*. A precision should be added regarding these two forces. Sometimes impetus or momentum (*vega*) succeeds to the action of gravitation (*gurutva*) and acts in the same way as the latter. For example, the falling of the pestle in the mortar. Gravitation is responsible for the first moment of the fall. Afterwards, it is the momentum (*vega*) which takes the relay. The *Nyāya Kośa* defines *vega* as the non-inherent cause of the second fall.[6] This applies to two elements affected by gravitation, earth and water. Sometimes the residual impetus

---

[5] *Vaiśeṣika Sūtra* (=VS) V.1,17-18.

[6] (NK=) *Nyāya Kośa*, article *vega*, § B, pp. 733–34.

counter acts against the gravitation and makes the fall of the motor or engine delayed. Examples—lancing of a javeline, of an arrow, or the flight of birds. When huge birds glide in the sky, gravitation does not activate their fall, because the residual impetus hinders it.[7]

We cannot simplify or demystify the problem by thinking that *vega* or impetus has nothing substantial so let us reduce it to motion or movement only. This is impossible because *vega* explicitly figures in the list of effects of movement—conjunction, separation, impetus (*vega*) are produced by movement.[8] And the movement cannot be auto generated, movement obtained by movement itself, this cannot be found.[9] This will end in the absurdity of perpetual movement. Though *vega* is one of the causes of motion, it is not reducible to motion. It possesses a directional and vectorial property.[10] Commentaries on Praśastapāda's VS explain without any ambiguity that *vega* is the cause of continuity of motion in a given or fixed direction.[11] The *Nyāya Kośa* defines *vega* as being nothing but a *saṃskāra* which generates motion.[12] It is the cause of the second movement and hence forward motion (*dvitīyādikrīyāhetuḥ*). In conclusion, impetus or *vega* is at the same time cause and effect of motion. It is an intermediary force between two punctual motions. It has in the mechanical order the same epistemological function of mediation which belongs to a *saṃskāra*.

---

[7] *ākāśāvasthiteṣu śakuniṣu gurutvaṃ na patanaṃ karoti saṃskārapratibandhat/ Vyomavatī*, sub-commentary by *Vyomaśivācārya* to the Commentary on Praśastapada, *Guṇagrantha, Gurutvanirūpaṇam*, p. 630.

[8] *Guṇagrantha: saṃyogavibhāgavegāḥ karmajāḥ*

[9] VS I, 1, 11: *karma karmasādhyaṃ na vidyate*

[10] See S.N. Sen, "The impetus theory of the Vaiśeṣikas", *Indian Association for the cultivation of science*, vol. 1, n° 1, pp. 34–35, Calcutta, 1965.

[11] *Guṇagrantha, Saṃskāranirūpaṇam*, p. 633: *niyatidikkriyāprabandhahetuḥ*

[12] Article vega § D: *karmajaḥ saṃskāraḥ* / See also NK *vega*, § C.

3. Definition of "elasticity"

Elasticity (*sthitisthāpaka*) is that which restitutes its previous state to an object that has undergone a deformation.[13] Just like *vega* it is a quality (*guṇa*) and not a substance (*dravya*). For example, a rolled mat unrolls by itself, a branch of tree if pulled regains its initial position, energy emmagnified in the bow-string, etc.[14] Elasticity is a form of *saṃskāra* as it is a factor of reproduction and restitution of a previous state. This is its "restorative tendency".

4. Psychological theories of *Vaiśeṣika* philosophy

In the psychological theories of *Vaiśeṣika*, the concept of *saṃskāra* is dealt with in relation to "memory-souvenir" (*smṛti*) and "dream" (*svapna*). Each of these is subdivided— though *smṛti* covers total memory phenomenon, in a narrower sense it designates "recall" or "rememoration", quite similar to *bhāvanā*. Besides dreams, "border-line dream states" (*svapnāntika*) are also treated in the *Vaiśeṣika Sūtras*.[15]

4.1 Memory: a particular conjunction between *ātman* and *manas*

Memory (*smṛti*) results from a particular conjunction between *ātman* and *manas*, as well as residual impressions (*saṃskāra*)[16]. This definition contains two parts and underlines two conditions, negative and positive, which make rememoration possible. Rememoration supposes a provisional disconnection from one's present sensori-motor environment, and a direct coming closer of *ātman* and *manas*. Thus *bhāvanā*, a variety of *saṃskāra*, factor of

---

[13] TS II. 24. 4 : *anyathākṛtasya punas tadavasthāpādakaḥ sthitisthāpakaḥ /* See also *Guṇagrantha*, *Saṃskāranirūpaṇam*, p. 636; and *Nyāya Kośa*, art. *Sthitisthāpaka*, 6 C2, p. 957; pargraphe A.

[14] This is Praśastapāda's favourite example. See *Karmagrantha*, *Śatpratyayakarma-nirūpaṇam*, pp. 663–64.

[15] (VS=) *Vaiśeṣika Sūtras* IX. 2. 6: *ātmamanasoḥ saṃyogaviśeṣāt saṃskārāc ca smṛtiḥ /*

[16] VS IX. 2. 6.

reproduction and reiteration, is the extraordinary power that only human beings possess—power of rendering the past acts once again in present. It is a supra-sensorial faculty (*atīndriya*).[17] Hence *bhāvanā*, which connects two disparate time-moments, is a means of making supple the *partes extra partes* principle or the localization phenomenon.

4.2 Memory: residual impressions and direct experience

As to the positive condition of memory (*smṛti*), it is the presence of residual impressions (*saṃskāra*) that distinguishes memory (*smṛti*) from direct experience (*anubhava*). Knowledge is of two kinds—memory and direct experience. Memory is that knowledge which is produced by a *saṃskāra* only,[18] deposited in the *ātman* by a direct or new experience (*anubhava*) in the past. The power of evocation (*bhāvanā*), born from *anubhava* cause of *smṛti* resides only in *ātman*,[19] not in *manas*, budging all the time, subject to modification.

4.3 Power of evocation: latent desires and unforeseen causes

Power of evocation (*bhāvanā*) is based on oblivion, forgetfulness, which is just the opposite of *smṛti*. This is to be understood in terms of "unconscious traces", "impregnations", "latent desires" (*vāsanā*). On *vāsanā*, the manner in which they model our "invisible destiny" or "unforeseen causes" (*adṛṣṭa*), without our knowledge, the *Padakṛtyam*,[20] gives interesting details, quite similar to those examined later in Western depth psychology. Invisible destiny (*adṛṣṭa*) is nothing but merit and demerit produced by prescribed and

---

[17] NK, article *bhāvanā*, § I, B and C, pp. 574–575: *sa tu saṃskāra-prabhedaḥ/ jīvamātravṛttiḥ / atīndriyaś ceti bodhyam* / Let me remind that *bhāvanā* is also a quality or property (*guṇa*) of the substance (*dravya*) and not a substance.

[18] See TS II bis, 1, 2: *sā dvividhā smṛtir anubhavaś ca saṃskāramātrajanya jñānaṃ smṛtiḥ* /

[19] TS II, 24, 3: *anubhavajanyā smṛtihetur bhāvanā ātmāmātravṛttiḥ* /

[20] Candrasiṃha's commentary on TS II, 22–23.

prohibited acts[21]. Both of them are born from *vāsanās,* which are nothing but a particular mode of reiteration or *saṃskāra,* left over by previous acts and experiences.[22] Alas! our actions are nothing but reactions. Compared to *saṃskāra, vāsanā* represents the passive, preserving and unconscious aspect of memory.

4.4 *Saṃskāra* and dream

Just as in memory (*smṛti*), residual impressions (*saṃskāra*) intervene also in dream (*svapna*).[23] In dream experience, *manas* comes in close contact with *ātman* in which *saṃskāras* are stored up. The conjunction of *ātman* and *manas* in dreams play the role of non-material cause (*asamavāyī-kāraṇa*), although immanent in the effect. The *ātman* as the seat of dream knowledge is the inherent and material cause (*samavāyī-kāraṇa*). Śaṅkara Miśra names three efficient causes (*nimitta-kāraṇa*) of dream knowledge (*svapnajñāna*). Firstly, it can be activated by the intensity of residual impressions (*saṃskāra-paṭava*). Second factor, dream content may depend on perturbations caused by disequilibrium of the three active elements of the body, wind, bile, phlegmn (*tridhātu—vāta, pitta, kapha* or *śleṣman*), liable to become morbid (becoming three "defects" *tridoṣa, dhātu-doṣa*). Thirdly, what is lived in dreams may equally depend on *adṛṣṭa,* invisible causes and effects of our past meritorious and demeritorious acts.

The *Nyāya Kośa* also puts accent on the mnemonic aspects of dream experience. Like the *Vaiśeṣikas,* this dictionary accords importance to previous vigil experiences upsurging in dreams because of rememoration. But it considers dream to be nothing but a procession of "false representations", "deprived of precise contours", which is

[21] TS II, 22–23: *vihitakarma janyo dharmaḥ / niṣiddhakarmajanyas tv adharmaḥ /*

[22] *Padakṛtyam,* Commentary on the *Tarka Saṃgraha* II, 22–23: *etāv eva adṛṣṭam iti kathyete vāsanājanyau ca vāsanā ca vilakṣaṇasaṃskāraḥ /*

[23] VS IX, 2, 6–7: *tathā svapnaḥ /*

due to the presence of the three "defects" (*tri-doṣa*).[24] The *Nyāya Kośa* quotes opinions of other authors, amongst whom, *Sāṃkhya* and *Vedānta* scholars, that dream states are due to mental traces (*vāsanā*) and residual impressions (*saṃskāra*), left over by wakeful experiences. All that is seen in dream is false according to those *Vedāntins* who profess the doctrine of cosmic illusion (*māyāvādin*). But this is not the opinion of Madhva, who is a dualist. His argument is that things or living beings seen in dream are true only on the condition that they were equally true in wakeful states, if not, they are false. Moreover, falsity of dreams would entail the falsity of vigil experience. In his commentary to the *Brahmāṇḍa Purāṇa*, Madhva says, the Lord (*Īśvara*) utilizes, all sorts of residual impressions (*saṃskāra*) in the mind, and make us see, according to his own sweet will, all that we see in dream. The Supreme Lord is thus the author of our dream, at least as a projectionist of *saṃskāras*, imprinted on our unconscious mental screen.[25]

4.5 *Saṃskāra*: oniric and para-oniric states

As to the difference between oniric (*svapna*) and para-oniric (*svapnāntika*),[26] it is explained in the following manner by Śaṅkara Miśra:

> **Dreams are caused by *saṃskāras* issued from experiences prior to dreams, which relate them to memory. A borderline, intra-or para-oniric state is activated by a *saṃskāra* coming from an experience concomitant to dream.[27]**

In his second interpretation, he situates these states on the border of wakeful and dream states.

---

[24] NK§ I, p. 968: *jāgradavasthāyāṃ bāhyavastuanubhavajanyaṃ yathārthaṃ smaraṇam /...tac ca nirākāram eva / (ibid.) mithyāpratyayapravāhaḥ / Ibid.*, §IIc.

[25] See NK p. 370: *īśvaro'nādimanogataṃś ca saṃskārān upādānīkṛtya svecchāmātreṇa pradarśayati (padārthān) (...) sa svapna itigīyate* / But the problem then is: if dreams are false, then this will lead to the falsity of vigil experiences also!: *yad anyathātvajāgarattvaṃ sā bhrāntis tatra tatkṛtā* /

[26] VS IX, 2, 8.

[27] *Ibidem*, Śaṅkara Miśra: *pūrvānubhavajanitāt saṃskārāt/ tat kālautpannānubhavajanita saṃskārād eva* /

5. *Saṃskāras* as factors of prolongation in space and time

From an existential and ontological point of view, this six-fold capacity of potentialisation and reiteration (*vega* and *sthitisthāpaka*, on the one hand; *vāsanā, bhāvanā, svapna* and *adṛṣṭa* on the other hand), brings about a certain suppleness in our attitude. This helps us to surpass spatio-temporal limits, considered as fixed. The notion of fixity of spatial limits is generated from our experience of solid bodies and accentuates the idea of separation (*bheda*) and multiplicity (*nānātva*). Now, without talking about *ākāśa*, vehicle of sound, or of fluids, phenomena such as momentum (*vega*) and elasticity (*sthitisthāpaka*) institute liaison and continuity in the spatio-temporal order. Factor of prolongation or maintenance in space and time can be a good definition of *saṃskāra*.[28]

5.1 *Saṃskāras:* factors of mediation and continuity

From an epistemological point of view, reference is always made by Indian thinkers to the concept of *saṃskāra* when they seek to restitute an intermediary chain between apparently heterogeneous phenomena at physical, mechanical or psychological level. Factors of mediation and continuity, *saṃskāras* are above all factors of intelligibility. Herein lies their major epistemological function. The common denominator between these three varieties of *saṃskāras* (*vega, bhāvanā, sthitisthāpaka*) is the persistency of the effect after the cessation of the initial cause. In this way, a *saṃskāra* guarantees perfect liaison between past and present or between conscious and unconscious phases of our psyche, just as *saṃdhi* guarantees perfect liaison between phonemes.

6. St. Augustine and the vast palacės of memory

In quite a different cultural context, reference can be made to some sublime passages from St. Augustine for whom memory is a sort of proof of divine immanence, the presence

[28] See Synoptic Tables at the end of the chapter.

of God in us. He compares it to a "spacious palace". The prolongation or persistency of the effect beyond the intial cause, well-explained through the concepts of *smṛti, vāsanā, bhāvanā*, etc., in the Indian context, a sort of reversibility of the *irreparable tempus*, find its echo in St. Augustine's *Confessions.* Here is an extract:

> So I must also go beyond this natural faculty of mine, as I rise by sages towards God who made me. The next stage is memory, which is like a great field of a spacious palace, a storehouse for countless images of all kinds which are conveyed to it by the senses. In it are stored away all the thoughts by which we enlarge upon or diminish or modify in anyway the perception at which we arrive through the senses, and it also contains anything else that was entrusted to it for safe keeping, until such time as these things are swallowed up and burried in forgetfulness. When I sue my memory, I ask it to produce whatever it is that I wish to remember. Some things it produces immediately, some are forthcoming only after a delay, as though were brought out from some inner hiding place, others come spilling from the memory, thrusting themselves upon us when what we want is something quite different [....]. They come and give place in their turn to others that follows up them, and as their place is taken they return to their place of storage, ready to emerge again when I want them. This is what happens when I recite something by heart.[29] I can recall at will all the images formed by different senses, recorded and laid up in the memory. I can distinguish the scent of lillies from that of violets, even though there is no scent at all in my nostrils, and simply by using my memory I recognise that I like honey better than wine and smooth things better than rough ones, although at the moment I neither taste nor touch anything".[30]

A very good explanation indeed of what a *vāsanā* ("impregnation") and a *bhāvanā* ("power of evocation", "creative imagination ") is. Similar to Proust's *madeleine,* (the cake he ate during his childhood), we can taste (and smell, etc.) something we liked during our first experience years after.

> All things goes on inside me, in the vast cloisters of my memory. In it are the sky, the earth, and the sea, ready at my summons, together

[29] See St AUGUSTINE, *Confessions,* X.8.12-15, Translated by R.S. PINE-COFFIN, Penguin Classics, Penguin Books, England, 1961, pp. 214–16.

[30] *Ibidem.* X.8.13.

with everything that I have perceived in them by my senses, except the things which I have forgotten. In it I meet myself as well. I remember myself and what I have done, when and where I did it, and the state of my mind at that time. In my memory, too, are all the events that I remember, whether they are things that have happened to me or things that I have heard from others. [....] If I say to myself in the vast cache of my mind, where all those images of great things stored, 'I shall do this or that', the picture of this particular thing comes into my mind at once. Or I may say to myself 'If only this or that would happen!' No sooner do I say this than the images of all things of which I speak spring forward from the same great treasure-house of the memory. [....] The power of the memory is prodigious, my God. It is a vast, immeasurable sanctuary. Who can plumb its depth? and yet it is a faculty of my soul.[31]

7. Synoptic Tables 1 and 2

SYNOPTIC Table 1

Saṃskāra	*Memory (smṛti)*
	saṃskāra-mātra-janyam jñānaṃ smṛtiḥ (*Tarka Saṃgraha,* II.I.2)
Factors of prolongation of the effect beyond the initial cause, potentialisation and with its two aspects: reiteration of the *Movement*	1. Power or faculty of conservation, of latency. "Engraving in memory" of the past. 2. Power or faculty of reactualisation of the past dynamism, capacity of reproduction and reiteration.

[31] *Ibidem.* X. 18. 00014-15.

SYNOPTIC Table 2

In The Mechanical Field	**In The Psychological Field**
Here the two faculties of conservation and reiteration are intimately related, nearly contemporary.	Here the two aspects appear to be united by their time gap (except for *Svapnāntika*).
Vega Elan, acquired speed, residual impulsion.	*Bhāvanā* Recall, either occasional, or active and voluntary.
Sthitisthāpaka Elasticity. Spontaneous return of a body which has undergone a deformation of its anterior shape.	*Svapna* Dream. Non-voluntary return of the past residual impressions.
Saṃskāra The phenomena of propagation of sound, of the resonance (*Nyāya Bhāṣya* II.2.35) explained by taking recourse to the concept of *saṃskāra*.	In *vāsanā* the conservation-oblivion aspect predominates. In *bhāvanā* the reproductive –reiterative aspect predominates. In *svapna* the reproductive-reiterative aspect predominates. In *adṛṣṭa* the repetitive aspect predominates. *Vāsanā*, *svapna*, *adṛṣṭa* constitute in the psychological field what inertia is in the physical field. It is our memory in the shape of slavery.
Vega applied to *Manas* An interlinking factor between the mechanical and the psychological fields.	*Svapnāntika* Limitrophe dream states. Irruption of residual impressions concomitant to dream.
Vāsanā Residual impregnations or impressions, dharmics and adharmics. Here the two aspects appear to be quite different by their time gap (except for *svapnāntika*)	*Adṛṣta* Invisible destiny. Non voluntary return of previous residual impressions (*vāsanā*), dharmic and adharmic, and of all that happens to us without our knowing.

CHAPTER V

Role of *Saṃskāras* in Theories of Language

1. Word, phonemes and verbal knowledge

The importance of revealed word through audition (*śruti*), hence, of its sonorous materiality is such that Brahmanical authors accord a due primacy to the significant. A word (*pada*) made of multiple phonemes (*varṇa*) is not only a sound, it is also a *śabda* having one particular meaning or significance and denotes an object, *artha*. How is verbal knowledge (*śabda-bodha*) possible? What sort of relation exists between sound and meaning (*śabda-artha-saṃbandha*) between phonetical diversity and semantic unity? This is the traditional enquiry, which can thus be situated on two levels, that of a word and that of a sentence. Contemporary development in the language sciences, encourages more interest in the ancient Indian theories.

1.1 *Varṇa-vāda* and *sphoṭa-vāda*

Two currents of thought, which are rather two interpretations, tackle the questions of *varṇa-vāda* and *sphoṭa-vāda*. In both these doctrines, references are made to *saṃskāras*, understood as linking factors.

2. *Saṃskāra* and *sphoṭa*

For Śabara, who is a *varṇa-vādin*, a word is nothing but a succession of phonemes.[1] It has no unity by itself. The invisible binder between phonemes are "mental dispositions" (*saṃskāra*) only, imprinted by previous phonemes. The last phoneme associated with mental impressions produced by previous ones, is that which makes us know (the object).[2] Thus, in case of audition and comprehension of a language, *saṃskāras* work like a sort of immediate memory. Just as there is a persistency of a luminous impression on the retina, similarly there is a sonorous impression on the ear. Thus a psychological type of the explanation (the fact of taking recourse in the concept of *saṃskāra*), allows to fill the gap between articulation of sound and its comprehension; between phonetics and semantics.

This kind of interpretation has its variants, for example, the one attributed to Upavarśa. Śaṅkara who follows him on this point[3] does not accord any privileged status to the last letter of the word heard (as does Śabara). Immediate memories deposited in the mental organ by each phoneme or letter makes for the comprehension of the word, which is thus based on a symbiosis between *varṇa* and *saṃskāra*.

2.1 *Saṃskāras* as factors of liaison

Amongst late Mīmāṃsakas (8th century A.D.), a split takes place between Prābhākaras and Bhāṭṭas. The first are mainly concerned with ritual injunctions, with a sentence, not a word. They are those who profess that designation appertains to things put in relation (*anvitābhidhāna-vādin*). On the contrary, the Bhāṭṭas are those who profess that relation appertains to things named (*abhihitānvaya-vādin*). In this case a word is a garland of phonemes (*varṇa-mālā*). The Bhāṭṭa interpretation concerning audition and comprehe-

[1] Commentary on *Jaimini Sūtra* I. I. 5, p. 46: *pūrvavarṇajanitasaṃskārasahito'nto varṇaḥ pratyāyaka iti* /

[2] *Śābara Bhāṣya* I. 1. 5, p. 47: *akṣarebhyaḥ saṃskārād arthapratipattir iti* /

[3] See *Brahma Sūtra Bhāṣya* I. 3. 28.

nsion depends equally on *varṇa-saṃskāra* synergy. The phonemes are the flowers, *saṃskāras* are the invisible thread. Taken together, they make a garland.

3. Dialogue between *varṇa-vādin* and *sphoṭa-vādin*

There is a polemical dialogue between a *varṇa-vādin* and a *sphoṭa-vādin* in *Tattvabindu* of Vācaspati Miśra about the multivocity of the word *saṃskāra*. The *sphota-vādin* asks his adversary what he means by impressions (psycho-physical saṃskāra) left by each phoneme or invisible sacrificial efficiency (*adrṣta, apūrva*). The *varna-vādin* replies that he uses it in a psychological sense. Vācaspati Miśra explains the exact nature of this psychological function:

> A word, because it has a relation with its meaning, works like an instrument of recall. The relation of meaning with the word is that of recalled (*smarya-smāraka-bhāva*). Recall is effectuated by means of reawakening of mental dispositions (*saṃskāra*)[4].

According to *sphoṭa-vāda* (mainly Bhartṛhari, 5th century AD), sonorous synthesis is *a priori*. A word, as an indivisible sonorous unity exists before its eclosion (*sphoṭa*) in concrete multiple phonemes. Same is true of a sentence (*vākya*). The rule that governs the discussion between a *varṇa-vādin* and a *sphoṭa-vādin* is very rational. It is a principle of economy (*lāghavatva*). The *sphoṭa-vādin* finds that the *varṇa-vāda* solution is quite complicated and wants to solve the problem of verbal knowledge (*śabda-bodha*) in one single stroke, by introducing the concept of *sphoṭa* (which is nothing but a metaphysical postulate in the opinion of a *varṇa-vādin*).

3.1 Bhartṛhari's contribution

Even Bhartṛhari, who believes in a pre-existent metaempirical sonorous unity of a word before its pronunciation (*sphoṭa*), does not exclude *saṃskāras* as factors of liaison. He admits their role at three levels[5]—Firstly, our senses (*indriya*) and the sensorial field (*viṣaya*) are affected

---

[4] See *Tattvabindu* 75; 64–65.

[5] See *Vākyapadīya* I. 78–80.

by *saṃskāras.* Secondly, latent speech-instinct in a new-born baby results from previous impressions (*saṃskāra*).[6] This is the psycho-cosmological register of the Law of *karman.* Thirdly, Bhartṛhari considers Grammar as the door to liberation.[7] A language, when purified and perfected (*saṃskṛta*),[8] in conformity with grammatical rules, bestows perfection on those who utilize it.

There is a sort of mythical prehistory in the mechanism of acquiring a *habitus,* the instinctive knowledge, in animals, e.g., birds making nests, spiders the net. There is no logical fault of *regressus ad infinitum* (*anavasthā*) in this kind of reasoning in the Indian thought because the world is without beginning (*anādi*). The dialectics of *aptitude* and *habitude* (habits) does not escape to this general rule.

4. Some parallels with the West

After having affirmed in §61:"All is one, all is diverse. How many natures in that of man!", Pascal writes in his *Pensées,* §63 about custom and then "the origin of our preferences and our choice of a profession" (§62). He continues:

> The most important thing in life is the choice of a calling: it is left to chance. Custom makes men masons, soldiers, tilers. [...] Our choice is made because in childhood we heard these callings praised and all the rest despised; for we naturally love truth and hate folly; we are stirred by the names; we only go wrong in applying them. Such is the force of custom that, out of those whom Nature has made merely men; for some districts are full of masons, others of soldiers and so on. Nature is certainly not so uniform. Custom is the cause, forcing Nature; and sometimes nature gets the upper hand and keeps man to his instinct in spite of the custom, whether good or bad.[9]

---

[6] *Vākyapadīya* I.122; II.145–52. Bhartṛhari, surprisingly enough, passes spontaneously from the strict Vedic and ritualistic theories of the Mīmāṃsakas concerning the domain of language to the psychological interpretations of the concept of *saṃskāra.*

[7] *Ibidem,* I.14: *tad dvāram apavargasya...*/

[8] *Ibidem,* I.10-12 and 131.

[9] See *Pascal's Pensées,* with an English Translation, brief notes and Introduction by H.F. STEWART, London, Routledge and Kegan Paul, 1950, p. 35.

Indian texts however extend the topic of nature/culture beyond one single life span to innumerable series of lives in which we learn (giving lieu to habits) or forget.

4.1 Hindu Philosophers are all *samskāra-vādin*

Hindu Philosophers, whether *varṇa-vādin* or *sphoṭa-vādin*, are all *saṃskāra-vādin*. This is the reason why both Maṇḍana Miśra, a partisan of *sphoṭa-vāda*, and Śaṅkara who is against it, make a frequent use of concepts such as *saṃskāra*, *vāsanā*, *bhāvanā*. As to the Buddhists, (the *Śramaṇas*), who refuses to give any priviledge to the Vedic revealed word (as do the *Brāhamaṇas*), they need not give priviledge to the *significant* because of "production" of words. In the Buddhist *Vijñānvāda* or Idealistic school, the object of thought is in the thought. There is an interesting echo of the discussion between a Buddhist (a *nirālambana-vādin*) and Kumarila Bhaṭṭa, (a Mīmāṃsaka) as reported in the *Ślokavārttika*.[10] Kumārila Bhaṭṭa clings to the "plural" reality and substantiality of letters and words. If everything is just an "idea" wherefrom generates the plurality of ideas? Kumārila's answer is that it is due to the plurality of objects in the exterior world. Unable to take recourse to the objects existing in the external world, the Buddhist Idealist retorts that the diversity of "ideas" come from the diversity of the latent impressions (*vāsanā*) deposited by previous experiences. But this also supposes the diversity of objects, retorts back Kumārila Bhaṭṭa. So there is a vicious circle.

4.2 Leibniz's repliqua

In an altogether different context, this discussion reminds me of Leibniz's repliqua about the Cartesian *Cogito*. There is no such thing as a one single "primary truth of resaon" like the *Cogito*. There are two truths of reason *cogito sed cogito cogitata*.

---

[10] *Ślokavārttika*, §167–68.

> As for primary truths of fact, these are inner experiences which are immediate with the *immediacy of feeling*. This is where the first truth of the Cartesians and St Augustine belongs: *I think, therefore I am*. That is, *I am a thing which thinks*. But we must realize that just as identities can be general or particular, and they are equally evident in either case (since A is just as evident as *A thing is what it is*), so it is with the first truth of fact. For not only is it immediately evident to me that I think, but it is just as evident that *I think various thoughts*: at one time *I think about A* and at another time *about B* and so on. Thus the Cartesian principle is sound, but it is not the only one of its kind. This shows that all of the primary truths of reason and of fact have in common that we cannot prove them by anything more certain."[11]

In a nutshell, let us conclude that in order to solve the fundamental problem of the One and Many, may it be on the language or any other level, Indian Philosophers take recourse to the concept of *saṃskāra*, dynamic scheme, which is in itself one of the directive schemes of the Indian way of thinking.

---

[11] G.W. LEIBNIZ, *New Essays on Human Understanding*, Book IV, chapter ii, §1, translated and edited by Peter REMNANT and Jonathan BENNETT, London, Cambridge University Press, 1981, pp. 367–68.

CHAPTER VI

The *Advaita Vedānta* Theory of *Saṃskāras*

1. Śaṅkarācārya's contribution to *saṃskāra*

Śaṅkarācārya's commentaries on Vedic *Upaniṣads, Brahma Sūtras, Bhagavad Gītā,* and also his *Upadeśasāhasrī* contain rich materials on the concept of *saṃskāra.* Reference is made to many other post-Śaṅkarian Vedāntic texts. Authors such as Abhinavagupta and Kṣemarāja (Kashmir Śaiva tradition), largely influenced by *Vedānta* (and by *Sāṃkhya-Yoga*) are also quoted. Surely, in India there is veritable master-disciple tradition (*guru-śiṣya-paramparā*) which keeps alive the eternal norm (*sanātana-dharma*) or set of laws. Still, we should not forget that fourteen centuries separate the Vedic *Upaniṣads* and the commentaries written on them by Śaṅkarācārya.

1.1 *Saṃskāra, saṃskṛta, asaṃskṛta*

The richness of Śaṅkara's contribution on this subject lies in the fact that he is familiar with the use of the verb (*saṃskṛ-*), of the noun (*saṃskāra*), and of the adjectives (*saṃskṛta, asaṃskṛta*), in the Brahmanical, Buddhist and philosophical contexts. He is aware of both the ritual and the psycho-moral connotation of the word *saṃskāra.* For example, we find reference made to *śarīra-saṃskāras* when he quotes the *Gautama Dharma Śāstra* in his commentary to the *Bṛhad*

Āraṇyaka Upaniṣad. IV.4.22. Also when he refers himself to the concepts of impetus (*vega*), or to acts which have started giving their consequences because the fruit is now ripe (*ārabdhakārya, prārabdha-karman*), to "residue of acts" (*karmāśaya*), "latent desires" or "impregnations" (*vāsanā*), "dormant subconscious tendencies" (*anuśaya*), etc., concepts quasi-synonymous with *saṃskāra*. Besides, Śaṅkara is familiar with Buddhist texts and all interminable debates among Brahmins, Buddhists and others as show his commentary on the *Brahma Sūtras* of Bādarāyaṇa.[1] He knows better than anybody else what a Buddhist has to say about rituals or about the concepts of *karman, saṃsāra, saṃskāra, vāsanā*. Śaṅkara's place in the history of Indian philosophy is interesting because he is also a renouncer like Mahāvīra, the Jīna, and Siddhārtha Gautama, the Buddha, although not the same kind of renouncer. He remains a *Brāhmaṇa*, a *Vaidika*, whose veneration for the *Veda* or the revealed text cannot be questioned. This does not mean that Śaṅkara has no critical sense. If the Veda says that the "fire is cold" he will rather not consent to its validity because of the contradiction the sentence contains.[2]

In the ancient Indian society, the *Brahmāṇa* and the *Śramaṇa* co-existed side by side and yet apart at the same time. In Brahmanism/Hinduism, the secular members of the socio-religious group are in the centre whereas the renouncer is in the margin. In Jainism and Buddhism, two monastic traditions, the renouncer is in the centre and the lay-members or the laity is in the margin of this big circle. This is the reason why approach and the interpretation of the concept of *saṃskāra* is so very different in their respective texts.

Śaṅkara uses the substantive *saṃskāra* and the adjectives *saṃskṛta/asaṃskṛta*. However, Śaṅkara never attaches pejorative value to these words. In Śaṅkara's writings *saṃskṛta*

[1] *Brahma Sūtra Bhāṣya* (=BSBH), II.2.18-II.2.33.

[2] *Bhagavad Gītā Bhāṣya* (=BHGBH), XVIII.66.

signifies "perfected", "purified", "embellished by rites", belonging to the sacred realm and *asaṃskṛta* just the opposite, "imperfect", "uncultivated", etc. Inversely, a-*saṃskṛta* will never be a synonym of *nirvāṇa* in his writings as it is in the Buddhist literature. As Śaṅkara represents the *Uttara Mīmāṃsā,* while facing Jaimini, author of the *Pūrva Mīmāṃsā Sūtra* or his opponent (*Pūrva-pakṣin*), his position to the valorisation of *saṃskāras* (purificatory rites or dynamic traces of acts and experiences left in the psyche) differs totally from the Buddhist criticism of the same. He defends his thesis from the point of view of a renouncer, the ultimate goal of life deliverance (*mokṣa, mukti*). The access to "heaven" or paradise (*svarga*) gained by sacrificial acts (*yajña*) is not satisfactory because the duration of the sojourn in the *svarga* is limited, depending on accumulated merits (and demerits). Therefore, the Buddhist criticism towards rituals is situated outside Brahmanical orthodoxy.

1.2 Renunciation, knowledge, deliverance

Renunciation (*saṃnyāsa* preceded by *vairāgya, virakti*), (true) knowledge (*jñāna*) and deliverance(*mokṣa, mukti*)—these three words can resume Śaṅkara's position and thus his philosophical and religious doctrine known as *Kevala Advaita Vedānta.* Amongst the human goals of life (*puruṣārtha*), he gives a due place to socio-religious laws (*dharma*), but according to him, it is only deliverance (*mokṣa*), which puts a final end to *saṃsāra,* that really counts. Now, deliverance is nothing but an intuitive or immediate knowledge of the *Ātman-Brahman* identity. Knowledge (*jñāna*) is always there, but only hidden and hindered by ignorance (*avidyā, ajñāna*). This non-dualistic intuition has nothing to do with ritual activity which supposes time factor and duality. Surely, some "preparation" is required to favour arising of this intuition which immediately annihilates space-time and subject-object notions.

Śaṅkara's hermeneutic philosophy is called *Brahma Mīmāṃsā, Vedānta Mīmāṃsā* or *Śārīraka Mīmāṃsā,* which is opposed to *Pūrva Mīmāṃsā*, also known as *Karma Mīmāṃsā* and *Dharma Mīmāṃsā*. According to him the most favourable stage for the "knowledge" of *Brahman* (*brahmajijñāsā*) is the Vedic student-life-period (*brahmacaryāśrama*). He stayed life-long with his master in *Veda* as a *naiṣṭhika brahmacārin*. Śaṅkara's dialogue with the *Pūrva-pakṣin*, very often a *Mīmāṃsaka*, needs to be interpreted in this context.

1.3 Sacralization and deliverance

A good comprehension of the concept of *saṃskāra* in the *Kevalādvaitavedānta* perspective results if reference is made to two opposite poles which govern the Indian thought "section of ritual actions" (*karma-kāṇḍa*) versus "section of pure knowledge" (*jñāna-kāṇḍa*); "inclination towards transactional actions" (*pravṛtti*) versus "cessation of transactional actions" (*nivṛtti*)); leading to "heaven" (*svarga*) and to "deliverance" (*mokṣa*) respectively. *Pravṛtti* "activity" or engagement in the world, equal to the "path of acts" (*karma-mārga*), is "cause of bondage" (*bandha-hetu*), whereas *nivṛtti* is the "path of renunciation" (*saṃnyāsa-mārga*), "cause of deliverance".[3]

In *Pūrva Mīmāṃsā* purificatory and perfective rites (*saṃskāra*), subordinated to sacrificial activity (*yajña*) are valorized. What about the status of *saṃskāras* in the *Uttara Mīmāṃsā*? Are they subordinated to deliverance (*mokṣa*) defined as immediate knowledge of *Brahman* residing in us (i.e., in our *ātman*)? This leads to the relationship between action and knowledge on the one hand, and between sacralization and deliverance on the other hand, in Śaṅkara's writings. These two topics are interrelated in his writings because sacralization (through *saṃskāras*) is a part of ritual actions and knowledge is the *conditio sine quo non* of deliverance (although deliverance does not depend on "conditions", "means", etc). Sacralization through ritual purification (*saṃskāra*) and release (*mokṣa*), actions

---

[3] See BHGBH. XVIII, 30; cf. *Nārada Parivrājaka Upaniṣad* III, 13.

(*karman*) and knowledge (*jñāna*), are incompatible.[4] In his concessions to the *Pūrva-pakṣin*, Śaṅkara however admits the value of "permanent" obligatory rites (*nitya-karman*) and also the solution offered by the *jñāna-karma-samuccaya-vāda*, "action-cum-knowledge-doctrine".[5]

Purification results either from the "addition of some quality" (*guṇādhāna*) or from the "removal of some defect" (*doṣāpanaya*).[6] Both these alternatives cannot apply to release since it is of the very nature of *Brahman* (*brahmasvarūpatvān mokṣasya*), eternally pure (*nityaśuddha*). If it is said that release is a quality of the Self (*ātman*) which becomes manifest when the Self is purified by ritual actions (such as bathing, wearing the sacrificial thread), Śaṅkara replies that in this case what is purified is the Self which is joined to the body (*śarīra, deha*) and is under the power of nescience. Release (*mokṣa*) does not belong to any of these four categories of action—production (*utpatti*), modification (*vikāra*), obtention (*āpti*) and purification (*saṃskāra, saṃskārya*).[7]

1.4 Deliverance is a state of disembodiedness

For Śaṅkara, deliverance (*mokṣa*) is a state of "disembodiedness" (*aśarīratva*),[8] a radical separation from the body (*śarīraviyogo hi mokṣa ātyāntikaḥ*).[9] This definition offers a clear comprehension of his attitude towards *śarīra-saṃskāras*.[10] The *Upadeśasāhasrī* (I.1.14-17) also explains that the Self is not characterised by the diversity of birth, lineage, purificatory or perfective rites (*saṃskāra*). Thus *śarira-*

---

[4] See BSBH I.1.4.

[5] *Bṛhad-āraṇyaka-upaniṣad-bhāṣya* (= BĀUBH) I.4.1; III.3.1.

[6] BSBH I.1.4.

[7] See BĀUBH III.3.1; IV.4.22; IV.5.15; BSBH I.1.4; *Naiṣkarmyasiddhi, śloka* 53 (of Sureśvara); *Mānasollāsa* = *Dakṣiṇāmūrtivārttika, śl*=1. 25.

[8] BSBH I.1.4.

[9] BĀUBH III.9.29 (7).

[10] See BĀUBH III.3.1; IV.4.22 where he quotes *Manu Smṛti* II.27–28 *and Gautama-dh.-sūtra* VIII.22.

saṃskāras are superfluous, based on the inherent tendency of superimposition (*adhyāsa, adhyāropa*), which has its root in ignorance. Śaṅkara's disciple Sureśvara is also of the same opinion that the perfective rites such as *jātakarman,* etc., concern the body only.[11] *Śaiva* authors were very much influenced by the *Advaita Vedānta.* Philosophers like Abhinavagupta or his commentator Yogarāja award same importance to this purification obtained by *saṃskāras* helping to get rid of the "cuirasses" (*kañcuka*).[12] Finally, the very idea of means and ends (*sādhya-sādhana*) has to be given up because deliverance cannot be an effect (*kārya*) of an action (*karman*). The auxiliary means (*sahakāri-kāraṇa*), the relation of attribution expressed by the grammatical dative (*sampradāna-kāraka*), the notion of difference (*bheda-buddhi*), etc., necessary in sacrificials proceedings are to be discarded in the final run. Surely, even for Śaṅkara, the obligatory and permanent acts (*nitya-karman*) are the sacred duties of a twice-born (*dvija*), specially audition (*śravaṇa*), reflexion (*manana*), prayer (*upāsanā*), and meditation (*nididhyāsana*). They purify the internal organ (*antaḥkaraṇa*) of latent desires (*vāsanā*).[13] However, Maṇḍana Miśra and Vācaspati Miśra, give more importance to *nitya-karman.*[14] For Śaṅkara deliverance (*mokṣa*) is not subject to space-time categories (*na ca deśakālanimitta.../*).[15] Pure Self-knowledge (*ātma-jñāna,* coinciding with *brahma-jñāna, brahma-sākṣātkāra*) is nothing but pure intuitive knowledge of non-duality (*advaita*), *hic et nunc.* Constant meditation on the "great phrase" (*mahāvākya*)—"That thou art" (*tat tvam asi*)[16] or "I am *Brahman*" (*aham brahmāsmi*)[17]

---

[11] See Mānasollāsa, Commentary on the *Dakṣiṇāmūrti Stotra,* Ch. V, *śloka* 4.

[12] See *Yogarāja ad Paramārthasāra, śloka* 84.

[13] See BHGBH XVIII.9-10.

[14] See *Brahmasiddhi* III, 51 and *Bhāmatī,* I.1.1 respectively.

[15] BĀU IV.5.15.

[16] See CHU VI.8.7. VI.16.3.

[17] BĀU I.4.10.

help the upsurge of this liberating intuition. These *mahāvākyas* are in the present tense, they do not mean that one fine day "I will become *Brahman*" or "Thou wilt become That". The adept is an aspirant of liberation (grammatically *mumukṣu* is a desiderative), desiring to be one with the *Brahman*. But the desire for deliverance is not exactly a "desire" (*kāma, rāga*), because it does not produce any new "fruit" (*phala*) in space or time for somebody.

Quoting the famous *Śruti* passage[18] on *devayājin* and *ātmayājin*[19] by this rite, this part of body is being purified or made perfect" (*idaṃ me anenāṅgaṃ saṃskriyate*)— Śaṅkara explains the *aṅgāṅgin* ("whole and parts") type of relation, not applicable to the real Self (*ātman*), which is partless (*niṣkala, akhaṇḍa*), like *Brahman*. In conformity with the *Kevala Advaita Vedānta* Śaṅkara defines an *ātmayājin*, who is (or becomes) capable of seeing the one same Absolute principle in everything, transcending differences and duality.

1.5 Purification and ritual qualification

In Śaṅkara's works the important point is the relation between *saṃskāra* and *adhikāra* in the general framework of the Law of *karman* and *saṃsāra*.[20] Both ritual and psycho-moral connotations of *saṃskāra* (purificatory rite; residual impressions) and of *adhikāra* (capacitation, ritual fitness, mission, task, office) are present in Śaṅkara's mind.[21] Is *adhikāra* necessary for *brahmavidyā*? On this point he agrees with Jaimini and Bādarāyaṇa that only one who is born in a high caste family and has received *upanayana* has the right or the qualification to study the

[18] ŚB XI.2.6.13.

[19] See BĀUBH III.3.1; IV.4.22.

[20] For the relationship between these two concepts see Ch. II. 5 and Chs. VII–VIII.

[21] See for example : BSBH I.3.36; III.4.34; 38; 51; BHGBH VI.45. In his BSBH I.3.25–26; 31; 38.

Veda. A *Śūdra* has no right to study the *Veda* or to devote himself to *brahmavidyā*. Śaṅkara comments:

> On account of the reference to ceremonial purification (in case of the higher castes) and on account of their absence being declared (in the case of the Sûdras)".[22] "That the Sûdras are not qualified, follows from that circumstance also that in different places of the vidyâs such ceremonies as upanayana and the like are referred to. [....] With reference to the Sûdras, on the other hand, the absence of ceremonies is frequently mentioned; so for instance, when they are spoken of 'as once born' only ('the Sûdra is the fourth caste, once-born'), Manu X.4, and 'In the Sûdra there is not any sin, and he is not fit for any ceremony.' The prohibition of hearing and studying the Veda already imply the prohibition of the knowledge and performance of Vedic matters.... .[23] *Manu Smṛti* X.126.

And Śaṅkara well aware of the denotation and connotations of the word *saṃskāra,* adds something very interesting:

> From those Sûdras, however, who, like Vidura and 'the religious hunter', acquire knowledge in consequence of the after effect of former deeds [*pūrvakṛtādsaṃskāravaśād*], the fruit of knowledge cannot be withheld, since knowledge in all cases brings about its fruit.[24]

Swami Gambhirananda translates this as follows:

> But from those to whom knowledge dawns as a result of (good) tendencies acquired in past lives, as for instance to Vidura, Dharmavyādha, and others, the reaping of the result of knowledge cannot be withheld, for the result of knowledge is inevitable.[25]

Here Śaṅkara takes into account both the ritualistic and the psychological meaning of the word *saṃskāra.*

1.6 Debate between a *Mīmāṃsaka* and the *Siddhāntin*

Are works relating to stages of life (*āśramakarma*) necessary for one who is desirous of knowledge (or aims at final

---

[22] *Brahma Sūtra* I.3.36: *saṃskāraparāmarśāt tadabhāvābhilāpāc ca* / Translation George THIBAUT, *Vedânta-Sûtras,* SBE, vol. XXXIV, Pt I, p. 227.

[23] BSBH I.3.38.

[24] BSBH I.3.38, Translation by George THIBAUT.

[25] *Brahma Sūtra Bhāṣya of Śrī Śaṅkarācārya,* Advaita Ashrama, Calcutta, 1972, p. 234.

release)?[26] Co-operativeness (*sahakāritva*) of the works towards the origination of knowledge is accepted by the *Sūtrakāra* (*sūtra* 33) and by *Śaṅkara* who quotes the *Smṛti* passage "He who is qualified by those forty-eight purifications",[27] required for Vedic works, with a view to the origination of knowledge in whom he has undergone those purifications (*saṃskāra*).[28] Now, persons not belonging to a specific *āśrama*, are qualified for knowledge or not? The opponent (*Pūrvapakṣin*) or the *Mīmāṃsaka* maintains that they are not qualified. But Bādarāyaṇa and Śaṅkara conclude:

> And the promotion (of knowledge is bestowed on them) through special acts.[29] Also for widowers & c., [*vidhurādi*] the favour of knowledge is possible through special acts of duty, such as praying [*japa*], fasting [*upavāsa*], propitiation of divinities [*devatārādhana*], & c., which are not opposed to their *āsrama-less* condition and may be performed by any man as such.[30]

Quoting the *Bhagavad Gītā* VI.45, Śaṅkara takes recourse to the concept of *saṃskāra* in order to justify this specific *adhikāra* or qualification:

> Thus Smṛti also declares, 'Perfected by many births he finally goes the highest way' [...]; which passage shows that the aggregate of the different purificatory ceremonies performed in former births promotes knowledge. [....] Hence there is no contradiction in admitting qualification for knowledge on the part of widowers and the like.[31]

In this passage also the concepts of *saṃskāra* and *adhikāra* can be rendered in their ritual and or psychological sense. Gambhirananda's translation differs from that of G. Thibaut's "particular mental impressions acquired in past lives also help knowledge" (*janmāntarasaṃcitān api saṃskāraviśeṣān* ...). In any case what interest us is that contrary to the *Pūrvapakṣin* Śaṅkara holds the opinion that previous acquisitions are

[26] See BS III.4.32.

[27] *Gautama Dharma Sūtra* VIII.8.

[28] See BSBH III.4.34.

[29] BS III.4.38: *viśeṣānugrahaś ca* /

[30] BSBH III.4.38.

[31] BHGBH VI.45.

preserved throughout the chain of lives. This conclusion comes out from his Commentary to the BS III.4.51, where he quotes the case of the *Ṛṣi* Vāmadeva,[32] and in his commentary to the BS III.3.32, where he discusses at length on this topic with his opponent. "Of those who have a certain office, there is subsistence (of the body) as long as the office lasts".[33] The question here is whether knowledge when reaching its perfection brings about complete isolation (*kaivalya*) of the Self from all bodies (stopping the transmigratory process once for ever) or not. The *Pūrvapakṣin* being totally sceptic, Śaṅkara replies in affirmative by quoting several passages from the *Śruti* and the *Smṛti*. There is the well-known case of the *Ṛṣi* Āpāntaratamas and that of Vasiṣṭha (Brahmā's son of mind). They assumed new bodies because they had not yet finished their task (*adhikāra*). "[....] Āpāntaratamas and others – who are entrusted with offices conducive to the subsistence of the worlds, such as promulgation of the Vedas and the like – depends on those their offices." This office (*adhikāra*) depending on previous residual impressions remains as long as those results of actions which have begun to operate come to an end. As to the works the consequences of which are already in operation, effecting a delay, they will necessarily come to an end after the death of the body, "just as an arrow (*iṣu*) discharged stops in the end owing to gradual cessation of its impetus (*vega*)." This point is largely treated elsewhere also by Śaṅkara.[34]

2. Previous acquisitions in the context of Law of *Karman*

The thesis concerning the existence of previous acquisitions supposes three other hypothesis: A. The belief in the existence of a subtle psychic body (*sūkṣma-śarīra, ātivāhika-śarīra*); B. The Law of *karman* and its corollary, the Doctrine of Transmigration (*saṃsāra*) and C. The conservation of the

[32] See BĀUBH I.4.10.

[33] BS III.3.32: *yāvad adhikāram avasthitir ādhikāriṇām /*

[34] See (CHUBH=) *Chāndogyopaniṣad Bhāṣya* VI.14.2.

remote past because of memory-rememoration. The relationship between *saṃskāra, smṛti* or *smaraṇa* is evident and needs no further explanation. The main idea is that we never start with a *tabula rasa*. The past is preserved in the guise of memory-rememoration because of the psychic continuity. This mechanism inherent to the concept of *saṃskāra* is quite similar to Bergson's *mémoire-souvenir.* Words or expressions used in the texts to designate this total ancient stock are: *saṃskāra, vāsanā, anuśaya, śeṣa, bīja, vega, prārabdha-karman, ārabdha-kārya, karmāśaya,* etc.

2.1 Positive or negative aspect of *saṃskāras*

Both these aspects account for our character (or *svabhāva, prakṛti*), all sorts of tendencies, inclinations, aptitudes, traits of character, habits, talents, etc., tantamount to past *karman, saṃskāras* or *vāsanās*, acquired during previous lives. This major topic is mainly studied with reference to Śaṅkara's commentaries on the *Brahma Sūtras*, on the *Upaniṣads*, and on the *Bhagavad Gītā*. Some important Vedāntic texts previous to Śaṅkara are also quoted, along with the *Śaiva* tradition influenced by *Vedānta.*

2.1.1 *Our intrinsic nature and the psycho-moral predispositions*

The intrinsic nature (*svabhāva, prakṛti*) of a person is in conformity with his psycho-moral and intellectual dispositions (*bhāva, saṃskāra*).

> Nature (*prakṛti*) is the *saṃskāra* (the latent self-reproductive impression of the past acts of *dharma* and *adharma*) manifesting itself at the commencement of the present birth. Even the man of knowledge acts according to his own nature; it needs no saying that an ignorant man acts according to his own nature. Thus all living beings follow their own nature.[35]

---

[35] BHGBH III.33 : *prakṛtirnāma pūrvakṛtadharmādharmādisaṃskārā vartamānajanmādāv abhivyaktāḥ sa prakṛtiḥ.../. The Bhagavad-Gītā with the commentary of Śrī Śankarāchārya,* translated into english by A. Mahādeva Śastri, Mysore, 1901. Diacritical signs and italics were added to Sanskrit words in Śāstri's translation.

Just as in this passage, the word "nature" (*prakṛti*) is quite often used as a synonym for *saṃskāra* or *svabhāva* in the context of the *Bhagavad Gītā* and in the *Śāṅkara Bhāṣya.* Commenting on threefold faith (*śraddhā*), which depends on its turn on the three attributes (*guṇa*) of the nature: *sattva, rajas* and *tamas,* Śaṅkara says:

> "Faith, of which thou hast asked, is of three sorts. It is born of the individual nature (*svabhāva*), *i.e.,* the *saṃskāra* or tendency made up of the self-reproductive latent impressions of the acts – good and bad, *Dharma* and *Adharma* – which were done in the past births and which manifest themselves at the time of death.[36]

And when the *Bhagavad-Gītā* explains that the faith of each person is in confomity with his intimate being (*sattvānurūpa*) and inner nature (*svabhāva*), Śaṅkara understands "conform to the internal organ with the particular residual impressions".[37]

In fact, Śaṅkara puts *prakṛti* in relationship with *vartamāna-janman* or actual present existence, and *svabhāva* with *janmāntara,* i.e., with previous births, (or in course of previous births), and with the ultimate mental dispositions at the time of death. These two crucial moments, the time of death, and that of a new birth, presupposes latent impressions or *saṃskāras,* not only by the Hindus but also by the Buddhists. In Buddhist vocabulary terms used for this linking thought at the birth are: *upapatti-citta, pratisaṃdhi-citta,* and for the thought at death is *maraṇa-citta.*

Or to interpret yet in another way:

> Nature (*svabhāva*) is the tendency (*saṃskāra, vāsanā*) in living beings acquired by them in the past births, and manifesting itself in the present birth by way of being ready to yield its effects: and this nature is the source of the *guṇas,* it being impossible for the *guṇas* to manifest them without a cause.[38]

---

[36] BHGBH XVII, 2: *janmāntarakṛto dharmādisaṃskāro maraṇakāle 'bhivyaktaḥ 'svabhāvaḥ' ucyate.../.* On the importance of the last thoughts of a person before dying, see *Bh.-gītā* VIII, 6.

[37] BHGBH XVII.3: *viśiṣṭasaṃskāropetāntaḥkaraṇānurūpā /*

[38] *Ibidem* XVIII.41: *athavā janmāntarakṛtasaṃskāraḥ prāṇinām vartamānajanmani svakāryābhimukhatvenābhivyaktaḥ svabhāvaḥ.../*

In the vocabulary of the *Bhagavad-Gītā* the terms *svabhāva, svadharma, sahajakarman, svakarman* and *prakṛti* are nearly identical. Specially the chapter XVIII, means that one's intrinsic nature and all past achievements determine one's sacred duties. The personal self-duties (*svadharma, svakārya, svakarman*) enjoined for the four castes *Brāhmaṇa, Kṣatriya, Vaiśya* and *Śūdra* are divided according to the natural qualities. Going back to the *Śruti,*[39] the *Puruṣa-sūkta* mentions only the names of the members belonging to the four castes and the related parts of the body of *Puruṣa,* with their specific functions. Medhātithi's commentary is quite interesting on this point. He establishes a rapport between the mouth of the *Puruṣa* (the *Brāhmaṇa*) and the function of studying and teaching belonging to the priest (*mukha-karmādhyāpana*). Next comes the *Kṣatriya* (*Rājañya* in the *Puruṣa Sūkta*), from the arms of the Cosmic Giant (*Puruṣa*), having the function of undertaking war with the force of his arms (*bāhu-karmayuddham*). From the thighs of the *Puruṣa* emanates the *Vaiśya* whose function is to look after the cattles (*ūrū-karma paśūn rakṣato gobhiś caranti*) and from the feet of the Cosmic Man emanates the *Śūdra,* whose function, related to this part of the body, is to serve others (*pada-karma śuśruṣā*).[40] The seer (*ṛṣi*) or the poet (*kavi*) of the hymn is perhaps not consciously concerned about the hierarchical order of the society.

2.1.2 *Just like the seasons (all) comes back again and again*

The cosmogonical scheme in the *Manu Smṛti* throws some light on these interrelated concepts.

> But to whatever course of action the Lord at first appointed each (kind of being), that alone it has spontaneously adopted in each succeeding creation. Whatever he assigned to each at the (first) creation, noxiousness or harmlessness, gentleness or ferocity, virtue or sin, truth or falsehood, that clung (afterwards) spontaneously to it. As at the change of the seasons each season of its own accord

[39] To the *Ṛg Veda* X.90.11-12 precisely.

[40] See Medhātithi ad *Manu smṛti,* I.31 (and also I, 87).

> assumes its distinctive marks, even so corporeal beings (resume in new births) their (appointed) course of action.[41]

This is in total conformity with the text of the *Bhagavad-Gītā*. There is a sort of consensus on this point. Like the seasons (*ṛtu*), living beings get back to their former activities, regaining their previous dispositions and capacities. There is a sort of unconscious scheme framed up in man as in the seasons. The nature of each and everyone is nothing but what was conserved beyond a limited life-period in the shape of habits or traits of character. Memory is not lost, even if ordinary persons do not always remember their past as does a *jāti-smara*.[42]

2.1.3 Karman *and caste*

Many changes had intervened in the mean time in the History of ideas. But there has always been a continuity in evolution in the Indian tradition (sometimes even a "revolution"), which should not be overlooked. In the *Ṛg Veda* X.90, words for castes (*varṇa, jāti*) or the hierarchical distinctions between them are not attested. Neither is there any trace (of the belief) in the Law of *karman* or in *saṃsāra* in the Vedic hymns. The word *karman*, synonym of "sacrifice", "rite" (*yajña*), appears in its psycho-moral acceptation only in the last portion of the *Śruti*, i.e., in the Vedic *Upaniṣads*.[43] Same is the case with the word *saṃsāra*.[44] The concepts of *karman* and *saṃsāra* are present in Jaina and Buddhist texts, can be dated around the period of the first Vedic *Upaniṣads*. With time, the *Dharma Sūtras* start showing an interest in these concepts resulting in a sort of synthesis between Brahmanical and Hindu tradition on the one hand and non-orthodox Indian traditions on the other. Hinduism had by

---

[41] *Manu Smṛti* I.28–30; cf. IX.38–39.

[42] On *jāti-smara*, see: *Manu Smṛti* IV.148; BSBH III.3.32; Caraka, *Śārīra Sthāna* III.3. The Buddha of course, (like all accomplished *yogins*), was capable of remembering all his past lives, where from the *Jātakas*.

[43] First occurrence in the BĀU III.2.13.

[44] Attested for the first time in the *Kaṭha Upaniṣad* III.7.

this time discovered the devotional trend (*bhakti*) along with its fascination for renunciation (*saṃnyāsa*). One can find in *Manu Smṛti* Ch. 12 ample materials on human destiny (*gati*) depending on one's past deeds (*karman*), in relation with one's psycho-moral and intellectual dispositions (*bhāva*), which are nothing else but *saṃskāras.*[45] These dispositions are good and favourable when predominated by the *guṇa sattva,* resulting in virtue, righteousness (*dharma*), knowledge (*jñāna*), dispassion (*vairāgya*), and lordship (*aiśvarya*). They are bad and unfavourable when predominated by the *guṇa tamas,* resulting in vice or unrighteousness (*adharma*), ignorance (*ajñāna*), passion or attachment (*avairāgya*), non-lordship (*anaiśvarya*). Only one of these eight *bhāva,* i.e., discriminating knowledge (*jñāna*) liberates the monad (*puruṣa*) from the bonds or seduction of the nature (*Prakṛti*). Thus the link established between *karman* and caste throws a new light on the concept of *saṃskāra* in its ritual and psychological aspects. The psychological aspect is treated in all Indian philosophical texts in the soteriological context.

While commenting on the relevant *Bhagavad-Gītā* verse, Śaṅkara quotes the '*Apastamba Dharma Sūtra*', II.2.2.3.

> These duties, respectively enjoined on the several castes, lead, when rightly performed to *Svarga* as their natural result, as stated in the *smritis,* such as following: Men of several castes and orders, each devoted to his respective duties, reap the fruits of their actions after death, and then by the residual (*karma*) attain to births in superior countries, castes and families, possessed of comparitively superior *dharma,* span of life, learning, conduct, wealth, happiness and intelligence. 'And in the *Purāṇa* also are specified the different results and worlds which several castes and orders attain".[46]

2.1.4 *The subtle body vehiculates the* saṃskāras

The relationship between *saṃskāra* and *smṛti-smaraṇa* in addition to the supposition that the subtle body (*sūkṣma-* or

---

[45] See my Chapter VII for the *Bhāva/Saṃskāra* theory in the *Sāṃkhya Kārikās.*

[46] BHGBH XVIII.44.

ātivāhika-śarīra)[47] preserves and transports these traces beyond death comes out from several passages. For example, an advanced adept of *Yoga* who had failed to achieve the final end (or liberation) in a given life, can obtain the highest perfection "due to the influence of previous dispositions" (*pūrvakṛtātsaṃskāravaśād*) in his forthcoming lives. These psychological dispositions or tendencies know no destruction even if they have remained dormant or inactive for a long time. Multiple births (and deaths) are a sort of receptacle for the acquirement of these perfective dispositions whose object or purpose is (liberating) knowledge.

Arjuna asks the Lord Kṛṣṇa as to what happens to the adept of *Yoga* who has failed to achieve his aim. Kṛṣṇa explains that nothing is lost because

> He gains touch with the knowledge that was acquired in the former body [....]".[48]
>
> By that very former practice is he borne on, though unwilling. Even he who merely wishes to know of Yoga rises superior to the Word-Brahman.[49]

Śaṅkara's comments are interesting:

> The man who failed in Yoga is borne on towards perfection by the force of the practice of the former birth. If he had done no unrighteous deed (*adharma*) which could overpower the tendency caused by the practice of Yoga, then, certainly, the tendency of Yoga prevails. If *adharma* be stronger, then, even the tendency born of Yoga is certainly overpowered by *adharma*. But on the exhaustion of *adharma* the tendency caused by Yoga begins to produce its effects: that is to say, it is not liable to destruction though it may have long been in abeyance.[50]

Here *saṃskāra* is translated by "tendency".

It should be added that *dharma* and *adharma*, which figure in the list of eight *bhāvas* should be overpassed in the final run because deliverance (*mokṣa*) surpasses *dharma*. "Even *dharma* is a sin, in the case of him who seeks liberation,

---

[47] BĀUBH IV.4.3 (Introduction).

[48] *Bh.-gītā* VI.43.

[49] *Ibidem* VI.44.

[50] BHGBH VI.44.

as it causes bondage. He is liberated from both (*dharma* and *adharma*), i.e., he is liberated from *saṃsāra*", explains Śaṅkara.[51] For Śaṅkara, even while he comments on the *Bhagavad-Gītā* where *bhakti* predominates, what counts above all is the pre-eminence of knowledge (*jñāna*) on works (*karman*) or duties (*dharma*). "At the end of many births, the man of wisdom comes to Me, (realising) that Vāsudeva is the all...." says Kṛṣṇa to Arjuna.[52] Śaṅkara interprets, "At the end of many births occupied in spiritual regeneration as preparatory to the attainment of wisdom, the man of mature wisdom resorts to Me, Vasudeva, the innermost Self".[53]

3. Previous acquisitions are helpful

Previous acquisitions are sometimes helpful. If one remembers, (thanks to *saṃskāra* cause of *smṛti-smaraṇa*), what should be done (because prescribed), what is forbidden it helps the person to react in a given situation.

> In fact, prohibitions have just that end in view, viz., to create an idea that the acts in question must not be done. When a hungry man is chastened by a knowledge of prohibited foods (*pratiṣedhajñānasaṃskṛtasya*) such as *Kalañja* (the meat of an animal killed with a poisoned weapon), or food coming from a person under a curse, his first notion is that the food can be eaten. This is however checked by the recollection that it is a forbidden food. This is similar to the notion that one can drink from a mirage, is checked by the knowledge of its true nature.[54]

The discovery of the real Self is nothing but disappearance of erroneous illusory notions.

---

[51] BHGBH IV.21. See also BSBH III.4.51; VII.19. Cf. Abhinavagupta's *Paramārthasāra, śloka* 90–91.

[52] *Bhagavad-Gītā* VII.19.

[53] BHGBH VII.19 : *'bahunāṃ janmanāṃ' jñānārthasaṃskārārjanāśrayṇāāṃ' 'ante' samāptau 'jñānavān' prāptaparipākajñāno 'māṃ' vāsudeva pratyagātmāṇm pratyakṣataḥ.../*

[54] BĀUBH I.3.1. Translation by Swāmī Mādhavānanda, *The Bṛhadāraṇyaka Upaniṣad with the Commentary of Śaṅkara*, Calcutta, Advaita Ashrama, 1965, p. 50.

Śaṅkara once again takes recourse to *saṃskāras* explaining the famous utterance: "I am That" (*So'ham asmi*).[55] The *ātman* in form of *Puruṣa* was one and alone in the origin.

> And because owing to his past impressions he first declared himself as *Aham,* therefore he was called *Aham* (*pūrvajanmaśrauta-vijñānasaṃskṛta*). Therefore, saying I or Me became possible only because of the mental perfection received in past life from Vedic science. Even the vision of unicity could be born in Prajāpati's mind because of the accumulated dispositions during previous lives.[56]

3.1 "Kārmic Residua" are cause of bondage

To be born and return to this world again and again (*punar-āvṛtti*) implies that one is a transmigratory being. All "Kārmic Residua", in the shape of millions of *saṃskāras, vāsanās* and *anuśayas* retain us in the *saṃsāra.* Quoting the *Chāndogya Upaniṣad* Śaṅkara establishes the ontological and psychological continuity of the Self (*ātmaṇ*), transcendent and immanent at the same time. Inspite of provisory discontinuities, previous acquisitions are not lost. All the creatures having merged into Being rediscover their identity:

> They become impressed with the tendencies of past cognitions and actions, and after having merged into Being (at death), they are born again in that same condition with the same tendencies; and returning from Being they become a tiger, or a lion, [....]; even though the two consecutive births of an evolving creature be separated by an interval of millions of time-cycles, the tendencies imprinted upon it during the preceding life do not cease to exist [....].[57]

Terms used are *vāsanā, bhāva, bhāvita,* etc. While the living Self or the body (*śarīra, jīvātman*) dies, the Self (*ātman*) never perishes. The Self is unborn and so neither dies nor transmigrates. This indestructibility of Being goes along with the conservation of memory traces,

---

[55] BĀU V.15.1.

[56] BĀUBH I.4.1-2: *janmāntarakṛtasaṃskārahetukam* /

[57] CHUBH VI.9.3; 11.3.

> because it is found that in case a man who has gone to sleep leaving the work in hand unfinished, on waking from sleep, he remembers his unfinished work and finishes it. Further, in the case of creatures just born, they are found to evince desire for milk from the mother's breasts, fears and such other feelings; and from this it is inferred that they remember the experience, in their previous births, of drinking milk from mother's breasts, and also unpleasant experiences.[58]

It is not possible for the whole "kārmic residua" of the man to be exhausted during a single life. The variety and quality of deeds have also to be taken into account.

> For instance, in a certain case the man's nature may be beset with numerous tendencies (and impressions) due to his previous births as *Man, peacock, ape,* etc., and if his coming birth happens to be brought about by that portion of his "kārmic residua" which is conducive to making him born as *ape*—the rest of his "kārmic residua" and tendencies—does not become entirely destroyed (or set aside). If all the tendencies and impressions conducive to other kinds of birth (as man or peacock, etc.) were entirely set aside or destroyed, then, in the case when the man has been born as an ape, by virtue of that "kārmic residua" which was conducive to his "apish" birth [....], then it would not be possible for the ape, immediately on birth, to acquire the capacity to jump from the tree, or remain clinging to the mother's breasts: because it has not had any practice of these arts during its present birth. [....] From all this it follows that just like the tendencies and impressions there can be no destruction of all the "kārmic residua" so that the remnant of such residue is quite possible".[59]

3.2 Former experience

The Śaṅkara Bhāṣya on the *Bṛhadāraṇyaka Upaniṣad* IV.4.2 contains same type of remarks which is explained as *pūrvaprajñā* or "former experience". The *Upaniṣad* passage describes how every organ becomes united with the subtle body of the dying man. When the vital force departs all the organs follow. "Then the self has particular consciousness, and goes to the body which is related to that consciousness.

---

[58] CHUBH VI.11.3. Cf. *Yoga Tattva Upaniṣad* V.131–33; and Bhartṛhari, *Vākyapadīya, Brahmakāṇḍa,* 121.

[59] CHUBH V.10.5, translation Ganganath Jhā.

It is followed by knowledge, work and past experience".[60] Quoting the *Bhagavad-Gītā* VIII.6 Śaṅkara comments:

> As a matter of fact, everybody has at that moment a consciousness which consists of impressions [*vāsanā*] in the form of particular modification of his mind (regarding the next life). [....] It has been stated that the departing self, loaded with materials, goes making noises like a cart [*śaṭaka*]. This load consists of impressions [....] the impressions of experiences regarding the results of past actions. These impressions take part in initiating fresh actions as also in bringing past actions to fruition; hence they too accompany. Without these impressions no action can be done, nor any results of past actions be achieved, for organs are not skillful in unpractised work. But when organs are prompted to work by the impressions of past experience, they can easily attain skill even without practice in this life. It is frequently observed that some are clever in certain kinds of work, such as painting, from their very birth, even without practice in this life, while others are skillful even in some very easy tasks. [....] Hence these three—knowledge, work and past experience—are the food on the way to the next world, corresponding to the load of the carter. Since these three are the means of attaining another body and enjoying (the results of one's past work), therefore one should cultivate only the good forms of them, so that one may have a desirable body and desirable enjoyments. This is the purport of the whole passage. [....] Therefore the impressions called past experience, under control of the person's knowledge and work, stretch out, like a leech [*jalāyukā*] from the body, retaining their seat in the heart, as in the dream state, and build another body in accordance with his past work; they leave their seat, the old body, when a new body is made.[61]

This leech illustration from the BĀU IV.4.3 describes how the transmigrating self passes on to another body by stretching out its impressions, creating a new body (which is a "dream body", *svapna-deha*), with the organs under the sway of past deeds (*karmavaśāt*).

3.3 In the beginning was the "Rest"

The formula "In the beginning was the Rest" (*śeṣa*), summarizes Śaṅkara's commentaries.[62] Every civilisation has

[60] BĀU IV.4.2: *taṃ vidyākarmaṇī samanvārabhete pūrvaprajñā ca /*

[61] BĀUBH IV.4.2.

[62] On CHUBH, BĀUBH, BSBH, BHGBH, etc.

its genesis. "In the beginning was the Verb", says the St. Jean, the evangalist. In the mytho-cosmological perspective of the Purāṇas, the serpent *Śeṣa* ("Rest") is considered as a reservoir of all virtues. A new cosmic cycle begins, after the "cosmic cremation" when the universe, destroyed by fire, had been provisionally reabsorbed in fertile waters. In the Hindu iconography, Viṣṇu is represented lying on the serpent *Śeṣa* during his yogic sleep. In other words, the world is *anādi*, just like ignorance (*avidyā*), the cause of "repetitive compulsion" for acts. Morally qualified deliberate acts (*karman*) get exhausted themselves after giving their "fruits" (*phala*). These fruits in their turn become fertile "germs" or "seeds" (*bīja*) for new actions. Indeed, our actions are nothing but reactions! In this way the complex mechanism of "ripening of fruits of acts" (*karma-phala-vipāka*) continues, with the necessity of "enjoying" or "experiencing" (*bhoga*) the "fruits", sweet or sour, for the responsible agent.

The word *śeṣa* is semanticaly very rich. Although the doctrine of transmigration is absent from the *Veda* and the *Brāhamaṇas,* the Vedic hymns recited during the cremation, last *saṃskāra,* we find survival of an idea corporeal components after death.[63] The "descendance" (*śeṣa*) of the person is that what survives after him.[64] All is not lost, the dead conserves his *iṣṭā-pūrta* (sacrificial offerings to Gods and the ritual fees given to the priest). In other words, his *kratu* ("project", "intention", "totality of merits accumulates by sacrificial acts") survives even after his death.[65]

The early part of the *Veda* ignores the doctrine of transmigration. But the idea of a "second death" (*punarmṛtyu,* dying once again or "repeated death") in the world beyond

---

[63] See *Ṛg Veda,* X.16.5 and 3.

[64] *Nirukta,* III.2 quoted in Charles MALAMOUD, "Observation sur la notion de 'reste' dans le Brāhmanisme", *Wiener Zeitschrift für die Kunde Südasiens,* XVI, 1972, p. 19.

[65] On *kratu, see Īśopaniṣad,* 15 (or 17, depending on the editions); and ŚB X.6.3.1. On *iṣṭapūrta,* see Ch. MALAMOUD, "Terminer le Sacrifice", dans *Le Sacrifice dans l'Inde ancienne,* pp. 156–66.

is however present in the *Śatapatha Brāhmaṇa* X.2.6.19. The early *Vedic Upaniṣads* are concerned about the "return" to this world once again after death, when the merits get exhausted. The word used in the *Upaniṣads* is now *punarāvṛtti.* The ŚB X.4.3.10 makes the transition possible between these two text stratas by the use of the expression "again and again" (*punaḥ punaḥ*) attested in this passage. The two "paths" solar and lunar, the path of Gods (*devayāna*) and the path of Manes (*pitṛyāna*) are also known to the *Brāhamaṇas.*[66] To these two, the *Upaniṣads* add a third "path" or "destiny" those who became worms, insects, etc.[67] This is the text with that of the CHU which marks a real transition between the early Vedic conceptions and the Vedantic conceptions of the *Upaniṣads.* The word *saṃsāra* occurs for the first time in the *Kaṭha Upaniṣad* III.7. The *Bṛhad-* and the *Chāndogya Upaniṣad* offer us a complete picture and comprehension of the transmigratory mechanism. Three categories of living beings corresponding to these three paths are—"those who know" and will never return to this world. Secondly, those who have accomplished meritorious sacrificial works and will sojourn in the heaven (*svarga*) till the merits are not exhausted. And thirdly, all those small little beings condemned to be born (and to die), again and again, i.e., those who neither take the solar nor the lunar path.

3.4 *Karma-vipāka* in the transmigratory process

Śaṅkara's commentaries[68] offer us full clarity on the transmigration mechanism (*saṃsāra*) which goes hand in hand with the maturation of acts (*karma-vipāka*). Specially on the following three points—Firstly, a "remainder" has to be postulated in order to explain the coming back from the lunar world. The concepts of *karmāśaya* or *anuśaya* replace those of *saṃskāra* or *vāsanā* we are interested in. Secondly,

---

[66] See ŚB I.9.3.2; CHU IV.3.2; BĀU IV.2.15: *devaloka, pitṛloka.*

[67] BĀU VI.2.15-16; CHU V.10.5-8.

[68] On CHU V.10.5-8; BĀU IV.4.2; and on *Brahma Sūtra* III.1.8-9 sq.

diversity in the destinies (animal, vegetable, semi-divine, etc.) supposes diversity in the deeds or acts. Thirdly, the Law of *karman* is distributive, not recapitulative. Here are some major texts, mainly on the third point:

> As a matter of fact, whenever any single person is born in the world, such birth may be the result of any of the numerous acts which are conducive to experiences to be gone through several mutually incompatible bodies. So that it is not possible for the whole "kārmic residua" of the man to be exhausted during a single life. Further, it has been declared that there are many such acts as Brāhmaṇa-murder and other heinous crimes which lead to the persons being born during several lives. Further, such persons as have come to be born as inanimate things (as a result of grave misdeeds), as these would be entirely dull and non-intelligent, there is no possibility of their doing any such act of superior merit as would lead to an improvement in their position. And lastly, for those who are in the embryo-stage, there would be no possibility for these to be born into the world, as there would be no "kārmic residue" during the time that they are coming through the womb. From all this it follows that the experience resulting from all one's acts cannot be gone through during a single life.[69]

3.5 Analysis of the *saṃskāra-saṃsāra* relation

The concept of *pratiniyataphalatva*[70] supports the idea that the Law of *karman* is distributive. It does not work like a credit/debit, of a bank account but like a cosmic *talis .... qualis.* "On the passing away of the works (the soul redescends) with a remainder, according to the scripture and *Smṛti,* as it went (i.e., passing through the same stations) and not thus (i.e., in the inverse order)".[71]

The analysis of the *saṃskāra-saṃsāra* relation results in a deeper comprehension of the doctrinal points, typical to Indian thought, that the conception of time is cyclical and circular, not linear. Moreover, ontological and psychological continuity of the Self (*ātman* transcendent as well as immanent) is a fact (and needs no proof in the Brahmanical

[69] CHUBH V.10. 5.

[70] Attested in BSBH III.1.8.

[71] BS III.1.8.

context). The Law of *karman*, in its authentic version, cannot be equated with fatality or blind destiny (thanks to its distributive nature), though interpreted as such by the masses. The agent/consumer (*kartṛ-/bhoktṛ-*) relation presupposes the presence of "kārmic residua". The mechanism of maturation or retribution of acts (*karma-phala-vipāka* and *bhoga*) is complex. Only knowledge (*jñāna*) can put an end to ignorance (*ajñāna*), and thus to *karman*, *saṃskara*, *saṃsāra*.

In any case, the problem is not simple. The intricacy of the Law of *karman* resides in the fact that there are two kinds of residues or "fruits" of acts which must be consumated by the responsible agent. A distinction is made between acts which have not yet started to produce their fruits, and those which are in course of producing their fruits or effects (*pravṛtta-phala, prārabdha-karman, ārabdha-kārya*). The first set is annihilated when *Brahman* knowledge dawns, but not the second set. The doctrine of "liberation-while-alive" (*jīvanmukti*) is based on this very distinction because the liberated sage continues to live even after knowledge has dawned because of the remaining *saṃskāras*. Nothing radically new or different is "achieved" by the *jīvanmukta* after his physical death. The liberation of the sage is thus called liberation without or after the death of the body (*videhamukti*). The *jīvanmukti/videhamukti* distinction is quite similar to the Buddhistic distinction between extinction (while alive = *bodhi*), complete extinction, and extinction with or without rest of conditions (*nirvāṇa/parinirvāṇa*; *sopādhiśeṣa-nirvāṇa/nirupādhiśeṣa-nirvāṇa*).

3.6 Previous acquisitions and *prārabdha-karman*

Establishing a neat relation between *saṃskāra* and *vega*, Śaṅkara explains with the help of "potter's wheel" (*kulāla-cakra*) and "arrow" (*iṣu*) comparisons, why the body of the liberated sage does not perish immediately after knowledge, but only after complete exhaustion of all "kārmic residues".

Deliverance was rightly termed "bodilessness" (*aśarīratva*) by Śaṅkara.[72] Knowledge (*jñāna*) and deliverance (*mokṣa, mukti, kaivalya*) are one and the same thing. Śaṅkara and Abhinavagupta in the East, Plotinus[73] in the West share the same opinion that wisdom is not psychological but of an ontological nature.

The negative aspect of previous stock of acquisitions, last obstacles to deliverance, comes out from some of these passages of the *Brahma Sūtra Bhāṣya*. Bādarāyaṇa says, "But only those former (works) whose effects have not yet begun (are destroyed by knowledge), because (scripture states) that (i.e., the death of the body) to be the term".[74] The *Pūrvapakṣin* maintains that "all actions whatever must be considered to have undergone destruction. Śaṅkara replies, "But only those whose effects have not begun. Earlier actions whether good or evil, accumulated in previous forms of the existence as well as in current form of existence are destroyed by the attainment of knowledge only if their fruits have not yet begun to operate. Those actions whose effects have begun and whose results have been half enjoyed, are not destroyed by that knowledge. This opinion is found in the following passage:

> For him there is delay only as long as he is not delivered (from the body) (CHU VI. 14. 2), which fixes the death of the body as the term for attainment of final release.

Reply to another objection as follows:

> The origination of knowledge can take place without dependence on an aggregate of works whose effects have already begun to operate, and when this dependence has once been entered into, we must–as in the case of the potter's wheel–wait until the motion. The knowledge of our Self being essentially non-active destroys all works by means of refuting wrong knowledge; but wrong knowledge–comparable to the appearance of a double moon–lasts for some time even after it has been refuted, owing to the impressions it has made [*saṃskāravaśāt*]. [....] The final decision

[72] BSBH I.1.4.

[73] See *Enneades* 1.4.9.

[74] BS IV.2.15: *anārabdhakārye eva tu pūrve tadavadheḥ* /

> therefore is that knowledge effects the destruction of those works only–whether good or bad–whose effects have not yet begun to operate.[75]

Same type of discussion between the opponent (*Pūrvapakṣin*), who introduces the clause of relationship and temporality in his interpretation, and the *Siddhāntin*, is found in Śaṅkara's commentary around the expression *atha sampatsye*' [VI.14.2] of the *Chāndogyopaniṣad*. "Not so; because what is meant by that expression is the final stage of process of embellishment, and not any interval of time. If it were so, then this phrase would set aside the idea conveyed by the 'That Thou Art'".[76]

In his commentary on the *Chāndogyopaniṣad* (section dealing with the *mahāvākya*: "That Thou Art" (*tat tvam asi*), Śaṅkara takes recourse once again to the concept of *vega*, identical with *saṃskāra*, while replying to the opponent. The opponent maintains that liberation should appear simultaneously with the attainment of knowledge. The distinction between two sets of "kārmic residua" is hence reintroduced as explanation with the arrow simile.

> These "kārmic residua" which have become operative, and to which the present body is due, can be exhausted by experience alone; just as in the case of the arrow that has been shot at a certain target, it comes to rest only when the momentum is exhausted, and not successively on its reaching the target on account of there being no purpose to be served by its going any further [....].[77]

It is worth noting that our *Siddhāntin* (Śaṅkara) prefers here the mechanical model of intelligibility (i.e., *vega*) rather than the intentional or finalist model of intelligibility (i.e., *prayojana*). Other "kārmic residua" which have not yet become operative (*āpavṛttaphala*), "all these are consumed

---

[75] BSBH IV.1.15 and 19.

[76] CHUBH III.14.4. Here I differ from Ganganath Jhā's translation and would rather read it as follows: "because the continuation of life consists in the operative residual impressions in course (of fruition)" (*ārabdhasaṃskāraśeṣasthiti.../*).

[77] CHUBH VI.14.2.

by true knowledge, in the same way as they are by expiatory rites; as says the *Smṛti*".[78] Śaṅkara quotes the *Bhagavad-Gītā* IV.37 where it is said that the fire of knowledge (*jñānāgni*) destroys the fertility of all acts by reducing them to ashes.

So the conclusion is "But having destroyed by fruition the two other (sets of work) he becomes one with *Brahman*" (BS IV.1.19). Śaṅkara reminds the *Pūrvapakṣin* about what the *Upaniṣads* declare on this fusion and quotes *tat tvam asi* of the *Chāndogyopaniṣad*, and *brahmaiva san brahmāpyeti* being nothing but *Brahman*, he enters into Brahman of the *Bṛhadāraṇyakopaniṣad*.[79] But the opponent makes a higher bid and uses the very arguments from Śaṅkara himself. But an objection is raised, even when perfect intuition [*samyagjñāna*] has risen the practical intuition of multiplicity [*bhedadarśana*]. This may continue after the death of the body, just as it continued before death; analogously to the visual appearance of a double moon [*dvicandradarśana*]. — Not so, we reply. After the death of the body there no longer exists any cause for such continuance [....]; since the seed of all such fruition is destroyed [*dagdhabījavat*]. [....] But such false knowledge [*mithyājñāna*] is completely destroyed by perfect intuition. When therefore the works whose effects have begun [*ārabdhakārya*] are destroyed, the man who knows, necessarily enters into the state of perfect isolation [*kaivalya*].[80]

This means that when there is no *karmāśaya* left, or when the *prārabdha-karman* is exhausted, in brief, when *saṃskāras, anuśayas, vāsanās,* etc. are no more encumbering the mind or the subtle body of the *vidvān*, the process comes to an end for this particular person who merges into *Brahman*. As says the Sūtrakāra: "(Of them) there is non-return, according

---

[78] *Ibidem.*

[79] BĀU IV.4.6. R.E. HUME translates: "Being very Brahma, he goes to Brahma", in *The Thirteen Principal Upanishads translated from the Sanskrit*, Oxford University Press, 1968 (seventh impression), p. 141.

[80] BSBH IV.1.19.

to the scripture".[81] Śaṅkara naturally quotes the famous *Śruti* passages relevant on this subject.[82] *Advaita Vedānta* texts abound in discussions around the problem of *prārabdha-karman, ārabdhakārya,* etc. which indicate the persistancy of residual traces (*saṃskāra*) or momentum (*vega*), explained with the help of arrow (*iṣu*) or potter's wheel (*kulāla-cakra*) similes. Same type of arguments are found in his *Bhagavad Gītā Bhāṣya.*[83] Abhinavagupta in his *Paramārthasāra* (*śloka* 93 and 95) also explains as to why a sage remains submitted to the vicissitudes of life for sometime.

3.7 Late *Vedānta* texts on *saṃskāras*

Late Vedāntic texts contain the message of ancient Upaniṣads and the quintessence of Śaṅkara's *Kevala Advaita Vedānta* philosophy. "Blown by the wind of the *saṃskāras*, the desireless, independent, free, liberated person moves about like a dry leaf".[84] The *Vedāntasāra,* chapter VI, describes the characteristics of a man who is liberated in this very life (*jīvanmukta laksaṇa*). No more real obstacles left for this sage who has realized the oneness through true knowledge, because:

> [....] After the exhaustion of the *Prārabdha* work, his vital force is absorbed in the Supreme Brahman, the Inward Bliss; and ignorance with its effects and their impressions [*saṃskāra*] is also destroyed. Then he is identified with the Absolute Brahman, the Supreme Isolation, the embodiment of Bliss, in which there is not even the appearance of duality.[85]

---

[81] BS IV.4.22: *anāvṛttiḥ śabdāt anāvṛttiḥ śabdād /*

[82] For *na punar āvṛtti,* see CHU VIII, 15, 1; BĀU VI.2.15 ("Of these there is no return": *teṣām na punar āvṛttiḥ /*).

[83] BHGBH XIII.23. See also BHGBH V.13.

[84] *Aṣṭāvakra-saṃhitā,* XVIII, *śloka* 21, translation by Swami NITYASVARUPANANDA, Advaita Ashrama, Calcutta, 1969.

[85] *Vedāntasāra of Sadānanda,* translation by Swami NIKHILANANDA, Advaita Ashrama, chapter VI.226, p. 123.

4. Positive aspects of latent impressions

When previous acquisitions are negative, they constitute an obstacle to deliverance. Without *saṃskāras* and *vāsanās,* there will however be no memory on the individual or collective (socio-religious) level, i.e., no transmitted tradition. Śaṅkara's close disciple Sureśvara analyzes the relation between *saṃskāra* and *smṛti* as follows:

> At the time of experience and at the time of recollection, *Ātman* recollects the thing which has persisted in Himself in the form of a *saṃskāra* or latent impression.

Moreover,

> When a former experience has disappeared, its memory springs from a cause abiding in Atman and called *saṃskāra,* the latent impression produced on the seat of that experience.[86]

In the *Mānasollāsa* the *ātman* is glorified as being persistant and permanent, unique, capable of recognising himself, instead of loosing his own identity. In other words *ātman* is capable of abstracting himself from the limiting adjuncts (*upādhi*): all accidental circumstances like time, space, etc. This power or capacity of auto-recognition (*pratyābhijñā*) which the *ātman* possesses — which in the Theater, as for example in Kālidāsa's *Abhijñānaśākuntala,* Drama of forgetfulness and recollection, or in Molière's Plays, occurs between two persons — occurs here, in the case of *ātman,* between oneself and oneself (and not between two different persons). So what happens is just the opposite of various accretions and superimpositions (*adhyāsa*), which cause the forgetfulness of the Self, lost in worldly passions.

Now what exactly is the relation between auto-recognition (*pratyābhijñā*) and latent impressions (*saṃskāra*) in this text?[87] The *ātman* experiences all external perceptions (*pratyakṣa*) by means of *saṃskāras.* These latent impressions

---

[86] *Mānasollāsa, śloka* 8 and 12, Sureśvara's commentary on the *Dakṣiṇāmūrtistrotra* attributed to Śaṅkara. See *The Vedānta Doctrine,* translation by Pandit A. Mahadeva Sastri, Madras, 1920, chapter VIII, p. 135 and 138.

[87] Quite an unexpected one and which evokes the *memoria sui of* Augustine. *Confessions* X.13; 48; *De Trinitate* IX.VI.9.

are stocked and continue to be in there. This intimate relation between *saṃskāra* and *smṛti* comes out clearly in *śloka* 12. From this angle, the memory to the eternal inner light of the *ātman* is known as self-luminous (*svayamprakāśa*). *Saṃskāras* function like a cog wheel between direct perception (*pratyakṣa*) and rememoration (*smaraṇa*). They are, like memory (*smṛti*), on the side of the Self, i.e., on the side of *pratyabhijñā* and final liberation. On the contrary, the limiting adjuncts (*upādhi*) are on the side of superimpositions (*adhyāsa*), illusion (*māyā*), mental distractions or aberrations (*moha*). Finally, the auto-recognition (*pratyabhijñā*) or recollection of *ātman* becomes the root and the foundation of all other norms of valid knowledge (*pramāṇa*).[88]

The texts quoted above consider the role of *saṃskāras* in the genesis of memory or remembrance (*smṛti*). Some others bring out the role of *saṃskāras* in the genesis of inclinations and tendencies, because the concept of *saṃskāra* covers both these types of memory. The second type is quite similar to what Bergson will name memory-habit, *habitus*, good or bad. In the Indian context these "habits" are transmitted from one life to another. These traces remain intact in the *manas* throughout the transmigratory process, over and above cosmic dissolutions. The *Śataslokī*, attributed to Śaṅkara, puts it as follows:

> The inner self neither comes in at the time of birth, nor goes away at the time of death; for, it is infinite. But it is the mind with the subtle body that enters thus and goes forth afterwards. The mind does not reproduce in itself the leanness or the stoutness of the gross body. But it departs, taking with it two sets of tendencies (*samskara*) and the measures of light (*tejo-matrah*), and returns again to this world along with these very appendages.[89]

The *manas* transmigrates in two directions—it descends in the womb and incarnates itself. It leaves the body and

---

[88] See *ślokas* 15–16.

[89] *Śataslokī* 28, *The Century of Verses*, See *Sri Sankara's Select Works*, translated by S. VENKATARAMAN, Madras, 1921, pp. 103–104.

flies away after death, but not the Self (*ātman*), because unborn, it never dies and knows no transmigration. The mind vehiculates the subtle latent impressions (*saṃskāra*), good or bad. Their dynamism pushes the mind or the subtle body to descend in a new body. The quality of *saṃskāras* determines the quality of each and every birth, human, animal, etc. This is well explained by Madhva in his *Anuvyākhyāna* III.2.5-7.

4.1 Role of *saṃskāra* and *vāsanā* in dreams

The enigmatic dream phenomenon (*svapna*) is also accounted for with reference to residual impressions (*saṃskāra*) and to latent or inarticulate desires (*vāsanā*). Texts use more frequently the word *vāsanā* than *saṃskāra* in the dream context because the former are the material cause of dreams whereas *saṃskāra* function as a catalysor or *facteur déclenchant*. In any case, Śaṅkara, in his polemics with the Buddhist, questions their identity. "Moreover, an impression is a kind of modification, and modifications cannot, as experience teaches, take place unless there is some substratum to be modified" (G. Thibaut). Gambhirananda's translation as follows : "Besides, what you call a tendency is a kind of impression (or predisposition); and from common experience it is known that a disposition cannot be imagined to exist unless...".[90]

At this or that moment of our life, we feel so many desires, and sentiments, unfulfilled. This urge comes in the subconscious-unconscious mind to actualize itself in dreams. There is a huge stock of forgotten experiences hidden somewhere in the mind. A complex work of rearrangement and organization of materials takes place in dreams, a setting or *montage* which escapes us.

4.2 Freud on dreams and on unconscious drives

Sigmund Freud is eloquent on the dream phenomena, specially on latent dream-thoughts unconscious to the

[90] BSBH II.2.30: *api ca vāsanā nāma saṃskāraviśeṣaḥ* /

dreamer. It is true that dreams are not a pure and simple reproduction of vigil psychological activity of the day before. Surely not. Had it been the case, we would know about their content beforehand and would say: I know about what I am going to dream tonight. But alas! This remains a dream, because we have no hold on them! Some parallels can be drawn between the Indian and the Freudian dream and deep sleep theories. For both, dreams are nothing but actualization of latent desires. Ancient Indian brahmanical texts meet on several points with the recent discoveries of psycho-analysis. However, there are two big differences. Indian authors believe that the content of dreams may be supplied not only from the present life (including childhood, or even from intra-uterine life), but also from numerous previous lives. This dream content includes the remote past fallen in oblivion and goes beyond the limits of early childhood. What is projected on the dream screen does not limit itself to the content of present life experiences only. Secondly, as far as Indian authors are concerned, their interest in oniric life is fundamentally ontological and soteriological, not purely psychological. This is the reason why the treatment of wakeful state, dream state, deep-sleep state (and the "fourth" state (which is not really a "state") takes place in the *ātman-brahman* identity context, i.e., in the context of deliverance (*vimokṣa*).[91] To quote from Sigmund Freud:

> I shall now describe these thoughts more strictly than before as the day's residues and the latent dream thoughts, and, in conformity with our earlier usage, I shall designate as latent dream-thoughts everything we learn in interpreting the dream, whereas the day's residues are only a potion of the latent dream-thoughts. Our view is then that something is added to the day's residues, something that was also part of the unconscious, a powerful but repressed wishful impulse; and it is this alone that makes the construction of the dream possible. The influence of this wishful impulse on the day's residues creates further portion of the latent dream-

[91] See for example BĀU IV.3.6-34; (MU=) *Māṇḍūkyopaniṣad* I–IV; VIII–XII.

thoughts—that which need no longer appear rational and intelligible as being derived from waking life.[92]

Freud makes use of an analogy for the relation of the day's residues to the unconscious wish.

> In every undertaking there must be a capitalist who covers the required outlay and an *entrepreneur* who has the idea and knows how to carry it out. In the construction of dreams, the part of the capitalist is always played by the unconscious wish alone; it provides the psychical energy for the construction of the dream. The *entrepreneur* is the day's residues, which decide how this outlay is to be employed.[93]

Freud rightly asks his readers to consider the complexity of the word "unconscious":

> 'Are the day's residues', you will ask, 'really unconscious in the same sense as the unconscious wish which must be added to them in order to make them capable of producing a dream?' Your suspicion is correct. This is the salient point of the whole business. They are *not* unconscious in the same sense. The dream-wish belongs to a different unconscious—to the one which we have already recognized as being of infantile origin and equiped with peculiar mechanisms [p. 210]. It would be highly opportunate to distinguish these two kinds of unconscious by different names.[94]

So there is no such thing as a "single unconscious" in Freud's opinion, just as there is a variety of unconscious phenomena according to Indian texts.

4.3 States of consciousness in the Vedic *Upaniṣads* and in late *Vedānta*

Let us come back to the *Upaniṣads*. Wakeful and deep-sleep states (*avasthā, sthāna*) are compared to this world and the other world respectively. Dreams nourished by *saṃskāras* and *vāsanās* constitute the intermediary state, a sort of "junction"

---

[92] Sigmund FREUD, *Introductory Lectures on Psycho-analysis* (Part I and II), translated from the German under the General Editorship of James STRACHEY in collaboration with Anna FREUD, volume XV (1915–16), London, The Hogarth Press and the Institute of Psycho-Analysis, 1963, 1964, p. 226.

[93] *Ibidem*, p. 226.

[94] *Ibidem*, p. 227.

(*saṃdhyā*) between the two.[95] This strengthens my opinion that *saṃskāras* and *vāsanās* are linking factors, assuring continuity.

> The second state, that of dream, is known by experience to be midway between waking and sleep. In that state the individual, having withdrawn all the senses, has only the light of the self remaining. The gross body having been laid down on a suitable bed, the inner self, experiencing the objects it likes in their subtle form, goes about as it pleases in the same manner.[96]

The *Upaniṣad* says: "*Taijasa* is the second quarter, whose sphere (of activity) is the dream state (....)". Śaṅkara comments:

> "The consciousness of the waking state, though it is a state of mental vibration, is associated with many means, and it appears to be engrossed in external objects, and thus it leaves in the mind the corresponding impressions. Under the impulsion of ignorance, desire, and (past) action, the mind, thus possessed of the impressions like a piece of painted canvas, makes its appearance (in the dream state) just as in the waking state, but without any external means.[97]

Late Vedantic texts, in conformity with Śaṅkara, account also for the role of *saṃskāras* and *vāsanās* in dream experience. "When the sense-organs are withdrawn, *Ātman* is conscious of the mental images generated by the impressions of *Jāgrat* experience. It is the *svapna-avasthā* or the dream-state".[98] This is in perfect accord with Śaṅkara's opinion, "Moreover, a dream is not a totally new [without precedent *apūrva*] experience",[99] for most often it is a memory of past experiences. "It is a remembrance or rememoration of what was seen before".[100] In conformity

---

[95] See BĀU and BĀUBH IV.3.9.

[96] *Śataślokī* 78: (...) *paśyansaṃskārarūpān abhimataviṣyān yāti.../*

[97] MUBH 4, translation by Swami GAMBHIRANANDA, *Eight Upaniṣads*, Volume Two, Advaita Ashrama, Calcutta, 1973.

[98] *Mānasollāsa* ad *Dakṣiṇāmūrtistotra*, *śloka* 24, translated by A. Mahadeva SASTRI. See also *Paiṅgala Upaniṣad*, in *Laghu Upaniṣad*, *Minor Upanishads*, First Series with sanskrit text and translation, K. Narayanaswami AIYAR, The Akhila Bharata Sankara Seva Samiti, 1967, pp. 91, 103.

[99] BĀUBH IV.3.9.

[100] *Ibidem: pūrvadṛṣṭasmṛtir hi svapnaḥ /*

with the Vedic *Upaniṣads,* Śaṅkara also insists on the creative aspect of dreams made of *saṃskāras* and *vāsanās.* The *puruṣa* creates through his own sweet will a world of his own with the help of variegated images.[101]

4.4 *Svapna-deha* and *saṃskāra-deha*

One dreams within the strict limits of the body called "dream body" (*svapna-deha*).[102] The dreamer moves around freely, like a *mahārājā,* in his own body, made of latent desires (*vāsanāmaya*). This is similar to a magically created, illusory body (*māyāmayam iva*).[103] The *Śataślokī* also uses the expression *saṃskāra-deha* (*śloka* 77).

> The mind, tired of external activities, draws them together, and carrying with it the tendencies [*saṃskāra*] resulting from them, ceases from them and turns inward in search of its own place. In the dream body, it enjoys dream-objects generated by the combination of those tendencies. Abandoning these, again, it longs for the inner self, reaching which it attains perfect rest (*śloka* 75).

From the falsity of dreams discovered on waking, one may infer or deduce the falsity of the world.[104] Except the sage, well-awakened and aware of the reality, the whole humanity participates in this common dream-world like illusion. In the West Calderón[105] shares this opinion in his *La Vida es sueño.* Dreams are caused by "latent impressions of ignorance" (*avidyā-vāsanā*)[106] deceiving (*mṛṣā*) alas![107] As shown above, instead of putting emphasis on the irreality of dreams and the world, the Vedic *Upaniṣads* on the creative power of the dreamer. They celebrate the freedom and the self-luminosity of *Puruṣa* (*ātman*), which although associated with the body-psyche is not really responsible for good or

[101] See BĀUBH IV.3.9-14.

[102] See *Śataślokī* 75 and 77. The BĀU II.1.18 says : *sve śarīre.*

[103] BĀUBH IV.3.9.

[104] See BS and BSBH III.2.3 on this point.

[105] CALDERON (1635), *La Vida es sueño* (*La Vie est un songe*), éd. bilingue Aubier-Flammarion, Paris, 1976.

[106] BSBH II.I.14; IV.3.14.

[107] BĀUBH IV.3.18; BSBH III.2.6.

bad dreams. Is one responsible for the good or bad deeds done in dreams?[108] Not really. In any case, the *Puruṣa* is without attachment (*asaṅga*),[109] free from mundane considerations. The *Bhagavad Gītā* distinguishes between the immutable (*kūṭastha*), imperishable (*akṣara*) *Puruṣa* and the perishable (*kṣara*) *Puruṣa.* It is the *Kṣara-puruṣa* which is considered to be "the seat of all the latent impressions or *saṃskāras*".[110] As to the Absolute (*Brahman*), when approached with the apophatic method, not this, not this, not so, not so (*neti, neti*), both aggregate of material elements (*bhūtarāśi*) and "aggregate of psychological impregnations" (*vāsanārāśi*) are eliminated from the *Brahman.*[111]

Description of three empirical states of consciousness–vigil life, dream life, deep sleep (without dreams)–specially the passage from one to another, is nothing else but a description of *saṃsāra.* This is well explained by Śaṅkara.[112] But what about deep sleep state without dreams (*suṣupti*) described as something so very positive? The BĀU IV.3.15 uses even the word *saṃprasāda* which suggest a luminous and calm state of felicity.

In deep sleep, without dreams, a provisional disconnection takes place. Exempt of desires and dualistic notions, the empirical self becomes pure and transparent, embraced by the Supreme Self.[113] This state of felicity (*ānanda*) is a good illustration of deliverance.[114] However, *saṃskāras* and *vāsanās* being always present the profound sleep (*suṣupti*) cannot be equated with true deliverance (*mokṣa*).

[108] For Śaṅkara's opinion on this point, see for instance: BĀUBH IV.3.15; IV.3.9 and 20; BSBH III.2.4; II.1.14.

[109] BĀU IV.3.15-17.

[110] See BHGBH XV.16.

[111] BSBH III.2.22. *For neti, neti, see* BĀU II.3.6; III.9.26; IV.2.4; 22; IV.5.15.

[112] Specially in BĀUBH IV.4.6; BSBH I.3.30; CHUBH V.10.6.

[113] BĀU IV.3.15; 19.21.23:32.

[114] See BĀUBH IV.3.34.

4.5 Psychological characteristics of sleep

Freud has also a lot to say on sleep and dreams.[115] He describes the psychological characteristics of sleep as follows:

> Sleep is a state in which I want to know nothing of the external world, in which I have taken my interest away from it. I put myself to sleep by withdrawing from the external world and keeping its stimuli away from me. I also go to sleep when I am fatigued by i. So when I go to sleep I say to the external world: 'Leave me in peace: I want to go to sleep.' On the contrary, children say: 'I am not going to sleep yet; I am not tired, and I want to have some more experiences.' The biological purpose of sleep seems therefore to be rehabilitation, and its psychological characteristic suspense of interest in the world. Our relation to the world in which we come so unwillingly, seems to involve our not being able to tolerate it uninterruptedly. Thus from time to time we withdraw into the premundane state, into existence in the womb. At any rate, we arrange conditions for ourselves very like what they were then: warm, dark, and free from stimuli. Some of us roll ourselves up into a tight package and, so as to sleep, take a posture much as it was in the womb. The world, it seems, does not possess even those of us who are adults completely, but only up to two thirds; one third of us is still quite like unborn. Every time we wake in the morning it is like a new birth. Indeed, in speaking of our state after sleep, we say that we feel as though we were newly born.[116]

4.6 States of consciousness in the *Śaiva* tradition

According to the *Śaiva* tradition, for instance in Yogarāja's commentary to the *Paramārthasāra*, dreamless deep sleep is described as a pure void, a soil of tendencies or latent impressions (*saṃskāra-bhūmi*). For Abhinavagupta, in the state of deep sleep (*suṣupti*), the predispositions or the unconscious tendencies (*saṃskāra*) remain as inactive germes (*bīja*). At the time of manifestation or expansion (of the world) they regain their dynamic capacity.[117] The *Śiva Sūtra* and the *Vimarśinī* of Kṣemarāja contain interesting materials on deep sleep state, a sort of reservoir of latent

---

[115] *Introductory Lectures on Psycho-Analysis*, pp. 88–89.

[116] *Ibidem*, pp. 88–89.

[117] See *Parātrīśikalālaghvṛtti*, French translation by A. Padoux, Diffusion De Boccard, 1975, p. 124, note 335. Cf. pp. 44, 61.

impressions (because of the presence of dreams), which need to be reabsorbed. In the *suṣupti-jāgrat,* the tendencies are liable to appear. In *suṣupti-svapna* they are much more abundant. In *suṣupti-suṣupti* the tendencies are appeased (*śānta*). In Yogarāja's opinion,[118] deep sleep exempt of dreams is a mass of pure consciousness, just like the "Fourth state" *(turīyāvasthā),* described in the *Māṇḍūkyopaniṣad* 12. It is not obscured by the predispositions that the universe had deposited after periodic dissolution (*viśvapralayasaṃskāra*) because it is pure consciousness.

This tallies with Śaṅkara's Commentary:

> Fourth, *Turīya,* merely the absolute Self [....]. The knower of Brahman, who has realized the highest truth, has entered into the Self by burning away the third state of latency; and hence he is not born again, since *Turīya* has no latency of (creation). For when a snake superimposed on a rope has merged in the rope on the discrimination of the rope and the snake, it does not appear again to those discriminating people, just as before, from the impressions of the past sticking to the intellect.[119]

4.7 Deep sleep and *jīvan-mukta*

Two fundamental points according to Śaṅkara are, firstly the Self (*ātman*) that is luminous, which explains how a blind continues to see images in dreams.[120] Although his eye-vision is lost, but the eternal (eye-) vision is permanent, *ātman* being the internal witness. A distinction is made between mundane (*laukikī-*) and supra-mundane vision (*pāramārthikī-dṛṣṭi*)[121]. Secondly, *ātman* is the core, the permanent ontologic thread-bare accounting for our personal identity making "rememoration of the self" (*ātmānusmaraṇa*) possible. Śaṅkara gives a challenging argument, "....and we awake from deep sleep with the remembrance that we slept happily

[118] *Ad Paramārthasāra, śloka* 35.

[119] *Māṇḍūkyopaniṣad Bhāṣya* 12.

[120] Discussion on the point in BĀUBH I.4.10; III.4.2; IV.3.6. BSBH III.2.3.

[121] See BSBH III.4.2.

and knew nothing".[122] In dreams (*svapna*) as in recollection (*smṛti*), whatever we experience can be nothing else but all that we had experienced before. The unique, self-luminous seer is of course the *ātman*. *Ātman*'s intervention in the body changes nothing as to its intrinsic nature.[123]

The vigil and sleep states can be compared to world creation and dissolution. A sort of micro-cosmogony takes place in our life each and every day during these states.[124] A late *Vedānta* text describes four sorts of cosmic dissolutions. Dreamless deep sleep state is compared to daily dissolution, in which *saṃskāras* are inhibited. Then it goes on explaining the difference between a man fast asleep (whose subtle body remains here itself, along with the *saṃskāras* imprinted in it) and that of a dead man, whose subtle body is in the other world."It cannot be urged that in that case a sleeping man would be indistinguishable from a dead man; for there is this distinction that the subtle body of the sleeping man remains here itself in the form of latent impressions, while that of a dead man remains in another world".[125]

As to the difference between a *jīvanmukta* and one who is fast asleep, the *Śataślokī* 70 adds something more:

> The disappearance of all gross and subtle existence, the cessation of the senses, and the attainment of bliss,—these three are common to liberation, while alive and deep sleep. There is however this difference that, whereas he who is asleep comes back to life again and again by virtue of the effects of his past actions [*saṃskāra*], he that has attained illumination and liberation, never comes back (to worldly life), because his past actions [*saṃskāra*] have been destroyed.

---

[122] BĀUBH IV.3.6: *sukham aham asvāpsaṃ na kiñcid avediṣam iti* / See also BSBH III.2.9.

[123] CHUBH VIII.12.1.

[124] See BSBH I.3.10 ; CHUBH VI.10.3.

[125] *Vedānta Paribhāṣā* VII.39.41, translation by Swāmī Mādhavānanda, Ramakrishna Mission Saradapitha, Belur Math, Howrah, India, 1972.

and knew nothing".[122] In dreams (*svapna*) as in recollection (*smṛti*) whatever we experience can be nothing else but all that we had experienced before. The ultimate self-luminous seer is of course the *ātman*. *Ātman's* intervention in the body changes nothing as to its intrinsic nature.[123]

The vigil and sleep states can be compared to world creation and dissolution. A sort of micro-cosmogony takes place in our life each and every day during these states.[124] A late *Vedānta* text describes four sorts of cosmic dissolutions. Dreamless deep sleep state is compared to daily dissolution, in which *saṃskāras* are inhibited. Then it goes on explaining the difference between a man fast asleep (whose subtle body remains here itself, along with the *saṃskāras* imprinted in it) and that of a dead man, whose subtle body is in the other world. "It cannot be urged that in that case a sleeping man would be indistinguishable from a dead man; for there is this distinction that the subtle body of the sleeping man remains here itself in the form of latent impressions, while that of a dead man remains in another world".[125]

As to the difference between a *jīvanmukta* and one who is fast asleep, the *Saṅgrahas* (?) adds something more:

> The disappearance of all gross and subtle existence, the cessation of the senses, and the attainment of bliss—these three are common to liberation, while dreamless deep sleep. There is however this difference that whereas he who is asleep comes back to life again and again by virtue of the effects of his past actions (*saṃskāra*), he that has attained the liberation, including *jīvanmukta*, never comes back (to worldly life), because his past actions (*saṃskāras*) have been destroyed.

---

[122] BAUBH IV.3.6; *na kiñcid avediṣam*...; *na kiñcid avediṣam*. See also BSBH III.2.9.

[123] CHUBH VIII.12.1.

[124] See BSBH I.3.10; CHUBH VI.10.3.

[125] *Vedānta Paribhāṣā* VII.39-41, translation by Swami Madhavananda, Ramakrishna Mission Saradapitha, Belur Math, Howrah, India, 1972.

CHAPTER VII

The *Bhāva/Saṃskāra* Theory in the *Sāṃkhya Kārikās*

1. The word *saṃskāra* in the *Sāṃkhya Kārikā*

The word *saṃskāra* is attested in the *Kārikā* 67 only. Otherwise, *bhāva*, inherent and acquired states of mind replaces it. Identity of *bhāva* with *saṃskāra* is established in the *Gauḍapāda Bhāṣya*[1], the (*Sāṃkhya*) *Tattva Kaumudī* of Vācaspati Miśra[2] and in the *Yuktidīpikā*[3] (anonymous).

1.1 Particular features of the classical *Sāṃkhya* philosophy

This particular vocabulary feature leads us to develop the classical *Sāṃkhya* system or *darśana*—the so-called dualism, realism, atheism and rationalism.

1.1.1 Sāṃkhya *and Dualism*

The *Sāṃkhya* is dualistic because it poses two distinct omnipresent principles, the *Puruṣa* and the *Prakṛti.* The first is masculine, the second feminine. The Spirit or the spiritual

---

[1] (= SKBH) 52, 67-68. (SK=) *Sāṃkhya Kārikā. Sāṃkhyakārikā* of Īśvarakṛṣṇa with the commentary of Gauḍapāda, translation into English with Notes by T.G. MAINKAR, Oriental Book Agency, Poona, 1972.

[2] (=TK) 52.67. *The Tattva Kaumudī*, Vācaspati Miśra's Commentary on the *Sāṃkhya Kārikā*, translation into English by Gaṅganātha JHĀ, Poona Oriental Series 10, Poona, 1934; 1965.

[3] (= YD) 67. Anonymous Commentary on the SK. Ed. P. CHAKRAVARTI, Calcutta Sanskrit Series 23, Calcutta, 1938. Re. ed. R.C. PANDEYA, Delhi, 1967.

monad is a male (*puṃs*).[4] They do not, however, form a "couple" in the real sense of the term, i.e., for procreation. They are quite contrasted because the *Puruṣa* is pure consciousness-awareness, whereas the *Prakṛti* is devoid of consciousness (*acetana, ajña, jaḍa*).[5] She has a sort of "borrowed" and reflected consciousness, coming from the *Puruṣa.* Compared to a magnet, his simple presence becomes sufficient to attract all that is alien to him and triggers off or launches the process of creation-emanation (*sarga*). All physical and psychological elements of the world or *tattvas* emanate from the *Prakṛti* with an admixture of the three "attributes" or "qualities" (*guṇa*) in different proportions, in the manifested (*vyakta*) and the non-manifested (*avyakta*) states. Nothing comes out of or is produced from the *Puruṣa,* "devoid of attributes" (*aguṇa*).[6] This dualism is however initial and not final. Isolated and independent, the *Puruṣa* remains in his ever luminous consciousness when the *Prakṛti* disappears by herself[7] from the "stage" (*raṅga*) like a dancing-girl (*nartakī*)[8], when the theater is over.[9] The mysterious "connection" (*saṃyoga*)[10] between the two is explained by the author of the *Sāṃkhya Kārikās* and by the commentators in reference to "human goals", or to "the goal of the Spirit" (*puruṣārtha*).[11] A special feature of this apparent dualism is that it goes with the thesis of pluralism, in conformity with the multiplicity of beings or monads.[12]

---

[4] SK 11 and 60.

[5] SKBH 11.

[6] SKBH 11: *triguṇaṃ vyaktaṃ avyaktaṃ cāguṇaḥ purusaḥ/*. See also SKBH 61.

[7] SK 61, 66.

[8] SK 59.

[9] SK 66.

[10] SK 20, 21, 66.

[11] SK 31, 42, 63, 69.

[12] SK and SKBH 18.

1.1.2 Sāṃkhya *and Realism*

The realism of classical *Sāṃkhya* philosophy consists in the fact that for Īśvarakṛṣṇa and his commentators, this world or the manifestations of the *Prakṛti* are not assimilated to pure "illusion" (*māyā*), except in one place.[13] Creation and evolution of *tattvas* is explained by the doctrine of causality, the *satkāryavāda*, in which the effect (residing in the cause) is considered to be real, the cause being real.[14] It goes along with the doctrine of transformation (of the cause in its effect), the *pariṇāmavāda*.

1.1.3 Sāṃkhya *and Atheism*

The atheism of classical *Sāṃkhya* philosophy consists in the fact that *Puruṣa* is not considered as God (*Īśvara*). The *Puruṣa* is simple witness-consciousness, compared to an ascetic, indifferent to mundane affairs.[15] Īśvarakṛṣṇa is an atheist, he advocates *nirīśvaravāda*, and explains the "why" of all that takes place in teleological terms.[16] He rather takes recourse to the theory of "human goals", or "the goal of the spirit" (*puruṣārtha*), interpreted in a new dimension, instead of taking recourse to God as creator of the universe. The creation-emanation takes place in order to fulfil the supreme goal of "each particular monad", this goal being nothing else but "liberation".[17]

1.1.4 Sāṃkhya *and Rationalism*

As to the rationalistic tendency of the classical *Sāṃkhya* philosophy, some reserves can be made. Even if the *buddhi* ("consciousness", "intellect", "intelligence", power of reasoning, judging and taking firm decisions) is a faculty

---

[13] SKBH 23.

[14] SK 9.

[15] SKBH 19.

[16] SK 56-58.

[17] SK 56, *pratipuruṣavimokṣārtham...*/

which can be translated by "reason",[18] it cannot be limited or assimilated to the latter. It overpasses the simple function of reasoning because one of the luminous "predispositions" (*bhāva*) of the *buddhi* is liberating knowledge or *jñāna*, which is not a product of the faculty of reasoning only.

2. The receptacle of the *bhāvas* is the *buddhi*

The receptacle and birthplace of *bhāvas* is the *buddhi*[19] (consciousness, intellect), first evolute of the *Prakṛti*. In the transmigration context, the subtle body (*sūkṣma-* or *liṅga-śarīra*)[20] is held to be their receptacle, called also "thirteen-fold instrument" (*trayodaśa-karaṇa*),[21] comprising: *buddhi*, I-principle or ego (*ahaṃkāra*), mind (*manas*), and ten sensorimotor faculties (*indriya*). Invested with *bhāvas* or *saṃskāras*, which represent the personal non-transferable acquisitions of each monad, the subtle body, surviving after death seeks to reincarnate itself in a gross body (*sthūla-śarīra*),[22] because, by itself, it is incapable of having an experience (*nirupabhoga*),[23] *i.e.*, enjoying the good or bad fruits of acts. Hence the interdependency between subtle and gross body, as well as between subtle body and "predispositions".[24]

2.1 The *Puruṣa* and the *Prakṛti*

Man and the world are made of twenty-three evolutes (*tattva*) emanating from the fundamental or Primordial

[18] See R. J. PARROT, "The Experience called 'Reason' in Classical Sāṃkhya", *Journal of Indian Philosophy*, vol. 13, n° 3, September 1985, pp. 235 sq.

[19] See SK and SKBH 23, SK 40, 43, 52.

[20] SK 20, 40–42, 52; SKBH 39–43; 55.

[21] SK 43; SK and SKBH 32; SKBH 42–43.

[22] SK 41. The subtle elements called *tanmātra* are permanent. The gross body born of parents is perishable and impermanent. "The elements which are born of the parents perish in this very world, leaving the subtle body at the time of death. At the time of death, the body born of parents is left behind and merges into earth and other gross elements", SKBH 39, translation T.G. MAINKAR.

[23] SK 40 and Commentaries.

[24] SK 40–41 and Commentaries.

Nature (24th *mūla-prakṛti*) also called *Pradhāna*, by a specific admixture of three attributes or qualities (*guṇa*). The *Puruṣa* (25th) devoid of attributes (*aguṇa*) and activity, is nowhere localized in the *Prakṛti*. In the atheistic or Godless doctrine (*nirīśvaravāda*) advocated by Īśvarakṛṣṇa, the *Puruṣa* is pure consciousness, void and devoid of all substances, and works like an absolute. Nevertheless the whole spectacle is enacted for him. The world is compared to a "stage" (*raṅga*), the *Prakṛti* to an actress or dancing-girl (*nartakī*), and the *Puruṣa* to a spectator.[25] Nothing comes out of the *Puruṣa* and nothing really happens to him. Creation or evolution takes place only when the equilibrium of three *guṇas* (residing in the Primordial Nature) is broken, always in the same manner, from *mahat* ("great" principle) or *buddhi* onwards till five subtle and five gross (or material) elements.

2.2 Three attributes inherent in the *Prakṛti*

All predispositions (*bhāva*) are tinged with the three *guṇa* (*sattva, rajas, tamas*), each of them possess a physical, psychological, moral and intellectual dimension, inherent in the *Prakṛti* or *Pradhāna*. The *Pradhāna* contains all sorts of virtualities, named "predispositions in movement" and "predispositions at rest" (*gati-* and *sthiti-saṃskāra*).[26] *Sattva* represents, on the physical level, all that is light and luminous, clear and transparent. On the psycho-moral and intellectual level it is joy, serenity, goodness, generosity, sympathy. On the intellectual level it is intelligence, the capacity of understanding and discriminating. *Rajas* is movement, agitation and activity on the physical level; passion, distraction, maliciousness, aggressivity, on the psycho-moral level. On the intellectual level it is agility and rapidity of the psycho-motor faculties. *Tamas* on the physical plane is heaviness, inertia, obscurity; on the psycho-moral level it is stupor, despondency, exhaustion, passivity, indifference. On the

---

[25] SK 66.

[26] See *Yoga Bhāṣya* (= YBH) and *Tattva Vaiśāradī* (= TV) II.23.

intellectual level it is lack of understanding or stupidity (just the contrary to *sattva*).

2.3 Two sets of predispositions: luminous and obscure

Sattva and *tamas guṇas* (*rajas* being always and everywhere present, specially in the human condition) determine "luminous" or good (*sāttvika*) and "obscure" or bad (*tāmasa*) predispositions (*bhāva*). Intellect (*buddhi*) is the determinative faculty. When goodness and intelligence predominate virtue (*dharma*), knowledge (*jñāna*), detachment (*vairāgya* "dispassion"), lordly powers (*aiśvarya*), constitute *sāttvika* form. Vice (*adharma*), ignorance (*ajñāna*), attachment (*avairāgya*), absence of lordly powers (*anaiśvarya*) constitute *tāmasa* form.[27]

Vyāsa in his commentary to the *Yoga Sūtras* of Patañjali[28] refers to this same *bhāva/guṇa* theory in relation to mental modifications (*citta-vṛtti*). Vācaspati Miśra in his *Tattva Vaiśāradī* equates *citta-vṛtti* with *buddhi-vṛtti*,[29] which are nothing but a conscious phase of *saṃskāra*.[30] In the *Mahābhārata*[31] also, *bhāva* and *guṇa* are held to be synonymous. In his commentary to the *Śvetvāśvatara Upaniṣad* and to the *Bhagavad Gītā*, Śaṅkara also interprets *bhāva, svabhāva, prakṛti* and *guṇa* in relation with *saṃskāras*. *Manu Smṛti*[32] and *Yājñavalkya Smṛti*[33] explain that our "states of mind" (*bhāva*) determine the quality of our future births. Thoughts at the moment of death (*maraṇa-citta*) have also their impact in rebirth (*upapatti-citta*).[34]

---

[27] See SK and SKBH 23.

[28] YBH I.2.

[29] TV I.2.

[30] See YBH I.5.

[31] XII.187; 239–240, Crit. edn.

[32] XII.1.

[33] III.133; 129; 132; 140.

[34] See my Chapter II. Rites along with the recitation of sacred texts prepare the last thoughts of the dying person. See *Bhagavad Gītā*, VIII.6. Rich materials on the subject in: F. EDGERTON, "The Hour of Death, its

2.4 The central directive line of the *bhāva* theory

Amongst the three directive lines of the *bhāva* theory, the central one is found in the following verse.[35]

> Intellect is determinative. Virtue, knowledge, non-attachment and majesty constitute its *sāttvika* form, when *sattva* (goodness) predominates. The *tāmasa* form, i.e., the form when *tamas* dominates is just the reverse.[36]

2.5 Eight *bhāvas* or *rūpas*

In the SK 63, *rūpa* (form) replaces *bhāva*. The general context is focused on the problem of bondage and release. Seven of these *bhāvas* bind. Only one, namely discriminating knowledge (*jñāna*) liberates. In reality, *Puruṣa* is neither bound nor released. It is the *Prakṛti* alone that is bound, migrates released. She liberates herself through one form (*rūpa*) in order to accomplish "the goal of the spirit" (*puruṣārtha*). "Verily, Spirit is neither bound, nor released, nor migrates. It is *Prakṛti*, the Primal Nature alone, abiding in manifold forms, that is bound, released, and migrates".[37] Gauḍapāda explains virtue, non-attachment, power, vice, ignorance, attachment and absence of power, these are the seven forms of the *Prakṛti*, the Nature. With these the nature binds herself by herself. The same *Prakṛti* with a view to accomplish the purpose of the Spirit, liberates herself through one form, namely knowledge".[38] "By seven forms *Prakṛti*, the Primal Nature binds herself by herself, by one form she releases herself for the deliverance of the spirit".[39] Gauḍapāda explains as to what "happens" to a particular monad, "In this manner the subtle body migrates till discriminative

importance for man's future fate in Hindu and Western Religions", ABORI 1926–27, vol. VII, part III, pp. 219–49. Also in E. Lamotte, *Traité de la Grande Vertu de Sagesse*, Louvain, 1970, t. III, pp. 1535–38.

[35] SK 23, 40, 43–44, 63–64 and Commentaries.

[36] SK 23.

[37] SK 62.

[38] SKBH 62.

[39] SK 63.

knowledge is attained. After the rise of this knowledge, the knower leaves the body and wins liberation".[40]

2.6 The concept of *puruṣārtha*

Īśvarakṛṣṇa introduces the concept of *puruṣārtha* (the "purposes of the Spirit") in all its novelty, by bringing them under two heads: "experience" (*bhoga*) and "liberation" "retreat" (*apavarga*)[41] and "perception", "vision" (*darśana*) and "isolation" (*kaivalya, mokṣa*).[42] His main concern is to explain how and why a mysterious "union" (*saṃyoga*)[43] institutes itself between the *Puruṣa* and the *Prakṛti* (two radically distinct, omnipresent, juxtaposed principles). So he takes recourse to a teleological argument. Creation takes place in order to accomplish these purposes and that is why a semblance of connection institutes between them. The ever free *Puruṣa* "works" like a catalyst or magnet only. This is his unique "contribution" in the cosmogenesis. Each particular monad gets the opportunity of going through all sorts of experiences and learns that the fundamental taste of these experiences is nothing but deception and suffering (*duḥkha*).[44] The only way of getting rid of suffering is disconnection, obtained through discriminating soteriological knowledge (*pañca-viṃśati-tattva-jñāna*).[45]

2.7 Details on predispositions (*bhāva*)

Let us refer ourselves to some of the *Kārikās* with commentaries where these predispositions (*bhāva*) or traits of character are described in the following order. There

---

[40] SKBH 39: *evam etan niyataṃ sūkṣmaśarīraṃ saṃsarati na yāvaj jñānam utpadyate / jñāne vidvān charīraṃ tyaktvā mokṣaṃ gacchati /*

[41] See TK 21, 62, 66.

[42] SK 21.

[43] Compared to that of a lame (*paṅgu*) and a blind (*andha*) in SK 21.

[44] Īśvarakṛṣṇa is in search of a radical and definitive means of eradicating the threefold suffering. See SK 1-2 and Commentaries.

[45] This discriminative wisdom consists in isolating the 25th, i.e., the *Puruṣa* from the 24 *other tattvas*. See SKBH 1, 2, 22, 44, 51, 55, Cf. 64, 69.

are the four *sāttvika* forms of the *buddhi* in which the *guṇa sattva* dominates over *rajas* and *tamas*. The distinctive mark of virtue (*dharma*) is compassion and donation (sacrificial and other gifts); restrictions and observances (*yama, niyama*), parts of the eightfold *yoga* (*aṣṭāṅga-yoga*) advocated by Patañjali. Virtue leads to prosperity (*abhudaya*) and the highest good (*niḥśreyasa*).[46] Knowledge (*jñāna*), second *bhāva*, has an affinity with light, understanding and manifestation. It is two-fold—knowledge extrinsic or external, which comprehends the knowledge of the *Veda* with its six "branches" (*Vedāṅga*: phonetics, ritual, grammar, etymology, metrics and astronomy), the *Purāṇas*, the philosophical "systems" such as *Nyāya* and *Mīmāṃsā*, and the *Dharmaśāstras*. The intrinsic or internal knowledge is the comprehension of the difference between the *Puruṣa* and the *Prakṛti*. Although external knowledge generates the admiration among the people, only internal knowledge results into liberation. Non-attachment (*avairāgya*) is also twofold—external (i.e., freedom from the senses), and internal (i.e., desire for liberation). Power is majestic. It is of eight kinds: *aṇimā, mahimā, garimā*, etc. (as described in the treatise of *Yoga*).

2.8 Predispositions and destinies

The four other predispositions (*bhāva*) or traits of character correspond to the *tāmasa* forms of the *buddhi* and are just the reverse of *sāttvic* form. Our destinies are determined by these psycho-moral predispositions as explained by the author of the *Sāṃkhya Kārikā*:

> By virtue is ascent to a region above; through vice to a region below: by knowledge is deliverance; by the reverse, i.e., ignorance, bondage.
>
> From non-detachment results merger in *Prakṛti*, the Primal Nature; migration is the result of passionate attachment; power assures non-obstruction; the reverse from the contrary.[47]

---

[46] See SKBH and TK 23 for details on these eight *bhāvas*.

[47] SK 44–45 and Commentaries.

3. Other two directives of the theory of eight *bhāvas*

The other two directives of the theory of eight *bhāvas* gravitate around the central one. They are subdivided under three heads—*saṃsiddhika* (original, innate, connate), *prākṛtika* (natural) and *vaikṛtika* (modified, acquired, incidental).[48] Virtue, knowledge, detachment and majesty are called *saṃsiddhika.* Latent dispositions (potentially present), those of mythical personalities–Sanaka, Sanandana, Sanātana, Sanatkumāra, sons of Brahmā–are named *prākṛtika.* Acquired dispositions (*vaikṛtika*) are obtained by personal efforts like, knowledge, detachment, virtue, majesty.

3.1 Relation between the fifty *pratyayas* and the eight *bhāvas*

The third directive of the *Sāṃkhya* theory of *bhāva* is found in SK 46–51. This is the "creation of the intellect" (*pratyaya-sarga*) or "volitional subjective evolution". The word *pratyaya* stands for the *buddhi.*[49] They are fifty in number (through the disparity of the influence of the *guṇas*), to comprehend 5 varieties of ignorance, 28 incapacities, 9 contentments, 8 attainments.[50] All of them are the "properties of intellect" (*buddhi-dharma*).[51] After quoting the verses SK 40–43 where eight *bhāvas* are described, Gauḍapāda and Vācaspati Miśra interpret *pratyaya-sarga* with reference to "creation of dispositions" (*bhāva-sarga*), and "creation of subtle body" (*liṅga-sarga*) with reference to "creation of subtle elements" (*tanmātra-sarga*).[52] The Chinese commentary of Paramārtha[53] furnishes an excellent example showing how these fifty

---

[48] See SK and SKBH 43.

[49] SKBH 46.

[50] SK and SKBH 46. On the *pratyaya-sarga,* see G.J. LARSON, *Classical Sāṃkhya,* Delhi, Motilal Banarsidass, 1969, p. 211, sq.

[51] TK. 46.

[52] SKBH and TK 52.

[53] See J. TAKAKUSU, *La Sāṃkhya Kārikā étudiée á la lumière de sa version chinoise,* BEFEO 4 (Hanoi, 1904).

pratyayas/ bhāvas intervene in our everyday behaviour. The *Yukti Dīpikā* (YD) introduces cosmological and cosmogonical themes in this context.

According to the YD, the *pratyaya-sarga* constitutes one of the aspects of the (primal nature) in the manifested phase (*vyakta*). These aspects are material "form" (*rūpa*), "action" (*pravṛtti*), and "fruit" (*phala*). The first accounts for the creation of elements (*tattva-sarga*), from *mahat* (or *buddhi*) till five gross elements (*mahābhūta*). In the YD scheme, action (*pravṛtti*) corresponds to eight "creation of dispositions" (*bhāva-sarga*), and consequences (*phala*) to "creation of ideas" (*pratyaya-sarga*), comprehending fifty *pratyayas* mentioned above.

4. The subtle body and the psycho-moral predispositions

The SK 52 offers a total appraisal of the *bhāva* theory: predispositions cannot function without the subtle body and the subtle body cannot function without predispositions. Therefore, a two-fold creation takes place. Gauḍapāda comments:

> There would be no subtle elements without dispositions and there would be no elaboration of dispositions without subtle elements. Creation, therefore, proceeds in two ways, the elemental and intellectual. (Further) without predispositions, i.e., without creation of intellect (*pratyaya-sarga*), there can be no *liṅga-* or no creation of subtle elements (*tanmātra-sarga*), because "every successive body is acquired by the residual impressions of actions performed in previous births".[54]

The *liṅga-śarīra* and the *bhāvas* are assimilated to two aspects of the psyche, amongst which the former accounts for our remote past about which we are unconscious. What is true on the cosmic level is also true on the individual level because the *pradhāna* is also a reservoir of virtualities inspite of cyclic creations and reabsorptions.[55] In the same way, the *liṅga-* is the reservoir of psycho-moral predispositions, residual

---

[54] SKBH 52: *pūrvapūrvasaṃskārādṛṣṭakāritvād uttarottara dehalambhasya /*

[55] See TV II, 24 (Vācaspati Miśra's Commentary on the *Yoga Sūtra*).

impressions, latent desires (*bhāva, saṃskāra, vāsanā*), since the primordial creation, because it is permanent. It preserves all these dynamic traces inspite of the periodical intervals of the universe. The *bhāva-sarga* represents the changing aspect of our psyche (conscious and unconscious) in a given lifetime. In any case both *liṅga-* and *bhāva-* are two inseparable aspects of our psychological life. Both of them are responsible for our implication in the transmigratory process (*saṃsāra*). Paramārtha explains this relation through comparisons as between "the fire and the heat", and as between the "two horns of a buffalo".[56] Gauḍapāda and Vācaspati Miśra introduces the thesis of *anāditva* in order to explain the reciprocity of these creations (*sarga*).[57] This mutual dependency is "similar to that of a seed and sprout" (*bījāṅkuravat*). The *anāditva* theory helps to cut short the philosophical problem of *regressus ad infinitum* and renders reciprocal causality intelligible.

Thus *bhāva* and *liṅga* taken together represent two aspects of our psychic life. *Liṅga* or the "permanent" subtle body accounts for the past, kept intact on the unconscious level, as dynamic traces of acts and experiences. Predispositions (*bhāva*) represent the changing aspect of our conscious and unconscious psyche, in the present life, our drives, new orientations, aspirations, etc.

4.1 The "why" of mysterious connection (*saṃyoga*)

The TK and YD 52 introduce here the teleological argument of two *puruṣārthas* (*bhoga, apavarga*), explain the mutual dependence of gross body, subtle psyche, and predispositions. The "creation made of union" or "due to connection" (*saṃyogakṛtasarga*) takes place for the fulfilment of these ends. The YD introduces the concept of *adhikāra* ("task", "mission", "authority") and refers to the disinterested mission which sages like Kapila and Hiraṇyagarbha accomplished.

---

[56] *Ad.* SK 46, TAKAKUSU, p. 1043.

[57] SKBH and TK 52.

Vyāsa takes recourse to the concept of *guṇādhikāra*,[58] task due to attributes. The unknown author of the YD adds that in the mythico-cosmogonical context this mutual dependency (*anyonyāśraya*) between the "grain" (*bīja*) and the "sprout" (*aṅkura*) does not constitute a fault or a fallacy in the reasoning.[59]

4.2 The right discriminative knowledge

Now, deliverance as "isolation" (*kaivalya*) is realized through one of the luminous dispositions (*bhāva*) of the intellect (*buddhi*, when *sattva* abounds in it), i.e., knowledge (*jñāna*). Thus *buddhi* appears to be the place of "conjunction" and of "disjunction" between the *Puruṣa* and the *Prakṛti*. The fire of knowledge burns and reduces the seeds of actions to ashes. This non-germination puts an end to *saṃsāra*. Eradication of suffering in its threefold aspects is made possible through therapeutical and soteriological knowledge, overpassing the *buddhi*. In fact, there is a double level of discourse in the *Sāṃkhya Kārikās* and its commentaries. From the transcendental point of view, the Spirit (*Puruṣa*) is always free.[60] From the empirical level, in order to account for the condition of every singular monad (*prati-puruṣa*),[61] the means to acquire discriminating knowledge are dealt with by the sages of these doctrines. Gauḍapada explains it clearly as to how long the Spirit suffers from misery (*duḥkha*):

> Till the cessation of the *Liṅga*, till the subtle body has ceased to be. As long as the Spirit is in the subtle body, composed of intellect and the rest, it is individualised and as long as migratory body does not cease, so long, in brief, does the Spirit experience pain due to decay and death in the three worlds. [....] Whenever knowledge of

---

[58] YBH II.23; IV.34. See also YS IV.34. for Patañjali's definition of "Isolation" (*kaivalya*).

[59] See YD p. 137.

[60] See SK 62.

[61] "This creation, from intellect down to gross elements, is brought about by *Prakṛti*, the Primal Nature, for the deliverance of each Spirit [*pratipuruṣavimokṣārtham*]. This is done for another's sake as for itself" (SK 56).

> the twenty-five principles, the characteristic of which is knowledge of the distinctness of the Nature from the Spirit, is attained; or whenever a person knows that this is the nature, this is the intellect, this is egotism, these are the five subtle elements, these the eleven senses, these the five gross elements and this the Spirit, separate and dissimilar, different and distinct from them all; then on account of such knowledge the subtle body ceases to be, and thence liberation.[62]

4.3 *Saṃskāra, vega, prārabdha-karman*

A liberated sage (*jīvanmukta*), even after having attained perfect knowledge may still continue to live, although his present actions will bear no more fruits. The compounds, *jīvanmukti* (liberation while living), and *videhamukti* (liberation after death) are not found in the SK and commentaries, but the idea is fully present. Hence, the problem of time-gap between these two "states" is raised. Īśvarakṛṣṇa introduces the concept of *saṃskāra* to explain the continuation of the body in the case of a liberated sage. Due to the force of residual impressions (*saṃskāra-vaśāt*),[63] responsible for the maintenance of the body, a yogin continues to live, or has to wait. The impetus (*vega*) retained in the potter's wheel (*kulāla-cakra*) is nothing else but the set of *prārabdha-karman* or *śeṣavṛtti* ("whirling of the rest","duration or persistency of the body").[64]

4.4 Soteriological purpose of knowledge

Gauḍapada and Vācaspati Miśra comment on the *Kārikā* 67.

> One may here wonder, if after the rise of knowledge a man wins liberation, then why do not I win it. To this it is replied. Though the attainment of perfect knowledge of the twentyfive principles is attained yet because of the past impressions, the sage continues in a bodily condition—how? like the whirling of a wheel. As a potter, having set his wheel whirling, fabricates a jar by putting a lump of clay on the wheel. After making the jar, he forsakes the wheel, but the wheel continues to rotate round. It does so on account of the

---

[62] SKBH 55.

[63] SK 67.

[64] The concept of *śeṣavṛtti* is introduced in the TK 71.

past momentum. Thus from the attainment of perfect knowledge virtue and the rest cease to be producers of any effects. These seven kinds of bonds are burnt by perfect knowledge. Just as seeds burnt by fire cannot germinate, so these forms of bondage (...) are not able to fetter the soul. But the body continues because of the past impressions and the spirit remains invested with that body. Why does not knowledge destroy virtue and vice of the present? Because they are of the present and are destroyed in the next moment. Knowledge destroys all future actions in his present body by following the actions prescribed by the scriptures. After the exhaustion of the previous impressions the body perishes and then liberation occurs.[65]

4.5 Bondage and release

Vācaspati Miśra rightly refers to the *Chāndogya Upaniṣad* and the *Brahma Sūtra* while commenting on this important and unique *kārikā* where the compound *saṃskāra-vaśāt* figures[66]. He has also in mind the *Yoga Sūtras* and commentaries.

> When true knowledge appears, the "kārmic residuum"– even though it is beginningless and its time for fruition uncertain – has its productivity destroyed and is unable to produce any "fruit" in the shape of "birth, life and life experiences". [....] Even so, when wisdom has been attained, the body continues for a while, on account of the previous impulse; just as, even after the action of the potter has ceased, the wheel continues to revolve on account of the momentum imparted to it. In due time, however, when the impulse becomes exhausted, it becomes *inactive.* In the continuance of the body, the impulse is supplied by such virtue and vice whose fruition has already commenced; as is declared in *Śruti*—"Having exhausted the others by means of experience, the soul attains beatitude" [*Brahma Sūtra* IV. 1.19] and "The delay is only so long as beatitude is not attained" [*Chāndogya* VI.14.2]. The "impulse" (to which the continuance of the Body is due) is in the remnant of that impulse which had been imparted by the disappearing ignorance; it is true that on account of the momentum of this impulse the Spirit continues to be invested with the body for a time.[67]

---

[65] SKBH 67.

[66] We saw the importance of these two passages from the *Śruti* and the *Smṛti* in my chapter VI. Śaṅkara takes recourse to the concept of *saṃskāra* in order to explain the delay for the liberated sage.

[67] TK 67.

Let us see how the practice of *aṣṭāṅga-yoga* helps the adept to get rid of *saṃskāra*, cause of bondage.

CHAPTER VIII

Ambivalence of *Saṃskāras* in the *Yoga Sūtras* of Patañjali

1. The Concept of *saṃskāra* in the eight *sūtras* of Patañjali

In the *Yoga Sūtras* of Patañjali, *saṃskāras* appear as one of the factors of bondage and release. The word *saṃskāra* figures in eight *sūtras* of Patañjali.[1] Translations used in the commentaries of Vyāsa,[2] Vācaspati Miśra,[3] Rāja Bhoja,[4] and Vijñānabhikṣu are, "residual or latent impressions", "(acquired) dispositions", "subliminal-impressions" (J.H. Woods), etc.[5] Correlative concepts such as "latent desire" or "impregnation" (*vāsanā*), "deposit of acts", "kārmic residua" (*āśaya* or *karmāśya*), "grain" or "seed" (*bīja*), "memory", "mnemonic traces" (*smṛti*) are also frequent and more or less synonymous. For instance Rāja Bhoja *ad* YS I.24 identifies *āśaya* with *vāsanā* and *saṃskāra*.

1.1 Residual impressions only

YS 1.18 describes the nature of non-notional concentration (*asaṃprajñātasamādhi*) in which the mind of the adept is

[1] In *Yoga Sūtra* (= YS) I.18 and 50; II.15; III.9-10; 18; IV.9; 27.

[2] *Yoga Bhāṣya* (=YBH).

[3] *Tattva Vaiśāradī* (=TV).

[4] *Rājamārtāṇḍa*.

[5] *Yoga Vārttika* (=Y.-vārt.).

perfectly stable, and is not conscious of objects. "The other (*asaṃprajñātasamādhi*) consists of residual impressions only (*saṃskāraśeṣo'nyaḥ*) having for antecedent repeated practice of cessation".[6]

J.H. Woods translates:

> The other [concentration which is not conscious of objects] consists of subliminal-impressions only [after objects have merged], and follows upon that practice which effects the cessation of [fluctuations].[7]

When all fluctuations of the mind (*citta-vṛtti*) cease, or are restricted for the time being, in this state, only *saṃskāras* are left over.

1.1.1 *The compound* saṃskāra-śeṣa

The compound *saṃskāra-śeṣa* is interpreted in two different ways by the commentators. Vyāsa explains:

> The concentration which is not conscious [of objects] is that restriction of the mind-stuff in which only subliminal-impressions are left and in which all fluctuations have come to rest. [....] Mind-stuff, when engaged in the practice of this [imperceptible object], seems as if it were itself non-existent and without any supporting-object. Thus [arises] that concentration [called] seedless [without sensation stimulus] which is not conscious of objects.[8]

So he equates *asaṃprajñātasamādhi* and *nirbīja-samādhi*. Unlike Vyāsa and Vācaspati Miśra, for whom in this concentration only *saṃskāras* are left, Bhoja in his *Rājamārtāṇḍa* ad YS I.18 understands the compound *saṃskāra-śeṣa* as "the end or extinction of psycho-cerebral dynamic tendencies" or *saṃskāras*. So let us try to determine the nature of this "rest" (*śeṣa*) or remainder, i.e., the subconscious-unconscious impressions (*saṃskāra*) left over

---

[6] YS 1.18: *virāma-pratyaya-abhyāsa-pūrvaḥ saṃskāra-śeṣo'nyaḥ /*

[7] YS I.18. I have mostly used the translation by J. H. WOODS: The *Yoga-System of Patañjali* Or *The Ancient Hindu Doctrine of Concentration of Mind*, First ed., Harvard University Press (1914, 2nd ed. 1927), reprint: Delhi, Motilal Banarsidass, 1966. For the Sanskrit text, see: *Patañjalayogadarśanam*, edited by Śrī Nārāyaṇa MIŚRA, Bhāratīya vidyā prakāśaṇa, Vārāṇasī, Sīma Press, 1971 (containing Commentaries from Vyāsa, Vācaspati Miśra, Vijñānabhikṣu.

[8] YBH I.18.

in the mind. It seems that this *śeṣa* corresponds to the *nirodha-saṃskāras* born of the yogic effort and act of suppression repeated several times. Even the *nirodha* leaves a "trace" which is a "blank", a "no", a "void". Now, will the "inhibitory disposition" (*nirodha-saṃskāra*) relaunch the *yogin* once again in the phenomenal flux?—No. The very nature of an inhibitory disposition is to redress itself against the "exteriorising dispositions" (*vyutthāna-saṃskāra*),[9] born out of ordinary acts and experiences (before the practice of *Yoga*). For this reason they are identified with "anterior residual impressions or dispositions" (*pūrva-saṃskāra*), anterior to yogic practices.[10] The psychological "pause" or "break" obtained for some seconds or minutes in the concentration without objects or notions (*asaṃprajñāta-samādhi*) is susceptible to be interrupted sooner or later due to the latent dynamism and pressure of *vyutthāna-saṃskāras.*

2. Sapience-made and residual impressions of emergence

YS I.50 deals with residual-impression made of (or in) deep insight (*prajñā-kṛta-saṃskāra*[11] or *prajñā-saṃskāra* : "dispositions made of insight or sapience"), pertaining to sapience or to knowledge. "The subliminal-impression produced by this [i.e., by the concentration with seed or notions] is hostile to other subliminal-impressions".[12] The latent or residual impression born of this knowledge acquired through "seeded concentration" (*sabīja-samādhi*) is hostile to other dynamic impressions of empirical life, tending towards exteriorisation (*vyutthāna-saṃskāra*).

> The subliminal-impression arising from concentrated insight inhibits the latent-impression from the emergent subliminal-impression. After emergent subliminal-impressions have been repressed, the presented ideas arising from them do not occur.

[9] See YS III.9; YBH and TV ad YS I.14; 50; III, 9 and 13; TV IV.27-28.

[10] See YBH and Y-vārt., IV.27-28.

[11] The expression *prajñā-kṛta-saṃskāra* is attested in Vyāsa, YBH I.50-51. See also TV and Y.-vārt.

[12] YS I.50: *taj-jaḥ saṃskāro'nya-saṃskāra-pratibandhī /*

> When presented ideas are restricted, concentration follows thereafter. Then concentrated insight, after that, subliminal-impressions made from insight. Thus latent-impressions from subliminal-impressions are reproduced again and again. Thus first comes insight and then [follow] subliminal-impressions.[13]

The gradual, progressive and repetitive aspect of *Yoga* practices is quite obvious here.

2.1 Latent impressions of emergence

Identified with anterior or afflicted tendencies (*pūrva-* and *kleśa-saṃskāra*),[14] these latent impressions of emergence or dispersal (*vyutthāna-saṃskāra*) represent the whole past stock of unconscious drives and afflictions. Five sorts of afflictions or "hindrances" (*kleśa*)[15] saturate the mind before the practice of "eight-fold" or *aṣṭāṅga-yoga* is undertaken (and starts producing its results).[16] Progressively, after having restricted all thought activity, including the impressions made by insight (*prajñākṛtasaṃskāra*), born of concentration (*samādhija*), the *yogin* attains "seedless concentration" (*nirbījasamādhi*).[17] This is realized through "subliminal impressions of restriction or suppression" (*nirodha-saṃskāra*). Existence of these yogic *saṃskāras* can be infered from the experience of lapse of time during which there is stability (*stithi*) of restriction.[18]

3. Three kinds of suffering

YS II.15 establishes an intimate relation between *saṃskāra* (previous impressions born from ordinary acts or experiences) and "pain" or "suffering" (*duḥkha*). "As being the pains which are mutations and anxieties and subliminal-impressions, and by reason of the opposition of the

---

[13] YBH I.50.

[14] See TV IV.27 and Y.-vārt., IV.28: *pūrvasaṃskārah prācīnaḥ kleśasaṃskāraḥ* /

[15] Mentioned in YS II.2-3 sq.

[16] On eight-fold *Yoga*, see YS II.29 *sq.*

[17] YS I.51.

[18] YBH I.51.

fluctuations of the aspects (*guṇa*), to the discriminating all is nothing but pain".[19] This endless painfulness of existence is due to the incessant "transformation of aspects", attributes or qualities (*guṇa-pariṇāma*), in the outer world, and in our inner mental life. This *sūtra* reminds us of some Buddhist texts and we find an echo of these in the commentaries to the YS. The relationship between psychological dispositions, subject to incessant transformations, and pain forms the general framework of the *Sāṃkhya* philosophy also.[20] Vyāsa enumerates three kinds of pains—pain due to transformations or to perpetual change (*pariṇāma-duḥkhatā*), pain due to anguish (*tāpa-duḥkhatā*), pain due to latent impressions (*saṃskāra-duḥkhatā*).[21] He defines the *saṃskāra-duḥkhatā* by taking recourse to the concepts of *āśaya* or *karmāśaya,* situating the problem in the context of *karma-phala-vipāka* and *bhoga.* The major root is of course "ignorance" (*avidyā*).

> But what is the painfulness of subliminal-impressions? There is a latent-deposit of subliminal-impressions of pleasure arising from the experience of pleasure; and there is a latent-deposit of subliminal-impression of pain arising from pain. Thus analogously (*evam*), while the fruition from the *karma* is under experience, there is an accumulation of a latent-deposit of *karma.* Thus this stream of pain from time without beginning, spreading wider and wider, agitates the *yogin* because its essence is counteractive. Why is this? It is because a wise man is like an eyeball. Just as a fine thread of wool fallen upon the eyeball by its touch gives pain, but not so when it falls upon other parts of the body, so these pains [from subliminal-impressions] hinder the *yogin* only, who is like an eyeball, but not any other perceiver.[22]

That's why the *yogin* seeks refuge in the "right vision" (*samyag-darśana,* "focused-insight").

---

[19] YS II.15: *pariṇāma-tāpa-saṃskāra-duḥkhair guṇa-vṛtty-a-virodhāc ca duḥkham eva sarvaṃ vivekinaḥ /*

[20] See SK 1-2; 55.

[21] On the pain due to latent impressions (*saṃskāra-duḥkhatā*), see for example *Abhidharma Kośa* VI.3, p. 875. Also the Buddhist para-canonic text *Visuddhi Magga* XVI.2.

[22] YBH II.15.

3.1 The quadruple scheme of Indian medical treatises

Explaining the painfulness due to latent impressions (*saṃskāra-duḥkhatā*), Vyāsa introduces the well-known quadruple scheme of Indian medical treatises (*cikitsā-śāstra*)—*roga, roga-hetu, ārogya, bhesaja.*

> Just as a system of medicine has four divisions [on] Disease [and on] Cause of Disease [and on] Health [and on] Remedy, Release, etc. so this system also has four divisions, [on] the round-of-birth [and on] the cause of the round-of-birth [and on] release [and on] the way to release. Of these [four], the round-of-birth with its mass of pains is that which is to be escaped; the conjunction of the primary-cause and of the Self is the cause of which is to be escaped (*heya*); the final destruction of the correlation is the escape (*hāna*); the means of escape is focused-insight.[23]

The first Sermon of the Buddha, the *Dhamma-cakka-pavattana-sutta,* known as the Sermon of Banaras, unfolds this same quadruple medical scheme in vogue at that time.

4. Residual-impressions of emergence versus residual-impressions of suppression

YS III.9-10 deals with "residual-impressions of emergence" (*vyutthāna-saṃskāra*) and "residual-impressions of suppression" (*nirodha-saṃskāra*), in the context of the last three limbs or members of the *aṣṭāṅga-yoga,* called "perfect control", "perfect restrain", "contention" and mastery (*saṃyama*), i.e., fixation of mind (*dhāraṇā*), meditation (*dhyāna*), deep concentration (*samādhi*).

> When there is a becoming invisible of the subliminal-impressions of emergence and a becoming visible of the subliminal-impresions of restriction, the mutation of restriction is inseparably connected with mind-stuff in the period of restriction. This [mind-stuff] flows peacefully by reason of the subliminal-impressions.[24]

---

[23] YBH II.15.

[24] YS III.9-10: *vyutthāna-nirodha-saṃskārayor abhibhava-prādurbhāvau nirodha-kṣaṇa-citta-anvayo nirodha-pariṇāmaḥ* / (9) *tasya praśāntavāhitā saṃskārāt* / (10).

5. Extraordinary or supra-normal powers

With the YS III.18 we enter in the domain of extraordinary or supernormal powers (*siddhi*) obtained by the *yogin* during his gradual progression towards liberation known as "isolation" (*kaivalya*). This *siddhi* consisting in the direct visualisation of past impressions (*saṃskāra-sākṣātkāra*), enables him to cross the threshold of present as well as intra-uterine life, and to see directly beyond them. By piercing the veil of time, the adept has to now access the whole unconscious psychic stock. Psycho-analysis does not pretend to go so far. Commentators develop here the famous relation between *saṃskāra* and *smṛti*. Memory of the past is valorized in this context, because obtained precisely through contention and control resulting in perfect mastery (*saṃyama*), and does not correspond to undesirable involuntary upsurge of vehement emotional drives.

5.1 *Saṃskāra* and *kleśa*

"As a result of direct perception of subliminal-impressions there is [intuitive] knowledge of previous births".[25] Vyāsa explains that these latent impressions (*saṃskāra*) are of two kinds—1. causes of memory and afflictions, in the form of *vāsanās* 2. causes of fruition (*vipāka*) in the form of merit and demerit (*dharma, adharma*).[26] Latent impressions produced by knowledge are causes of memory; whereas latent impressions produced by ignorance are causes of afflictions (*kleśa*)[27]. First amongst the five *kleśas, avidyā* is the source of all other *kleśas.*[28] The *yoga* of action (*kriyā-yoga*) helps to attenuate these afflictions.[29] For example, the will-to-live (*abhiniveśa*) which expresses itself in the instinct

---

[25] YS III.18: *saṃskārasākṣātkaraṇātpūrvajātijñānam /*

[26] YBH III.18.

[27] TV III.18 : *jñānajā hi saṃskārāḥ smṛtihetavaḥ/ avidyādināṃ kleśānāṃ hetavaḥ/*

[28] See YS II.3-9.

[29] YS II.1-2.

of self-preservation is a *kleśa* common to all living beings. Vācaspati Miśra explains that *abhiniveśa* is nothing else but the memory of anguish at the moment of death (*maraṇa-duḥkha, maraṇa-trāsa*), experienced before, in one of our previous lives.[30] At least the hypothesis of one previous life has to be admitted. If not, it becomes rather difficult to account for the fear of death which can be observed even in a newborn baby. From sages till insects, *abhiniveśa* is invariably present in all creatures. But in the case of a sage, the seed of afflictions (*kleśa-bīja*) is totally destroyed, and his acts are now "neutral", devoid of moral qualification. Precisely, colourless, neither white nor black (neither good nor bad).[31] He will not accumulate the fruits of his acts anymore. No "fruition" or "retribution" (*vipāka*) means no more rebirth or re-incarnation.

6. *Saṃskāra, smṛti, vāsanā*

The YS IV.9; 27, deal equally with *saṃskāra* in relation with *smṛti* and *vāsanā*.

> There is an uninterrupted [causal] relation [of sub-conscious-impressions], although remote in species and point-of-space and moment-of-time, by reason of the correspondence between memory and subliminal-impressions.[32]
>
> In the intervals of this [mind-suff] there are other presented-ideas [coming] from subliminal-impressions.[33]
>
> These are "previous subliminal impressions" (*pūrva-saṃskāra*), identified with "dwindling seeds" (*kṣīyamāṇabīja*).[34]
>
> The escape from these [subliminal-impressions] is described as being like [the escape from] the hindrances.[35]

Vyāsa comments:

---

[30] TV II.9.

[31] See YS IV.7 and Commentaries.

[32] YS IV.9: *jāti-deśa-kāla-vyavahitānām apy ānantaryaṃ smṛti-saṃskārayor eka-rūpatvāt /*

[33] YS IV.27: *tac-chidreṣu pratyaya-antarāṇi saṃskārebhyaḥ /*

[34] See YBH IV.27.

[35] YS IV.28.

> The hindrances are the condition of burned seed which are unfit for generation. Just so a previous subliminal-impression, does not generate presented-ideas. The subliminal-impressions of [intuitive] knowledge are dormant until the task of the mind-stuff is completed.[36]

7. Two facets of *saṃskāras*: positive and negative

The attempt of locating the eight *sūtras* in their respective contexts brings to light the two facets of *saṃskāras*: positive and negative. Moreover, this analysis results in a better comprehension of the abrupt definition of *yoga* given by Patañjali, "*Yoga* is the (gradual but total) suppression of the fluctuating activities of the mind".[37] Vyāsa had already declared in his commentary to the first *sūtra*—"*Yoga* is (perfect) concentration".[38] The fluctuating activities of the mind (*citta-vṛtti*) comprehend the whole content of our experiences. Influenced by the three attributes or qualities (*guṇas*) of the Primal Nature and the five afflictions or "hindrances" (*kleśa*), cause mental agitation and instability.[39] Amongst the five "states" or "stages of mind" (*citta-bhūmi*), only last two : "single-in-intent" (*ekāgra*) and "restricted" (*niruddha*) are favourable for *yoga* practices.[40] "The restricted mind is that in which all fluctuations are restricted and in which nothing remains but residual-impressions".[41] Freed from all turbulences, the *yogin* abides in himself, just as the Seer.[42] In the West, Leibniz observes that thoughts keep on coming and going. The passage from a *perceptio* to another accomplishes itself under the influence of an *appetitio*.[43] To start with, Patañjali and his commentators are of the same

---

[36] YBH IV.28.

[37] YS I.2: *yogaś cittavṛttinirodhaḥ* /

[38] YBH I.1: *yogaḥ samādhiḥ* /

[39] YBH I.1: the restless (*kṣipta*), the infatuated (*mūḍha*), the distracted (*vikṣipta*), the "single-in-intent" (*ekāgra*) and "restricted" (*niruddha*).

[40] YBH I.1.

[41] TV I.1: *niruddha-sakalavṛttikaṃ saṃskāramātraśeṣaṃ cittaṃ niruddham* /

[42] YS I.3.

[43] See *Monodology* § 15, cf. § 10.

opinion, but they go much further while explaining the nature of the *appetitio.* The modifications or fluctuations (*vṛtti*) of the thinking substance represent our psyche in act, uprising from latent impressions (*saṃskāra*) deposited in the mind by past experiences. Thus *saṃskāras* account for all that is potentially present on the psychological level, impulsions and compulsions.

7.1 The *vṛtti-saṃskāra-cakra*

Afflicted (*kliṣṭa-*) or unafflicted (*akliṣṭa-*), the fluctuating activities of the mind (*citta-vṛtti*) are of two sorts.[44] Similarly the *saṃskāras* left over by *vṛttis* are also of two types: conscious phase of mental activities, and a "latent impression" (*saṃskāra*), unconscious phase of the same, expressed in terms of "wheel of fluctuations and subliminal impressions" (*vṛtti-saṃskāra-cakra*) which ceaselessly rolls until the highest concentration is attained.[45] Fifteen centuries before W. James, Vyāsa renders very well the idea of "stream of thought" by comparing the mind to a river (*citta-nadī*),[46] which flows in both good and bad directions: *kaivalya-prāgbhāra and saṃsāra-prāgbhāra.*

7.2 The natural state of the "psychic soil"

Dispassion (*vairāgya*) and repeated practice (*abhyāsa*) are unaflicted or *akliṣṭa-vṛttis.*[47] Without them, non-notional concentration (*asaṃprajñāta-samādhi*) cannot be attained (YS I.18). So ultimately, what counts for the *yogin* is to discriminate between the *Puruṣa* and the *citta.* The latter is on the side of the *Prakṛti.*

All these *kliṣṭa-/akliṣṭa-vṛttis, kliṣṭa-/akliṣṭa-saṃskāras,* are like "seeds" (*bīja*), scattered and sown on the psychic soil (*citta-bhūmi*), rendering it fertile. An advanced *yogin* seeks to stop the germination process by reducing these seeds to

---

[44] YS I.5.

[45] YBH I.5.

[46] YBH I.12.

[47] YS I.12-14.

ashes with the fire of knowledge (*jñānāgni*) and render the psychic soil sterile (*vandhya*). Only repeated "seedless concentration" (*nirbīja-samādhi*), apogee of *asaṃprajñāta-samādhi*, can totally suppress all psycho-intellectual activities. This "work" is done by the *nirodha-samskāras.* The yogic act of suppression, by definition, does not imprint the mind (with a content). More precisely, this "imprint" or "trace" is just a "blank", a "not", a "void". These anti-*saṃskāras*, a "barrage" which stops the flow of the psychic river (*citta-nadī*), put an end not only to *vyutthāna-saṃskāras* but also to the *prajñākṛta-saṃskāras* and are rightly called "conducive to Isolation", *lit.* "having a share in..." (*kaivalyabhāgīya*).[48] Made during unconscious concentration, working unconsciously, traceless, the specificity of *nirodha-saṃskāras* is to fade by themselves, which means that there is no need for a *nirodha-saṃskāra-nirodha.* They can be compared to a "draw-bridge" between the *Puruṣa* and the *Prakṛti.* Just like "knowledge" (*jñāna*), one of the *bhāvas* of the *buddhi*, *nirodha-saṃskāras* (a particular yogic functioning of the *citta*), are also on the side of the *Prakṛti.* As "means" to *kaivalya*, they are only "factors of mediation."

7.3 Five mental "states" or "stages"

The *Yoga Bhāsya* I.1, contains the description of the *citta-bhūmi,* in case of an ordinary man, as well in case of a *yogin.* Existence creates conflict because of incessant modifications in the proportion of the attributes, due to constant change in their equilibrium (*guṇa-pariṇāma*). These variations in the proportions of each *guṇa* has its repercurssion on the physical and psychological level, in the external and the internal world. Vyāsa mentions five mental "states" or "stages"—

> The stages of the mind-stuff are these: the restless (*kṣipta*), the infatuated (*mūḍha*), the distracted (*vikṣipta*), the single-in-intent (*ekāgra*), and the restricted (*niruddha*). Of these [stages the first two have nothing to do with *yoga* and even] in the distracted state of mind [its] concentration is [at times] overpowered by [opposite]

[48] YBH and TV.I.51.

distractions and consequently] it cannot be properly be called *yoga*. But that [state] which, when the mind is single-in-intent, fully illumines a distinct and real object and causes the hindrances (*kleśa*) to dwindle, slackens the bonds of *karma*, and sets before it as a goal, the restriction [of all fluctuations], is called *yoga* in which there is consciousness of an object (*saṃprajñāta*). This [conscious *yoga*], however, is accompanied by deliberation upon coarse objects, by reflection upon subtle objects], by joy, by the feeling-of-personality (*asmitā*). This we shall set forth later. But when there is restriction of all fluctuations (*vṛtti*) [of the mind-stuff], there is the concentration in which there is no consciousness [of an object]".[49]

8. *Saṃskāra* and *adhikāra*

These are correlative concepts with that of *karman*, coming from the same verbal root *Kṛ*-. The *nirodha-saṃskāras* do not encumber the mind of the *yogin* anymore with a "task", "mission", "office" (*adhikāra*) to be accomplished. On the contrary, they put an end to the "office of the attributes" (*guṇādhikāra*) and to the "office of the mental organ" (*cittādhikāra*) as explained in the commentaries to the *Yoga Sūtras.* Vyāsa explains the mechanism as follows:

> How is it that this excess of subliminal-impressions will not provide the mind-stuff with a task? [The answer is]: these subliminal-impressions made by the insight do not provide the mind-stuff with a task since they cause the dwindling of the hindrances. For they cause the mind-stuff to cease from its work. For the movement of the mind-stuff terminates at [the time of] discernment (*khyāti*).[50]

8.1 Seedless concentration (*nirbīja-samādhi*)

Vyāsa comments on the next *sūtra*:

> "This [seedless cocentration] is opposite not only to concentrated insight but is opposed even to subliminal-impressions made in insight. Why? Because the subliminal impressions produced by restriction inhibits the subliminal-impression produced by concentration. [....]. Together with the subliminal-impressions which arise out of the emergent and restricted concentrations and which are conducive to Isolation, the mind-stuff resolves itself into its own permanent primary-matter. Therefore, these

[49] YBH I.1.

[50] YBH I.50.

subliminal-impressions are contrary to the mind-stuff's task and are not causes of its stability. Consequently, its task ended, together with the subliminal-impressions which are conducive to Isolation, the mind-stuff ceases [from its task]. When it ceases, the Self abides in himself and is therefore pure and liberated".[51] Vyāsa explains further that unhindered *vṛttis* have discriminative discernment as their object and thus obstruct the task (*adhikāra*) of the aspects (*guṇa*). "Authority (*adhikāra*) is the competency to initiate effects. For it is as the result of this that the correlation (*saṃyoga*), which is the reason for the round-of-existence (*saṃsāra*), is produced".[52]

8.2 Isolation (*kaivalya*) is the "inverse generation"

We can now rejoin the final *sūtras* and understand them better—"When as a result of this the aspects (*guṇa*) have fulfilled their purpose, they attain to the limit of the sequence of mutations".[53] "Isolation is the inverse generation [*prati-prasava*] of the aspects, no longer provided with a purpose by the Self, or it is the Energy of Intellect grounded in itself".[54] The concept of "inverse generation" (*prati-prasava*),[55] sometimes *prati-sarga*,[56] is very typical to *Sāṃkhya-Yoga* Philosophy. There is a sort of *micro-pralaya*. The phenomenal world (*saṃsāra*) comes to an end for each liberated person, who could operate a sort of inverse or counter generation, only way of abolishing time.

9. Difference between *asaṃprajñāta* and *nirbīja samādhi*

Let us discuss the subtle difference between (non-notional) *asaṃprajñāta*- and *nirbīja-samādhi* (seedless concentration), in order to determine the nature of the "rest" in *saṃskāra-śesa*. The concept of *saṃskāra-vipāka*, carries the same idea (contained in *karma-phala-vipāka*), as well as between *deva*

---

[51] YBH I.51. See also YBH I.5,

[52] Declares rightly Vācaspati Miśra, TV ad YS II.23, while explaining the "office of the attributes (of the Nature)", *guṇādhikāra*.

[53] YS IV.32.

[54] YS IV.34.

[55] See YS II.10; YBH II.2; 27; III.50; IV.34.

[56] YBH III.51.

(=*videha*) and *prakṛtilaya*.[57] In his introductory phrases to YS.I.19, Vyāsa explains that the non-notional concentration (*asaṃprajñāta-samādhi*) is of two kinds:

> It is produced either by [spiritual] means [i. 20] or by worldly [means]. Of these two, that produced by [spiritual] means is the one to which *yogins* [who are on the way to Isolation] attain. The discarnate, that is, the gods attain to the concentration [not conscious of objects] caused by worldly [means]. Their mind-stuff uses only their own subliminal-impressions they experience a quasi-state of Isolation,[...] during which the fruit corresponding to their own subliminal-impressions ripens [for their enjoyment]. [But at the end of this period they must return to the world]. Likewise those whose bodies are resolved into primary-matter, experience a quasi-Isolation, during which the mind (*cetas*), is resolved into primary-matter. But this lasts only till the mind-stuff, under the pressure of its [unfulfilled] task returns [to the world].[58]

9.1 The *Videhas* and the *Prakṛtilayas*

The distinction between *asaṃprajñāta-samādhi* and *nirbīja-samādhi* is now quite clear. The *asaṃprajñāta-samādhi* dealt with in YS I.18 is attained by technical means and needs an intense yogic training detailed in YS I.20. This concentration leads the *yogin* to *kaivalya*. This *samādhi* can also be obtained by non-technical or non-yogic methods, as explained by Vyāsa.[59] But the gods (*deva*, without gross body or *videha*) and those who are engrossed in the Nature (*prakṛtilaya*) will still be involved in the process because their psyche contains ordinary latent impressions (*saṃskāra*). So what differs is the nature of the "rest" or the "remainder" (*śeṣa*) in the case of a *yogin* because his psyche contains only the trace of *nirodha-saṃskāras*. In the case of *devas* and *prakṛtilayas*, the traces in shape of "seeds" (*bīja*, identified with *saṃskāra*) are still fertile and so there will be germination and fruition. In the case of a *yogin*, they are like burnt seeds (*dagdha-bīja*), incapable of germination or fruition. The expressions

[57] See S. BHATTACHARYA, "The Concept of *videha and prakṛtilaya* in the *Sāṃkhya-Yoga* system", ABORI 39, pp. 307–12.

[58] YBH I.19.

[59] In YBH I.19.

"in a state of burnt seeds" (*dagdhabījabhāva*), "seeds of afflictions burnt" (*dagdhakleśabīja*), "infertile generation" (*vandhyaprasava*), etc. are attested in Vyāsa's Commentary[60]. Vācaspati Miśra sums up:

> The subliminal-impressions of emergent insight are resolved into mind-stuff. Thus the mind-stuff contains the subliminal-impressions of emergent insight. But the subliminal-impressions from restriction lies just uprisen in the mind-stuff. Although [this] subliminal-impression from restriction is [uprisen], the mind-stuff has no task [to fulfill]".[61]

When reiterated, at the summit of its achievement, the *asaṃprajñāta-samādhi* is identical with "seedless concentration" (*nirbīja-samādhi*), as well as with *dharmamegha-samādhi* (the "rain-cloud of knowable things", Woods). Gradually and progressively, it results from "supreme detachment" (*para-vairāgya*).[62]

9.2 The deliverance of the mental organ

Describing the "deliverance of the mental organ" (*citta-vimukti*)[63] or *cittanivṛtti*,[64] commentators explain what "good health" or "mental balance" means in the *Yoga* Doctrine expounded by Patañjali. The idea of *jīvanmukti* is introduced with reference to the third sort of *cittavimukti*.[65] In this stage, even while alive, the Self is called fortunate [and] released, since [this] is his last body". Commentators explain that this particular man (*kiṃcit puruṣa*),[66] i.e., the *yogin*, after having crossed the seven "stages" becomes *kuśala*: "well", "healthy", "integral" ("fortunate" translates Woods).[67] Perfect good

---

[60] YBH II.2-4; 13; 26; III.50; 55.

[61] TV I.51 : [...] *nirodhasaṃskāras tu pratyudita evāste citte/ nirodhasaṃskāre saty api cittam anadhikāraṇvat/*

[62] See YBH and TV I.18.

[63] YBH II.27.

[64] YBH II.24.

[65] TV II.27.

[66] TV IV.34.

[67] See YS and YBH II.27.

health results from the cessation of turbulences and afflictions.[68] Thus, the "normal" healthy man, the *yogin* whose afflictions have perished, is said to be in his last body.[69] "For this exalted [*yogin*], released yet alive in the body, whose present body is his last, has as his sole aim the resolving of the mind-stuff [into the primary cause]".[70] False conception (*viparyaya*), cause of becoming (*bhavasya kāraṇam*) once disappeared, the sage is liberated (*vimukta*), while alive (*jīvann eva*). Vyāsa confirms the same: "Upon the cessation of the hindrances and of *karma*, the wise man, even while alive, is released. Why is this? Because misconception is the cause of the world (*bhavasya*). For surely no one has ever seen the birth of any one whose misconceptions have dwindled away".[71] So deliverance is nothing but the total suppression of the psyche.[72]

10. *Yoga* and Psycho-analysis

Psycho-analysis does not pretend to go so far. In fact, on this point *yoga* and Psycho-analysis diverge completely. The true name of *yoga* ("union", "junction"), advocated by Patañjali is *vi-yoga*: "disunion", "dis-junction", "dis-connection", "separation". The "union" or "correlation" (*saṃyoga*) between the *Puruṣa* and the *Prakṛti*, which was instituted for practical "purposes" has now to be undone, because the real purpose, i.e., isolation (*kaivalya, apavarga, mokṣa*) is now prominent (inspite of the time-gap or "delay" required). "The Self as proprietor becomes correlated for the purpose of sight with the object-for-sight as property. That aperception of the object-for-sight which results from this correlation (*saṃyoga*) is experience. Whereas the aperception of what the seer is, is liberation. Since the

---

68 See YBH II.4.

69 YBH 11.4; IV.7: *ataḥ kṣinakleṣaḥ kuśalaś caramadeha ity ucyate /*

70 TV III.51: *tasya hi bhagavato jīvanmuktasya caramadehasya cittapratisargasya eko'rthaḥ /*

71 YBH IV.30.

72 YBH II.24: *tatra cittanivṛttir eva moksaḥ* / Cf. Caraka, *Śārīra Sthāna*, I.137.

correlation lasts until sight is effected, sight is said to be the cause of discorrelation (*viyoga*)".[73] We find here the two finalities regrouping the four human goals (*puruṣārtha*) under two heads: "experience" (*bhoga*) and "deliverance" (*apavarga*), typical to the *Sāṃkhya-Yoga* doctrines. Vyāsa explains: "The practice of (eight-fold) limbs (or aids) to *yoga* is the cause of disjunction with impurity, just as an axe (is the cause of disjunction of a tree) which is to be cut (from its root)".[74] Woods translates: "The following aids to *yoga* is the cause of discorrelation (*viyoga*) with impurity, just as an axe [is the cause of the disjunction (*viyoga*) of a tree] which is to be cut [from its root]."

Based on renunciation, *rāja-yoga*, in all its rigour, does not aim at better integration in the social world, nor amelioration of relations, which are supposed to result from a successful analytical cure. Though harmonization with the universe is obtained through *samāpattis*, a wonderful experience indeed, in this non-fusional perspective the *yogin* is expected to go far beyond, towards: *asaṃprajñāta-nirbīja-*, and *dharmamegha-samādhi*, resulting in isolation (*kaivalya*).

10.1 Divergence between *Yoga* and Psychoanalysis

A comparison between Patañjali's *yoga* and Freudian psychoanalytical approach[75] reveals very few similarities. Although divergences are more numerous. Healing mental diseases and their symptoms is the initial motivation and final aim of analytical cure. On the contrary, psychosomatic ailments are considered to be hindrances in the path of

---

[73] YBH II.23.

[74] YBH II.28 : *yogāṅgānuṣṭhānam aśuddher viyogakāraṇam yathā paraśus cheddasya... /*

[75] I have made an attempt to renew the question and add some precisions on the subject. See also Pal Kumar, "A comparitive Study of Psycho-Therapeutic Techniques and Yoga", *Vedanta Kesari*, vol. 33, no 4-5, Aug.-Sept. 1946. Pal Kumar, "Yoga and Psycho-analysis", *Prabuddha Bharata*, vol. 52, no 3-5. Coster G., *Yoga and Western Psychology*, First edn. London, 1934; Reprint, Delhi, Motilal Banarsidass, 1974.

Yoga.[76] Though it is said that a *yogin*, after having discriminated between the *Puruṣa* and the *Prakṛti* becomes *kuśala* or *śuddha* ("good", "healthy", "pure", "immaculate"), this does not mean that an apprentice *yogin* or all adepts of *yoga* are sick (or "abnormal") people, — except, if by sickness, *kleśas*, causes of entanglement in the phenomenal world, are meant. Noteworthy also is the word *svastha* (well "established in one's own self") used in SK 65, which means to be in "good health" and indicates the fact of getting back to one's initial, integral form (that of the *Puruṣa*).

Methods differ too. The way of acceding to the unconscious level is not the same in *Yoga* and in Psycho-analysis. Leaving aside the *siddhi* consisting in direct perception of subliminal impressions accumulated throughout past life series, *saṃskara-sākṣātkāra*, the *yogin* becomes capable of mastering the unconscious forces, even without the help of his master, *saṃyama* onwards of course. Attachment to supernormal powers should however be discouraged.

The unconscious can be unveiled through the work undertaken by the analyst/analysand, in which "language" or speech intervenes a lot. The analyst interprets the content of dreams, also missed acts, slips of tongue, etc. No such method is detailed in the *Yoga Sūtras*. There is a difference in the depth of the cure and consequently in the methods employed. It is just passing by that the master wants to hear or the disciple wants to let the unconscious "talk". The final aim is to reduce it to silence, both verbal and mental. In the analytical cure, the analyst listens for hours, years, his patient "talk". Without putting in question the immense merit of Psycho-analysis, a *Yoga* practician will say : you believe that you are listening to the unconscious, but it is not exactly so! What you are receiving is the translation of what intellect (*buddhi*) or mind (*citta*) lived or experienced. The unconscious is never accessible on the conscious level,

[76] See YS I.30-31.

through deliberate or discursive thinking put in language, followed by a hermeneutical deciphering. So the great lesson that one learns from yogic methods is that in the last analysis, only the unconscious can really "encounter" the unconscious, treat with it, master and liberate it.

10.2 The ultimate aim of *Rāja Yoga*

The ultimate aim of *Rāja Yoga* is deliverance, termed "isolation". Thus the difference with didactic Psycho-analysis, undertaken sometimes for curiosity sake, or in order to know oneself better and to give relief to others who are in difficulty, is apparent. The field of investigation is of course the *Ich*, ego, the *citta*, of each particular person (*prati-puruṣa*). But unlike in texts on Psycho-analysis, the *Sāṃkhya-Yoga* texts explicitly mention about the final disappearance of ego (*ahaṃkāra*)[77] and the cessation of all psycho-cerebral activities.[78]

10.3 The genius of Patañjali

Surely, the level of effort should lean on the empirical self. The adept has to start with the preliminary phase of the *kriyā-yoga*, and then practice the *asṭāṅga-yoga* resulting in complete mastery of *yoga* and spiritual autonomy. *Yoga* is a real means of deconditioning man, a packet of habits. The genius of Patañjali and the tradition that he represents lies in the conviction that combating against unconscious tendencies, with the help of conscious and willful effort only, belongs to preliminary stages. After this, the *yogin* delegates this task to *saṃskāras*. Only the unconscious can unveil the unconscious. This new set of yogic "habits" functions automatically. Just as a car driver has not to think about or remind himself of his driving lessons once he has learnt to drive, similarly a *yogin* does not consciously think about the subtle mechanism that he has installed. The genius of *yoga* is to make use of the unconscious mechanism—which are

---

[77] SK 64.

[78] YBH II.24.

normally responsible for bondage—in view of release. In *asaṃprajñāta-samādhi,* and *dharmamegha-samādhi* (in which *nirodha-saṃskaras* are produced and function), the *yogin* looses all reference to himself. It is not he who burns and reduces to ashes the seeds of kārmic flux. It would be a contradiction in terms, because he will constitute himself as a "doer" (*kartṛ-*), which he has fortunately ceased to be.

CONCLUSIONS

Philological and Historical Issues

Considering the threefold human activity of body, speech and mind, how come that the presence of *saṃskāras* in them is highly praised in Brahmanical and Hindu thought, but looked down upon in Buddhist thought? The semantic content remains the same but how to explain this contrasting value judgements?

The answer concerning this axiological difference is that the denotation of the word *saṃskāra* is fundamentally identical from one school of thought and epoch to another but it is the connotation that changes, to the extent of becoming just the reverse. Apart from these two extreme poles some *darśanas,* such as the *Advaita Vedānta,* classical *Sāṃkhya* and *Yoga,* only sharpen the problematics.

Denotation

In the *Brāhmaṇas* (Fire altar rite), *saṃskṛ-* refers to the act of reconstructing the scattered parts of Prajāpati's body by assembling them together. This applies to the sacrificer's *ātman* also.

Amongst the seven purposes of *śarīra-saṃskāras,* n°s. 3-6 belong to denotation.

In Buddhism, *saṃskṛ-* denotes in the causal chain, two facets—psycho-physical "compositions" and all that is composed (caused, conditioned).

In Mechanics and Psychology of *Vaiśeṣikas, saṃskāras* designate *vega, bhāvanā* and *sthitisthāpaka.*

In the Theories of Language, *saṃskāras* denote the same activity of making a whole out of parts, forming a word out of various phonemes, a sentence out of words.

In the *Advaita Vedānta*, *saṃskāra* sometimes designates purificatory rites, sometimes in a psycho-soteriological context, where just like *vāsanā* it designates residual impressions, remanences. Both these concepts are inherited from Buddhist literature. A *saṃskāra* is a certain potentiality residing in mental states, a link between act and force, a subjacent continuity between the three time dimensions, an unconscious upsurge of the forgotten past, a certain reversibility of time, which for the psyche is quite similar to what elasticity is in the material context.

In the *Sāṃkhya-kārikā* 67 the word *saṃskāra* can be understood in the sense of *vega*. Rather than applying to the prolongation of the trajectory of an arrow, the impetus explains here the prolongation of the bodily existence of a sage liberated-in-life. Otherwise it is equal to predispositions (*bhāva*) engraved in the psyche.

Finally, the *Yoga Sūtras* bring out the ambivalence of residual impressions, classified under three heads, *vyutthāna-*, *prajñākṛta-* and *nirodha-saṃskāra*. Inherited from past acts or experiences, they are capable of remodelling the total psychosomatic moral and intellectual dimensions of adept's personality and finally leading him to total spiritual autonomy. In fact, given the definition and aim of *rāja-yoga*, the issue is not so much to make a whole out of disparate parts (on the physical and psychological level), but to become this integral whole, totally concentrated. This is what takes place in different grades of *samādhi*, in which yogic or disciplinary *saṃskāras* work like factors of cohesion.

A review of texts and contexts proves that in domains as different as rituals, anthropology, ethics, epistemology, soteriological philosophy, the concept of *saṃskāra* works like a universal key in the mind of Indian authors to unify the diverse heterogeneous materials.

Nevertheless, sometimes the linking of factors, in the objective and subjective world, is understood with reference to the past (in relation of course with present events). In this case, a *saṃskāra* is interchangeable with *vāsanā*. Here, the passive aspect of relation between sequences predominates. Sometimes, when mind is turned towards the future, the link between factors is felt as loaded with dynamic productive forces, in that case a *saṃskāra* is nothing else but a "seed" (*bīja*) full of multiple possibilities.

Moreover, the linking up of psychological consequences can take place either in a conscious deliberate mode or in a subconscious, nay unconscious mode.

Connotation

Human reactions, whether emotional or axiological, depend on the diversity of forces. The human resonator regulated by *pravṛtti-dharma*, engaged in worldly pursuits, or *nivṛtti-dharma*, which presupposes renunciation of family and social ties is not the same. This corresponds to the option *Kṛ/Jñā*.

Human reactions of approbation and disapprobation are determined by *saṃskāra*. Purification/perfection is the criterion par excellence. It applies to man (the only animal who participates in sacrificial activity), to language (Sanskrit = *saṃskṛta*, distinguished from *Prākrit* forms) as well as to Indian culture and civilization (*bhāratīya-saṃskṛti*). Maintenance of cosmic and socio-religious order (*dharma*) is possible through imposition of norms, which regulate the total conduct of man-in-the-world and help the perpetuation of *sanātana-dharma*.

In the epistemological domain of the *Vaiśeṣika* system, *saṃskāras* belong to the category of "qualities" (*guṇa*). Candrasiṃha in his commentary to the *Tarkasaṃgraha* feels himself obliged to put *vāsanās* (a particular species of *saṃskāra*) in relation with merit (*dharma*) and demerit (*adharma*).

For Buddhist monks, more generally for all renouncers, purity is important to a certain extent. A distinction is however introduced between mundane and supra-mundane purity. This does not correspond to the Christian distinction between bodily cleanliness and purity of soul. What is pure, beneficial, auspicious, from mundane point of view, may be esteemed from a supramundane point of view as subject to suppuration, an impure flow (*āsrava*), like all that participates in universal flux (*saṃsāra*). Naturally, the deprecatory attitude of the Buddhists towards *saṃskāra* is strictly speaking that of monks, not of laymen. The Law (*dharma*) that the Buddha preaches has for horizon *nirvāṇa*, not pertaining to socio-religious order.

In classical *Sāṃkhya* also the axiological criterion holds good because *bhāvas* are classified under two heads—four luminous (*sāttvika*) and, four tenebrous (*tāmasika*).

Brahmanical and Buddhist texts, in their treatment of *saṃskāra*, reveal diametrically opposite evaluations. The Buddhists prefer the healing path to that of rituals. Activity expressed by *saṃskṛ-* is disappointing in their opinion due to the very fact that it has to be recommenced again and again. They look for a more radical solution, in order to eliminate human suffering.

For the *Brāhmaṇas, Gṛhya-* and *Dharma-Sūtras, saṃskāras* are factors of maintenance of his own person, his family circle are affable. They constitute his feeling of security. For a renouncer, *saṃskāras* appear as the texture of the phenomenal tissue, an instrument of bondage. Object of trust for some, of distrust for others, such are alas *saṃskāras*!

This dichotomy needs however to be refined and made supple. Happily enough, in the history of Indian thought an intermediary place was made for the attitude called "metaritualist". The concept of "mental sacrifice" (*manoyajña*) is a good example of this synthesis.

A sort of synthesis between rituals and gnosis is also found in Śaṅkara's Works, for instance in his interpretation of *nitya-karman*. For a renouncer like him (though a *Vaidika*) the connotation of the word *saṃskāra* in the last analysis is negative. There remains however a big difference between a renouncer belonging to the *Advaita Vedānta* tradition and a Buddhist renouncer. Śaṅkara and others never utilize the word *asaṃskṛta* (*nirvāṇa*), indicative of Absolute in Buddhism, to designate the impersonal neutral absolute *Brahman.* There is a sort of linguistic taboo, an anthropo-cultural barrier that cannot be overstepped as far as *asaṃskṛta* is concerned, although so many other vocabulary exchanges have taken place between Buddhists and Brahmanical thinkers.

Originality of the concept of *Saṃskāra*

Precedent connotation and value-judgement problems constitute the intra-Indian debate-ground. On the contrary, the effort of conceptualization, properly speaking, raises few questions relative to Comparative Philosophy and Psychology. In fact, the concept of *saṃskāra* has no exact equivalent in Western dictionaries.

Therefore, the issue is, in what measure the pan-Indian Concept of *Saṃskāra* is a cultural phenomenon, more generally, to what extent exercise of intelligence can be fashioned by a culture? Presuppositions, acquisitions, methods, twists of thought, and above all the presence of tradition cannot be denied.

The insistent look for intermediary links has some consequences. Thus motion described by the *Vaiśeṣika* philosophers is not properly speaking due to "speed" (*vega*) phenomenon.

Thus motion described by the *Vaiśeṣika* philosophers is not properly speaking due to "speed" (*vega*) phenomenon. Pushing things to their extreme limits Nāgārjuna shows that it is impossible to seize motion in a phrase or to establish a verbal proceedings about it. Moreover, an absolute real value cannot be attached to a point of time, neither to its irreversibility, because of memory phenomenon. An immutable status cannot be ascribed to material forms (*rūpa*) either, because elasticity has to be taken into consideration.

The second consequence applies to conceptual systems. When one has understood that every thing is interrelated, the pretention of enclosing the truth in one single system fades away. This is the reason why the Indian *darśanas* are ways of looking and apprehending the reality, not exclusive, the ones from the others. This awareness of relations saves Indians from "isms".

Another consequence pertains to the idea of beginning at the level of cosmogony or ontogenesis. "In the beginning was the rest" (see Ch. VI), keeping in mind the famous iconographic data, the Lord *Viṣṇu* lying on the serpent *Śeṣa*, so called because the world (*like avidyā*) and is *anādi*; *śeṣa* and *anādi* go hand in hand. Just because mediation is everywhere, absolute is nowhere in the *saṃsāra*.

Same is the case with the mythical prehistory of a human being. An advanced *yogin* is capable of having the knowledge of his previous births. Even in the strict limits of a given human life, *saṃskāras* play an important part in the organization of psychic sequences.

Inspite of the originality of the concept of *saṃskāra*, some partial encounters with Western Philosophy and Psychology can be made.

The Kantian schematism

As we have seen, *saṃskāras* play an important role in the organization of psychic sequences. In as much as *saṃskāras* are factors of liaison and mediation, existing in the mode of potentiality and displaying essentially in time, these three characteristics evoke the Kantian transcendental schema: In his *Critique of Pure Reason*, Kant assigns two different sources radically distinct to the human nature: sensibility and understanding. He takes the opposite view of Leibniz for whom there is only a difference of degree between these two faculties. But once one has de-stiched, one has to re-stich and the Kantian theory of schematism of pure concepts of understanding corresponds to this necessity (of re-stiching). While an image is a product of an empirical power or force of productive imagination, a scheme is a sort of monogram of pure *a priori* imagination, i.e., transcendental imagination. This one works like a bridge between sensibility and understanding, between receptivity and spontaneity. And its product, the scheme, which is neither a pure concept nor an image traced on a board, serves as a link and as a binder between the two. Hence, it makes the human knowledge possible in act. Let's take the number seven. The scheme of the number seven is neither a pure concept defined abstractly, nor an image of the number seven as seven points traced or figured in the space. It is the rule or the procedure which has to be followed in order to compose this image: as when one teaches to a child how to count on his fingers (or on his phalanxes as in India) by stopping at the right number. Thus a scheme is the rule of fabrication of images of a determined type. Now, as we have seen for example, a scheme is something immaterial because it cannot be spread in space like an image. It displays itself in time. Here are some extracts from Kant's *Critique of Pure Reason*:[1]

> The Schema is, in itself, always a product of the imagination. But as synthesis of imagination has for its aim no single intuition, but merely unity in determination of sensibility, the schema is clearly distinguishable from the image. This if I place five points one after another,..... this is an image of the number five. [....] In truth, it is not images of objects, but schemata, which lie at the foundation of our sensuous conception. No image could ever be adequate to our conception of a triangle in general. [....] The schema of the triangle can exist nowhere else than in thought, and it indicates a rule of synthesis of imagination in regard to pure figures in space. [....] This schematism of our understanding in regard to phenomena and their mere form, is an art, hidden in the depths of human soul, whose true modes of action [*Handgriffe*] we shall only with difficulty discover and unveil. This much only we can say—the image is a product of the empirical faculty of the productive imagination—the scheme of sensuous conceptions (of figures in space, for example) is a product, and, as it were, a monogram of the pure imagination *a priori*, whereby and according to which

[1] *Critique of Pure Reason*, Immanuel KANT, translated by J.M.D. MEIKLEJOHN, Mineola, New York, 2003.

images first become possible, which, however, can be connected with the conception only mediately by means of the schema which they indicate, and are themselves never fully adequate to it." For example, the pure *schema of quantity* is *number*, and "number is nothing else than the unity of the manifold in a homogeneous intuition, by means of my generating time itself in my apprehension of the intuition".[2]

Heidegger[3] also considers the transcendental imagination as the centre of gravity of the human nature. This is the reason why he prefers the second edition of the *Critique of Pure Reason* to the second. In the second edition, Kant gives a less important place to schematism and comes back to the dualism between sensibility and understanding.[4] But the first edition and in its prolongation Heidegger's interpretation seems much more important when one knows, since Stcherbatsky,[5] that the theme of transcendental imagination with its corresponding Sanskrit concept of *kalpanā* furnishes one of pertinent occasions of encounter between the European and the Indian theories of knowledge. The *Einbildungskraft* and the Sanskrit *kalpanā* have in common the fact of being (the faculty of) imagination before images.

The "Psychology of Tendencies"

The Bergsonian dynamic schema can also be evoked for a comparative study. But reference should above all be made to André Burloud.[6] He is in search for a middle path between the internal observation and the analysis of behaviour. He seems to find out this intermediary in the concept of "tendency", half way off from the "abstract subject of

[2] *Ibidem*, pp. 102–103.

[3] See Martin HEIDEGGER, *Basic Writings, From Being and Time* (1927) *to the Task of Teaching* (1964), Revised and Expanded Edition by David Farrell KRELL, Harper Perennial Modern Thought, 2008, pp. 66–71.

[4] See *Kant et le problème de la métaphysique*, trad. A. de WAELHENS et W. BIEMEL, Paris, Gallimard, pp. 183–257, and 217–27.

[5] See *The Buddhist Logic*, 2 vols., New York, Dover Publications, 1962.

[6] Author of *Principes d'une psychologie des tendances*, Paris, Alcan, 1938.

knowledge"—that of Philosophers—and the theses of the behaviourists and reductionist schools. His discovery was that there is a "psychological causality", (discovery which may seem banal to Indologists). This is sort of "causality of tendencies", so to say, a set of distinct forces, each one having its history, its proper coefficient of energy, in consequence, its own individuality. Burloud declares that the real psychological forces are the internal factors, properly subjective, called intentions, tendencies, schemes, dynamic schemas, etc. In the field of psychopathology, Dr J. Lacan[7] also uses the concept of "psychological causality" in the field of the process of identification, with the minor phase and the apparition of the *imago*.

In any case, the concept of *saṃskāra*, reveals, that it is itself one of the dynamic schemes of Indian thought. From a psychological point of view, it reflects a secondary temperament.

Synchrony and Diachrony

In the difference of appreciation concerning the concept of *saṃskāra*, when one shifts from Brahmanical to Buddhist world, synchronic coefficients seem to have the upper hand on diachronic coefficients. Some reversal of values can be observed not only for the noun *bāla*[8] but for the adverb *tūṣṇīm* "in silence". A *saṃskāra* confered in silence (Vedic *mantras* are not uttered in case of females, except during marriage ceremony),[9] represents a minor form of the same. On the contrary, in Buddhism, the noble silence (*āryas tūṣṇībhāvaḥ*)

---

[7] See "Propos sur la causalité psychique", in *Ecrits*, Paris, Seuil, 1966, pp. 151–93.

[8] The word *bāla*: "infant", "child" also means "ignorant", "puerile", equal to *puthujjana/pṛthagjana* in Buddhism. See MN III.63; DN II.305; *Dhammapada* 63; *Viṃśaṭikā Vṛtti*, pp. 6, 11, 17–18; *Laṅkāvatāra Sūtra*, pp. 77–79. Moreover, appreciation goes to "childlike innocence" (*bālya*) in the context of renunciation and release, not to book learning and ritualistic knowledge, *pāṇḍitya*. See *Bṛhadāraṇyaka Upaniṣad* III.5.1; IV.4.22 with Śaṅkara's Commentary.

[9] See *Manu Smṛti* II.66; IX.18.

refers to the ultimate sense (*parmārtha*), the last word of all that is.[10]

Diametrically opposed value-judgements are dependent on two optional styles of life—man engaged in familial and socio-religious life; and the renouncer who looks for disentangling himself from the network of relations, considering them to be full of deception. Between two extreme poles *pravṛtti/nivṛtti; kṛ-/jñā-*, the *Bhagavad Gītā* advocates disinterested, selfless action, sustained by ardent devotion (*bhakti*).

The evolution of Indian thought reflects a movement of interiorisation with respect to four major pan-Indian notions related to that of *saṃskāra*: *karman, ātman, dharma, bhakti.*

Though belonging to the category of *naimittika-karman, saṃskāras* are not without relationship with *nitya-karman.* In its psycho-moral acceptation also, the concept of *saṃskāra* is identical with *karman.* The concept of *niṣkāma-karman* brings a nuance worth considering.

In the *Brāhmaṇas, ātman* refers to the central part of the sacrificial altar (*vedi*) and to the central, concrete, entire person of the sacrificer (*cf. ātmānaṃ saṃskṛ-*). In Vedic *Upaniṣads* and *Vedānta darśana, ātman* is the pure subject, the ontological kernel, *Brahman.* Though Śaṅkara uses the compound *ātma-saṃskāra* instead of *śarīra-saṃskāra, ātman* need not be purified or perfected. As to the *ātma-saṃskāras* of the *Śaiva* tradition, they depict how strong the sectarians reaction were against Vedic rites.

Dharma, solemn and domestic rites, ensure cosmic and socio-religious order. In the *Brāhmaṇas saṃskṛ-* clearly refers to a normative activity. As to *śarīra-saṃskāras,* they belong to the general rubric of *varṇāśramadharma.* In Buddhist thought the connotation of the word *dharma* is quite different (cf. *dharma saṃskṛta*). *Dharmas* are the evanescent spatio-temporal kārmic process. They are linked amongst

[10] *Paramārtho 'hy āryāṇāṃ tūṣṇīm, Madhyamaka Vṛtti,* p. 57.

themselves through the efficiency of imagination and constituting precisely *saṃskāras*. The *dharma* is the law of things, i.e., the succession of fleeting energetic points-instants and it is also our submission to this Law taught by the Buddha.

Finally, with the growing success of the devotional movement (*bhakti*), the relation between *saṃskāra* and *adhikāra*[11] loses its importance. Ritual qualification for Vedic study and rites were reserved for high or pure castes, the twice-borns. But Lord Kṛṣṇa or the beneficial Śiva do not refuse their grace to their true devotees, whether they are from high or low-caste, male or female, rich or poor.

Besides the theory of *āśramas* contributes a lot in this effort of making supple the tearing dichotomy between two life-styles. In this perspective, pursuit of all four human goals in one single life becomes at least theoretically possible. Entry in each *āśrama* is marked by a *saṃskāra*, for example, *upanayana* for *brahmacaryāśrama*, *vivāha* for *gṛhasthāśrama*. The *Upadeśasāhasrī* I.21 even mentions the *saṃskāras* confered to a *tapasvin*, to those who enter in the third and the fourth *āśrama*. Though rituals have no place in the *saṃnyāsāśrama*, entrance in this stage presupposes that the renouncer has been consecrated beforehand by means of forty-eight *śarīra-saṃskāras*. Thus, according to this ideal scheme of Hindu life, one could pass through all positive and negative, valorizing and devalorizing reactions raised in and around oneself in relation to *saṃskāras* and styles of life. Reconciled in this way, these two life-styles give a cross-sectional view of the Indian man, who carries in himself this two fold aspiration.

---

[11] Studied in my Chapters II and VI. See *guṇādhikāra*, *cittādhikāra*, in Chapters VII–VIII.

themselves through the efficiency of imagination and constituting precisely *saṃskāras*. The *dharma* is the law of things, i.e., the succession of fleeting energetic points instants and it is also our submission to this law taught by the Buddha.

Finally, with the growing success of the devotional movement (*bhakti*), the relation between *saṃskāra* and *adhikāra*[1] loses its importance. Ritual qualification for Vedic study and rites were reserved for high or pure castes, the twice-borns. But Lord Kṛṣṇa or the beneficial Śiva do not refuse their grace to their true devotees, whether they are from high or low-caste, male or female, rich or poor.

Besides the theory of *āśramas* contributes a lot in this effort of making supple the arising dichotomy between two life-styles. In this perspective, pursuit of all four human goals in one single life becomes at least theoretically possible. Entry in each *āśrama* is marked by a *saṃskāra*, for example, *upanayana* for *brahmacaryāśrama*, *vivāha* for *gṛhasthāśrama*. The *Upaniṣadbrāhmaṇa*, 1.21 even mentions the *saṃskāras* conferred to a *brāhmaṇa*, to those who enter in the third and the fourth *āśrama*. Though rituals have no place in the *saṃnyāsāśrama*, entrance in this stage presupposes that the renouncer has been consecrated beforehand by means of forty-eight *śarīra-saṃskāras*. Thus, according to this ideal scheme of Hindu life, one could pass through all positive and negative, valorizing and devalorizing reactions raised in and around oneself in relation to *saṃskāras* and styles of life. Reconciled in this way, these two life-styles give a cross-sectional view of the Indian man, who carries in himself this two-fold aspiration.

[1] Studied in my Chapters II and VI. See *guṇasthāna*, *nirdhāraṇa*, in Chapters VII–VIII.

BIBLIOGRAPHY

Texts and Translations

Abhidhammattha Saṅgaha, A Manual of Abhidharma, 2 vols., Pali-English, Bangalore, 1956, Pondichery, 1957. ––Tr. by AUNG and Rhys DAVIDS : *Compendium of Philosophy,* PTS 1910, revised 1956, London, Luzac.

Abhidharmakośa and Bhāṣya of *Ācārya Vasubandhu with Sphutārtha Commentary by Ācārya Yaśomitra,* critically ed. by Swāmī Dwarikādās ŚĀSTRĪ, Varanasi, (Bauddha Bharati Series, 5-7, 9), 1987. ––French tr. *Abhidharmakośa, de Vasubandhu,* trad. et annoté par L. de LA VALLEE POUSSIN, Paris, Geuthner ; Louvain, J. B. Istas, 1923–31 ; rééd. 1971.

Āgama Śāstra (see *Māṇḍūkya Upaniṣad*)

Aitareya Brāhmaṇa, 2 Vols. ed. by V.G. APTE, (Ānandāśrama Sanskrit Series = ASS 32) Poona, 1930). ––Tr. by A.B. KEITH, *Rigveda Brāhmaṇas. The Aitareya and Kauṣītaki Brāhmaṇas,* Cambridge Mass, Harvard Oriental Series (= HOS 25, pp. 107–343), 1920. (Reprint, Motilal Banarsidass, Delhi, 1977).

––*The Aitareya Brahmanam of the Rigveda,* 2 vols., Martin HAUG, Bharatiya Publishing House, Bombay, 1853; second edn., Delhi 1976–77.

Agniveśa's Caraka Saṃhitā, 2 vols., (Text with English Tr. and critical exposition based on Cakrapanidatta's *Āyurveda-dīpikā*) by Ram Karan SHARMA and Vaidya Bhagwan DASH. Vol. I: *Sūtra Sthāna*, Varanasi, *Agniveśa's Caraka Saṃhitā*, (Chowkhamba Sanskrit Series = CSS XCIV), 1976. Vol. II : *Nidāna Sthāna, Vimāna Sthāna, Śārīra Sthāna*, 1977.

Amarakośa, with the commentary of Maheśvara (...), ed. by Ch. Sh. THATTE, under the superintendence of F. Kielhorn, 2nd edn., Bombay, 1882.

Aṅguttaranikāya, 6 vols., ed. by R. MORRIS, E. HARDY, M. HUNT, C.A.F. Rhys DAVIDS London, PTS, 1885–1910. — Tr. by F.L. WOODWARD and E.M. HARE : *Gradual Sayings*, 5 vols. (PTS), London, 1932–36. Reprint, 1960.

Āpastamba Gṛhya Sūtra, ed. by WINTERNITZ, Vienna, 1887, —Tr. by H. OLDENBERG, Oxford University Press 1892. Reprint, Motilal Banarsidass, Delhi, (SBE vol. XXX, Part II, pp. 247–97), 1964, 1967.

Aṣṭaśāhasrikā Prajñāpāramitā Sūtra. See E. CONZE, *The Gilgit Manuscript of the Aṣṭa...*, Roma, Ismeo, 1962, reprint 1974. – —E. CONZE, *The Large Sūtra on Perfect Wisdom*, U.C. Press, Berkeley, 1975.

Aṣṭāvakara Saṃhitā. Text and translation by Swami NITYASWARUPANANDA, Advaita Ashrama, Calcutta, 1969.

Āśvālayana Gṛhya Sūtra (*Rules of Vedic Domestic Ceremonies*), —Tr. by H. OLDENBERG, Oxford University Press, 1886. Reprint, Motilal Banarsidass, Delhi, (SBE vol. XXIX, Part I), 1964, 1967, 1973.

Atharva Veda, tr. by W.D. WHITNEY, 2 vol., HOS, 7-8, 1904. Reprint, Delhi, Motilal Banarsidass, 1962, 1971.

Ātmabodha, ed. with Madhūsūdana Sarasvatī's commentary by D.C. BHATTACHARYA, Calcutta Sanskrit Series, 1961. —Text and tr. by S. VENKATARAMANAN in *Select Works of Sri Sankaracharya*, Natesan, Madras, 2nd edn. 1921, pp. 155–175.

Baudhāyana Dharma Sūtra, ed. by A. Chinnaswami SHASTRI, Banaras, 1934 (Kashmir Sanskrit Series = KSS 104) —Tr. by G. BÜHLER, Oxford University Press, 1882. Reprint, Motilal Banarsidass, Delhi (SBE vol. XIV, Part II, pp. 143–336), 1965, 1969.

Bhagavad Gītā, 2 vols., Sanskrit text and tr. by F. EDGERTON, Cambridge (Harvard University Press), 1948.

Bhagavadgītā-bhāṣya, Srīsaṃkaragranthavalīḥ, 10 vols., Complete Works of Sri Sankaracharya in the original Sanskrit (=CWS). vol. VI, Samata Books, Madras, 1981–83.—(The) *Bhagavad-Gītā* with the commentary of *Śrī Śankarāchārya,* tr. into English by A. Mahādeva ŚĀSTRĪ, Mysore, India, 1901. —*Śrīmadbhagavadgītā Śaṅkarabhāṣya* (with Hindi *anuvāda*), Śrīharikṛṣṇa Goyandaka, Gita Press, Gorakhpur, saṃvat 2009.

Bhāmatī (Vācaspati's commentary on the *Brahmasūtrabhāṣya* of Śaṅkara), ed. by N.S. Anantakrishna SASTRI and W.L.S. PANSĪKAR, 2nd edn., Nirnayasagar Press, Bombay, 1938. —Partial tr. (*Catussūtrī* section) by S.S. Suryanarayana SASTRI and C. Kunhan RAJA, Madras. The Theosophical Publishing House, Madras, 1933.

Bodhicaryāvatāra (Śāntideva's), ed. by P. MINAYEEF, St. Petersbourg, 1890.

Bodhisattvabhūmi (Asaṅga's), ed. by U. WOGIHARA, Tokyo, 1930–36.

Brahmasiddhi (by Maṇḍana Miśra), ed. by S. Kuppuswami SASTRI, Madras Government Oriental Series 4, 1937.

Brahmasūtraśaṅkarabhāṣyam with the Satyānandī Dipikā, Vārāṇasī, saṃvat 2028.—*Brahma-sūtra-bhāṣya of Śrī Śaṅkarācārya,* tr. by Swami GAMBHIRANANDA, Advaita Ashrama, Calcutta, 1972.

Bṛhadāraṇyakopaniṣad-Bhāṣya, in CWS, vol. X, Samata Books, Madras, 1981–83.—*Bṛhadāraṇyaka Upaniṣad* with the *Commentary of Śaṅkarācārya,* tr. by Swāmī MĀDHAVĀNANDA,

4th edn., Advaita Ashrama, Calcutta, 1965. —*Bṛhadāraṇyakopaniṣad* (sānuvāda *Śaṅkarabhāṣyasahita*), Gita Press, Gorakhpur, saṃvat 2029.

Canon bouddhique pāli (*Tipiṭaka*), Text and French tr. *Suttapiṭaka, Dīghanikāya*, t. I, fasc. I : BLOCH, L. RENOU et J. FILLIOZAT, A. Maisonneuve, 1949.

Chāndogyopaniṣad-Bhāṣya, CWS, vol. IX, Samata Books, Madras, 1981–83. —*Chāndogya Upaniṣad*, translated with the Commentary of Śaṅkara by G. JHĀ, Poona, POS 78, 1942. ––*Chāndogyopaniṣad* (sānuvāda *Śaṅkarabhāṣyasahita*), Gita Press, Gorakhpur, saṃvat 2028.

Daśabhūmika Sūtra, ed. by R. KONDO, Tokyo, 1936 ; ed. by P. L. VAIDYA, (Buddhist Sanskrit Series), Mithila Institute, Darbhanga, 1967.

Daśaślokī, in Select Works of Sri Sankaracharya, tr. by S. VENKATARAMANAN, Natesan, 2nd edn., Madras, 1921, pp. 26–31.

Dhammapada, ed. and tr. by C. Rhys DAVIDS (*Minor Anthologies*, no I). London, 1931. —Ed. and tr. by S. RADHAKRISHNAN, 1950. —Tr. by Narada THERA, The Wisdom of East series, 1954.

Dhammasaṅgani, PTS, London, 1885 ; J. KASHYAP, Nalanda, 1960. Transl. —*The Buddhist Manual of Psychological Ethics*, by C.A.F. Rhys DAVIDS, London, 1900, 2nd edn. 1923. —French tr. by A. BAREAU, Centre de Documentation Universitarire, Tournier et Constant, Paris, 1951.

Dīghanikāya, 3 vols., ed. by T.W. Rhys DAVIDS and J. Estlin CARPENTIER, London, PTS, 1889–1910. Tr. by Rhys DAVIDS : *Dialogues of the Buddha* (Sacred Books of the Buddhists = SBB, no 2, 3, 4), 1899–1921. Reprint, 1965–69.

Dīpikā, Auto-commentary by Annambhaṭṭa. See *Tarka Saṃgraha*.

Divyāvadāna, ed. by COWELL and NELL, Cambridge, 1886; ed. P. L. VAIDYA, Mithila Institute, Darbhanga, (Buddhist Sanskrit Texts 20), 1959.

Eight Upaniṣad, with the commentary of Śaṅkarācārya, 2 vols., tr. by Swami GAMBHIRANANDA, I : *Īśā-, Kena-, Kaṭha-* and *Tattirīya Upaniṣads*; II : *Aitareya-, Muṇḍaka-, Māṇḍūkya- and Kārikā, and Praśna Upaniṣads*, 2nd edn., Advaita Ashrama, Calcutta, 1965–66.

Garbhopaniṣad in One hundred and eight Upanishads (Īshâ and others) with various readings, ed. by Wasudev Laxman SHASTRI, PANSIKAR, 3rd edn., Bombay, 1921. —Paul DEUSSEN, *Sixty Upaniṣads of the Veda*, tr. from German by V.M. BEDEKAR and G.B. PALSULE, Pt 2, pp. 639–44.—French tr., *Garbhopaniṣad (Upaniṣad de l'embryon)*, translittérée et traduite par L. KAPANI, Collection fondée par. L. RENOU, XXI, Paris, A. MAISONNEUVE, 1976, pp.1–19. —L. KAPANI, "Upaniṣad of the Embryo, Note on the *Garbha-Upaniṣad*", in *Fragments for a History of the Human Body*, Part Three, Zone, ed. by Michel FEHER, New York, Feb. 1989, pp. 177–96.

Gauḍapādabhāṣya and Maṭharavṛtti, Allahabad University Series 7, 1931.

Gautama Dharma Sūtra, ed. by Umesh Chandra PANDEY, Banaras 1966 (KSS 172); tr. by G. BÜHLER, Oxford University Press, 1879. Reprint, Motilal Banarsidass, Delhi, Srinivasacharya, 1965, 1969, (SBE vol. II, Part I, pp. 175–310). —*Gautama Dharmasūtra with Maskari Bhasya*, ed. by L., Mysore, Government Oriental Library Series, Bibl. Sanskr. 50, 1917.

Gobhila Gṛhya Sūtra, ed. by Chintamani BHATTACHARYA, Calcutta, 1936 ; tr. by H. OLDENBERG, Oxford University Press 1892. Reprint, Motilal Banarsidass, Delhi (SBE vol. XXX, Part II, pp. 13–132), 1964, 1967.

Hiraṇyakeśi Gṛhya Sūtra, ed. by J. KIRSTE, 1889, tr. by H. OLDENBERG and F. Max MÜLLER, Oxford University Press, 1892. Reprint, Motilal Banarsidass, Delhi (SBE vol. XXX, Part II, pp. 137–246).

Jayamaṅgalā, ed. by H. SHARMA, Delhi, Calcutta Oriental Series 19, 1926.

Jaimini Mīmaṃsā Darśana, 7 vols., (containing *Jaiminī Sūtra, Śabara Bhāṣya, Tantra Vārttika, Kumārila Bhaṭṭa's Tupṭīkā*), (ASS 97), Poona, 1953 sqq. —*Sūtras and Bhāṣya* 3 vols., tr. by Ganga-Natha JHA, Baroda, (Gaekwad's Oriental Series, LXVI, LXXIII), 1933–36.

Jaiminīya Upaniṣad Brāhmaṇa, in *Jaminīya Ārṣeya, Jaiminīya Upaniṣad Brāhmaṇa*, ed. by Bellikoth Ramacandra SHARMA, Tirupati, (Kendriya Sanskrit Series 5-6), 1967. —English tr. by H. ORTEL, Jaos, 1894.

Jīvanmuktiviveka (*Liberation in Life*) *of Vidyāraṇya*, ed. with English tr. by Pandit S. Subramanyam SASTRI and T.R. Srinivasa AYYANGAR, The Adyar Library and Research Centre, Madras, 1978.

Kathavatthu, ed. by A.C. Taylor, 2 vols., London, PTS, 1894–97. Ed. by J. Kashyap, Pali Publication Board, Nalanda, 1961. —Tr. by *Points of Controversy* by C.A.F. Rhys DAVIDS and S. Z. AUNG, London, PTS, 1915.

Kauṣītaki Brāhmaṇa, ed. by Lindner, Iena, 1887. —Tr. by A.B. KEITH, in *Rigveda Brahmanas, The Aitareya and Kauṣītaki Brāhmaṇas*, Cambridge, Mass., (HOS 25, pp. 347–530), 1920. —*The Kauṣītaki Brāhmaṇa Upaniṣad* with the *Dīpikā*, Commentary of Śaṅkarānanda, ed. and tr. by E.B. COWELL, Varanasi, (CSS 64), 1968.

Khādira Gṛhya Sūtra, tr. by H. OLDENBERG, 1st edn. Oxford University Press, 1886. Reprint, Motilal Banarsidass, Delhi (SBE vol. XXIX, Part I, pp. 371–435), 1973.

Lalitavistara, Calcutta, 1897; ed. by P.L. VAIDYA, Mithila Institute, Darbhanga, BST I, 1958. —French tr. by E. FOUCAUX, *Le Développement des jeux*, 2 vols., *Annales de Musée Guimet*, Paris, 1884, 1892.

Laṅkāvatāra, ed. by Nanjio, Kyoto, 1923 ; ed. by P.L. VAIDYA, Mithila Institute, Darbhanga, BST 3, 1963. —Tr. by D.T. SUZUKI, London, Routeledge and Kegan Paul, 1932, reprint 1968.

Madhyamakāvatāra de Candrakīrti, Version tibétaine éd. par LA VALLEE POUSSIN. —French tr. by LA VALLEE POUSSIN, Muséon 8 (1907), pp. 249–317 ; 11 (1910), pp. 271–358 ; 12 (1911), pp. 235–327.

Mahābhārata, edited with the commentary of Nīlakaṇṭha, Chitrashala Press, Poona, 1929–36. —Tr. by P.C. ROY, 11 vols., Calcutta, 1883–1896.

Mahāprajñāpāramitāśāstra, de Nāgārjuna, 5 vols., French tr. by E. LAMOTTE : *Le Traité de la grande vertu de sagesse*, Institut Orientaliste, Louvain, 1944, 1949, 1970, 1976, 1980.

Mahāyānasaṃgraha, 2 vols., ed. and French tr. by E. LAMOTTE. T. 1 : texte. T 2 : trad. et commentaire : *La somme du Grand Véhicule d'Asaṅga*, Bureaux de Muséon, Louvain, 1938–39.

Mahāyānasūtrālaṃkāra, d'Asaṅga, ed. and French tr. by S. LEVI. T. 1 : texte. T 2 : traduction, introduction, index, Champion, Paris, 1911.

Maitri-, or *Maitrāyaniya Upaniṣad*, in *Upaniṣadāṃ Samuccayaḥ*, pp. 385–515 ; —German Tr. by Paul DEUSSEN, *Sechzig Upanishad's*, pp. 315–70. —English tr., *Māṇḍūkya Upaniṣad and Kārikā* (See Eight Upanisads, vol. II, p. 173–404). French tr. —*Māṇḍūkya Upaniṣad et Kārikā de Gauḍapāda*, publiée et traduite par Emile Lesimple, Paris A. Maisonneuve, 1944, rééd. 1981. —Christian BOUY, *Gauḍapāda L'Āgamaśāstra. Un traité vedāntique en quatre chapitres*, texte, traduction et notes, Collège de France/Institut de Civilisation Indienne, fasc. 69, Édition-Diffusion De Boccard, Paris, 2000.

Mānava Dharma Śāstra = *Manu Smṛti*, ed. by MANDLIK (with seven commentaries, by Medhātithi, Kulluka, etc.), Bombay, 1885.—French tr. : *Lois de Manu*, by A. LOISELEUR-DESLONGCHAMPS, Garnier, Paris, 1833. —English tr. by

G. BÜHLER, Oxford University Press, 1886, Reprint, Motilal Banarsidass, (SBE vol. XXV) 1964, 1067, 1970. —English tr. of the text with the commentary of Medhātithi by Gaṅgānātha JHĀ, Calcutta, 1920.

Mānsollāsa or *Dakṣiṇāmūrtistotra* attributed to Sureśvara, in *The Vedānta Doctrine of Śrî Śaṇkarâchârya*, tr. by A. Mahādeva ŚĀSTRĪ, 1899, 2nd edn. Madras, 1920

Mūlamadhyamakakārikās de Nāgārjuna, avec la *Prasannapadā*, commentaire de Candrakīrti, éd. L. de LA VALLEE POUSSIN, St. Petersbourg, (Bibl. Buddhica, no 4), 1903–13. —Nouvelle édition, Madras, Adyar, 1977 par J.W. De Jong, d'aprés un 4e manuscrit de la *Prasannapadā* découvert au Nepal par TUCCI. —English tr. (of the *Kārikās*) by D.J. KALUPAHANA, *Nāgārjuna : The Philosophy of the Middle Way*, State University of New York, 1986. —French tr. (trad. fsc. partielles de la) *Prasannapadā* : J. MAY, *Candrakīrti, Prasannapadā Madhyamakavṛtti* (*Commentaire limpide au Traité du milieu*). Douze chapitres (II-IV, VI-IX, XI, XXIII-XXIV, XXVI-XXVII) traduits de sanscrit et du tibétain, accompagnés d'une introduction, de notes, et d'une édition critique de la version tibétaine, Préface de Paul DEMIEVILLE. (Collection Jean PRZYLUSKI, II), A. Maisonneuve, Paris, 1959. —E. LAMOTTE : dans *Le Traité de l'acte*, de Vasubandhu (chap. XVII, pp. 265–88), *Mélanges chinois et bouddhiques*, 4, 1946, pp. 151–288. —Guy BUGAULT, *Stances du milieu par excellence* (*Madhyamaka-kārikās*) de Nāgārjuna, traduit de l'original sanskrit, présenté et annoté, Gallimard, 2002.

Majjhimanikāya, ed. by V. TRENCKNER and R. CHALMERS, 3 vols. London, PTS, 1888–89. English tr. by R. CHALMERS : *Further Dialogues of the Buddha*, 2 vols. (SBB n° 5-6), 1926–27. Reprint, 1967.

Nāradaparivrājakopaniṣad, in *Laghu Upaniṣad* (*Minor Upanishads*), second series with Sanskrit text and translation by K. NARAYANASWAMI, Madras, 1967.

Nyāya Bodhinī, Govardhana's Commentary on the *Tarka Saṃgraha*. See *Tarka Saṃgraha*.

Nyāya Kośa, by Bhīmāchārya JHALAKIKAR, Poona, 1874 ; 3rd edn. (Bo. Skt. Series), 1928.

Nyāya Sūtra (Gautama's) with the Commentary of *Vātsyāyana*, edn. Gaṅgā-Nātha JHĀ, POS 59, 1939.

Pañcaviṃśa Brāhmaṇa, ed. by Chinnaswami SHASTRI, Banaras, 1935, Tr. by W. CALAND, Calcutta, (Bibliotheca Indica 255), 1931.

Pañcaviṃśati-śatasāhasrikā-prajñāpāramitā-sūtra, ed. by N. Dutt, London, (Calcutta Oriental Series 28), 1934. —Tr. by E. CONZE, *The Large Sūtra on the Perfect Wisdom*, Part I, London, 1961 ; Parts II and III, Madison, 1964.

Pañjikā (*Bodhicaryāvatārapañjikā*), éd. L. de LA VALLEE POUSSIN, Calcutta, (*Bibliotheca Indica*), 1901–14.

Paiṅgala Upaniṣad, in *Minor Upanishads*, first series, text and tr. by K. Narayanaswami AIYAR, Madras, Akhila Bharata Sankara Seva Samiti, 1967, pp. 87–109.

Paramārthasāra, (Abhinavagupta's). Tr. (with the commentary) by L.D. BARNETT, in *The Journal of Royal Asiatic Society*, 1910. —French tr. : *Paramārthasāra*, texte sanskrit édité et traduit par L. SILBURN, Publ. ICI., fasc. 5, Édition-Diffusion De Boccard, Paris, 1957.

Parātriśkālaghuvṛtti d'Abhinavagupta, texte traduit et annoté par A. PADOUX, ICI., fasc. 38, Édition-Diffusion De Boccard, Paris, 1975.

Pāraskara Gṛhya Sūtra, ed. by A.F. STENZLER, Leipzig 1876 (*Abhandlungen der Deutschen Morgenländischen Gesellschaft*, VI, 2). —Tr. by H. OLDENBERG, Oxford University Press, 1886. Reprint, Motilal Banarsidass, Delhi, (SBE vol. XXIX, Part I, 261–368), 1964, 1967, 1973.

Pātañjalayogadarśnam, ed. by Śrī Narayana MIŚRA (with the three principal commentaries): the *Yoga Bhāṣya* of Vyāsa, the *Tattva Vaiśāradī* of Vācaspati Miśra, the *Yoga Vārttika* of

Vijñānabhikṣu, Sima Press, Varanasi, (Bharatiya Vidya Prakasana), 1971. See *Yoga-sūtra.*

Piṇḍopaniṣad, Unpublished Upanishads, Poona, (ASS, no 29), 1895. —Paul DEUSSEN, *Sixty Upanishads of the Veda,* Part I and II, tr. from German by V.M. BEDEKAR and G.B. PALSULE, Motilal Banarsidass, Part II, Delhi, 1980, pp. 653–654.

Praśna Upaniṣad, ed. with the Commentary of Śaṅkara, 2nd edn. Poona, 1922 (ASS 8). —R. D. HUME, *The Thirteen Principal Upanishads,* tr. from the Sanskrit (...), 1921 (...), 1968, Oxford University Press, pp. 378–90.

Praśastapāda Bhāṣya, Commentary on the *Vaiśeṣika Sūtra,* ed. by TARKACHARYA, Calcutta, 1925.

Prasannapadā de Candrakīrti. See *Mūlamadhyamaka-kārikās.*

Ṛg Veda Saṃhitā, ed. by Th. Aufrecht, 3 vols.; 2nd edn. Bonn, 1877.

Śabda Kalpa Druma = Shabda-Kalpadrum, or. *An Encyclopaedic Dictionary of Sanskrit* by Raja Radha Kanta DEVA, 5 vol., Calcutta, 1886. Reprint Banaras, 1967 (CSS, n° 93).

Śābara Bhāṣya. See *Jaimini Mīmāṃsā Darśana.*

Saddharmapuṇḍarirīka, éd. H. Kern-B, Nanjo (Bibl. Buddhica, n° 10). St.-Petersbourg, 1908–12. Tr. by H. KERN, *The Lotus of the True Law,* Oxford, Calderon Press, 1909.

Sāṃkhya Kārikā of Īśvarakṛṣṇa with Gauḍapādabhāṣya, ed. and translation by T.G. MAINKAR, POS 9, Poona, 1964, 2nd edn. 1972. —French tr., *Les Strophes du Sāṃkhya* (*Sāṃkhya-kārikā*) avec le Commentaire de Gauḍapāda. Texte sanskrit et traduction annotée par A.M. ESNOUL, Paris, Les Belles Lettres, 1964. —*La Sāṃkhyakārikā étudieé á la lumière de sa version chinoise,* traduction par J. TAKAKUSU, BEFEO, Hanoï, 1904, pp. 978–1054. —*The Sāṃkhya Philosophy containing Sāṃkhya Pravacana Sūtra with the Vṛtti of Aniruddha and the Bhāṣya of Vijñānabhikṣu* (...), tr. by N. SINHA, Allahabad, Sacred Books of the Hindus 11, 1915.

Saṃskāratattva of Raghunandana, tr. by H. CHATTERJEE, *in Studies in some aspects of hindu saṃskāras in ancient India in the light of Saṃskāratattva* (...), Calcutta, Sanskrit Pustak Bhandar, undated.

The Saṃnyāsa Upaniṣad-s, with the commentary of Śrī UPANIṢAD-BRAHMAYOGIN, ed. by T.R. Chintamani DIKSHIT, Madras, Adyar, 1929, reprinted 1966. Translation by A.A. RAMANATHAN, Adyar, 1978.

Saṃyuttanikāya, ed. by L. FEER, 5 vols. London, PTS, 1884–98. —Translation by C. Rhys DAVIDS and F.L. WOODWARD: *Kindred Sayings,* 5 vol. London, PTS, 1917–30. Reprint, 1950–56.

Śāṅkhāyana Gṛhya Sūtra, criticaly ed. by S.R. SEHGAL, Delhi, 1960. —English tr. by H. OLDENBERG, Oxford University Press, 1886. Reprint, Motilal Banarsidass, Delhi. (SBE vol. XXIX, Part I, pp. 3–150)

The Sarva Darśana Saṃgraha (Mādhva's), tr. by E.B. COWELL and A.E. GOUGH, London, Kegal Paul, reprint 1914.

Śatapatha Brāhmaṇa ed. by A. WEBER, Berlin-London, 1855 Mādhyaṃdina recension, Tr. by J. EGGELING, 5 vols., Clarendon Press, 1882–90. Reprint, Motilal Banarsidass, Delhi. (SBE vols. XLI–XLII, Part III–IV, Books VI–X), 1963–92.

Śataślokī, ed. and tr. by S. VENKATARAMANAN, *Select Works of Sri Sankaracharya.* Madras, Natesan, 2nd edn., 1921, pp. 85–154.

Śivasūtra et Vimarśinī de Kṣemarāja, trad. et introduction par L. SILBURN, ICI., fasc. 47, De Boccard, Paris, 1980.

Ślokavārttika (Kumārila Bhaṭṭa's), ed. by Rama SASTRI, (CSS 11), Varanasi, 1898. Translation by G. JHĀ, *Bibliotheca Indica,* Calcutta 1906.

Sphoṭasiddhi (Maṇḍana Miśra's), ed. by S.K. Rāmanātha ŚĀSTRI, Madras University Sanskrit Series 6, 1931, ed. by N. R. BHATT. —French tr. by Madeleine BIARDEAU, Publication de l'Institut Français de Pondichery, 1958.

Sutta Nipāta, PTS, 1884-93, 2nd edn. 1948 ; ed. by J.KASHYAP, *Khuddaka Nikāya*, vol. I, Pāli Publication Board, Nalanda, 1959. —Translation by E.M. HARE, *Wooven Cadences*, Oxford, SBB 15, 1948.

Śvetāśvataropaniṣad (*sānuvāda śaṅkarabhāṣyasahita*), Gorakhpur, Gita Press, saṃvat 2030.

Somaśambhupaddhati, Troisième Partie, Rites occasionnels, II, texte, traduction et notes par H. BRUNNER-LACHAUX, Institut Français d'Indologie, Pondichéry, 1977.

Taittirīya Brāhmaṇa, ed. by V.G. APTE, 3 vols., Poona, (ASS 37), 1934–38.

Taittirīya Saṃhitā, ed. by A. WEBER, Indische Studien XI and XII, Berlin, 1871–72. —Tr. by A.B. KEITH, 2 vols., Cambridge Mass (HOS).

Taittirīya Upaniṣad, with the Commentary by Śaṅkara and glosses by Ānandagiri, Śaṅkarānanda, Vidyāraṇya, ed. by Dinker Vishnu Gokhale, Bombay 1914. —Tr. by R.E. HUME, *The Thirteen Principal Upanishads*, Oxford University Press, 1887; 1921 (...), 1968, pp. 275–93.

Tantra Vārttika (Kumārila Bhaṭṭa's), Commentary on the *Śabarabhāṣya*, 2 vols., Tr. by G. JHĀ, *Bibliotheca Indica* 161, 1924. See *Jaiminī Mīmāṃsā Darśana*.

Tarkasaṃgraha and autocommentary Dīpikā, ed. and tr. by J. R. BALLANTYNE in his Lectures on the *Nyāya Philosophy*, Allahabad, 1849. 2nd edn., *Hindu Philosophy*, Allahabad, 1879. —French translation by A. FOUCHER, *Le Compendium des topiques d'Annambhaṭṭa, avec des extraits de trois Commentaires indiens : la Dīpikā autocommentaire, la Nyāya-bodhinī de Govardhana, le Padakṛtyam de Candrasiṃha*, Paris, A. Maisonneuve, 1949.

Tattvabindu (Vācaspati Miśra's), ed. by Gangadhara SASTRI, in *The Pandit*, n. s. 14, 1892 : 49, 105, 217, 273. 2nd edn., ed. by Kasinath Sarma, reprinted Bombay 1917. —French (critical ed., tr. and Introduction) by Madeleine BIARDEAU, Institut Français d'Indologie no 3, Pondichery, 1956.

Tattva Kaumudī, Vācaspati Miśra's Commentary on the *Sāṃkhya Kārikā*, ed. and tr. by G. JHĀ, Poona, POS 10, 1934 (3rd revised ed.).

Tattva Vaiśāradī of *Vācaspati Miśra* (See *Yoga Sūtra*).

Udāna, London, PTS, 1885 ; ed. by J. KASHYAP, *Khuddaka Nikāya*, Vol. I, Pāli Publication Board, Nalanda, 1959. —Tr. by F.L. WOODWARD, *The Minor Anthologies of the Pāli Canon*, Part 2, *Udāna : Verses of Uplift and Itivuttaka : as it was said*, Oxford, SBB, 8, 1935, reprint 1948.

Upadeśasāhasrī of Sri Sankaracharya (*A Thousand Teachings*) ed. and tr. by Swami JAGADANANDA, Mylopore, Madras, Sri Ramakrishna Math, 1973.

Upaskāra, Śaṅkaramiśra's Commentary on the *Vaiśeṣika Sūtra*. See *Vaiśeṣika Sūtra*.

Vaikhānasa Smārta Sūtra (=*Vaikhānasa Dharma Sūtra* and *Vaikhānasa Gṛhya Sūtra*), critically ed. by W. CALAND, Calcutta, 1927 (Bibliotheca Indica 242) and tr. by W. CALAND, (BI 251), 1929.

Vākyapadīya (Bhartṛhari's), *Vākyapadīya of Bhartṛhari, with the Vṛtti and the Paddhati of Vṛṣabha Deva, Kāṇḍa* I-III, Critical ed. by K.A. Subramania IYER, Deccan College Monograph Series, Poona, 1963, 1965–66 ; 1973. —*Kāṇḍa* I : English tr. with Introduction and critical and exegetical notes based on Helārāja's commentary by K.A. Subramania IYER Deccan College Building Centenary and Silver Jubilee Series, 26, Poona, 1965. *Kāṇḍa* III, Poona, 1971. —French tr. : (*Brahmakāṇḍa*), *with the Vṛtti* by Harivṛṣabha. Traduction, introduction et notes par M. BIARDEAU, ICI, fasc. 24, Édition-Diffusion De Boccard, Paris, 1964.

Vāsiṣṭha Dharma Sūtra, ed. by A.A. FÜHRER, Bombay, 1883 (Bombay Sanskrit Series XXIII), Tr. by G. BÜHLER, Oxford University Press, 1882 (SBE XIV, pp. 1–140).

Vedānta Paribhāṣā by Dharmarāja Adhvarin, ed. and tr. by S. S. Suryanarayana SASTRI, Madras, Adyar Series 34, 1942. Reprinted 1971. —Ed. and tr. by Swāmī MĀDHAVĀNANDA, Ramakrishna Mission, Belur Math, 1942, 4th edn. 1972.

Vedānta Sāra of Sadānanda Yogīndra, ed. and tr. by Swami NIKHILANANDA, Calcutta, Advaita Ashrama, 1949; 6th edn., 1974.

Vedanta-sutras, with the commentary by Śaṅkarācārya, tr. by Georges THIBAUT, Motilal Banarsidass, Delhi, SBE, vol. XXXIV and XXXVIII, Part I and II, 1962, 1968, 1972.

Viṣṇu Purāṇa, ed. Veṅkateśvara, Bombay, 1921, tr. by H.H. WILSON, 2nd edn., London, 1888.

Works of Śaṅkarācārya, Published under the aspects of the Government of India, 3 vols., Delhi, Motilal Banarsidass, 1964. Tome I : *Ten Principal Upaniṣads with Śaṅkarabhāsya* (*Īśā-*, *Aitareya-*, *Kaṭha-*, *Kena-*, *Chāndogya-*, *Taittirīya-*, *Māṇḍūkya-*, *Muṇḍaka-*, *Bṛhadāraṇyaka-Upaniṣad*). Tome II : *Brahmasūtra with Śaṅkarabhāṣya*. Tome III : *Bhagavad-Gītā with Śaṅkarabhāṣya*.

Vaiśeṣika Sūtra of Kaṇāda, with the Commentary of Candrānanda, critically ed. by Jambuvijaya, Baroda, (Gaekwad's Oriental Series, 136) 1961.

Vaiśeṣika Sūtra (Kaṇāda's), Sri Venkatesvar Press, Bombay, 1953. —*The Vaiśeṣika Sūtra of Kaṇāda, with the commentary of Śaṅkara Miśra*, tr. by N. SINHA, Allahabad, Sacred Books of the Hindus 6, 1923.

Vajracchedikā prajñapāramitā, ed. and tr. with Introduction and Glossary by A. CONZE, Is. M. E. O., Roma, 1957 ; 2nd edn. 1974.

Vimalakīrtinirdeśa. Introduction, traduction et notes par E. LAMOTTE : *L'Enseignement de Vimalakīrti,* Publications Univ.-Institut Orientaliste, Louvain, (Bibl. du Muséon, vol. 51), 1962.

Vinaya Piṭāka, ed. by H. OLDENBERG, 5 vols., London, 1879–83, ed. by H. KASHYAP, 5 vols., Pāli Publication Board, Nalanda, 1956–58. —Tr. : *Vinaya Texts,* by Rhys DAVIDS and OLDENBERG, SBE, vol. 13, 17, 20, Oxford, 1881–85. *The Books of Discipline* (*Vinayapiṭāka*), L.B. HORNER, SBB, vols. 10, 11, 13, Oxford, 1938–42.

Visuddhimagga (Buddhaghosa's), ed. by Rhys DAVIDS, 2 vols., London, PTS, 1920–21. —Tr. by P. M. TIN : *The Path of Purity,* 3 vols. 1923–31. —Tr. by NANAMOLI Bhikkhu : *The Path of Purification,* Colombo, 1956.

Vyomavatī (Vyomaśiva's sub-commentary on the *Praśastapādabhāṣya*), ed. by Gopinath KAVIRAJ and Dundhiraja SASTRI, Banaras, CSS 61, 1924–31.

Yājñavalkya Smṛti, with the *Mitākṣarā* (Vijñāneśvara's commentary), ed. by Narayan Ram ACHARYA, Bombay, 1949.

The Yoga Aphorisms of Pātañjali, with the commentary of Bhoja Rāja and an English tr. by R.L. MITRA, Bibliotheca Indica 93, Calcutta, 1883. —French tr. (*The Yoga Bhāsya*). *Patañjala-yoga-sūtram. Vyāsa-bhāṣya-sametam. Le Yoga-bhāṣya de Vyāsa sur le Yoga-sūtra de Patañjali,* traduit du sanskrit par Pierre-Sylvain FILLIOZAT Āgamāt, Paris, 2005.

Yoga Philosophy of Patañjali by Swami Hariharānanda ĀRAṆYA, Revised and tr. by P.N. MUKERJI, University of Calcutta, 1963.

Yogācārabhūmiśāstra, ed. by U. WOGIHARA, Tokyo, 1930–36. Ed. by V. BHATTACARYA, *The Yogācārabhūmi of Ācārya Asaṅga,* Calcutta, 1957.

Yoga Sāra Saṃgraha (*Vijñānabhikṣu's*), ed. by G. JHĀ, Bombay, 1894 ; Adyar, 1923. Tr. by G. JHĀ, Adyar, 1933.

Yoga Sūtra : *Pātañjalayogadarśanam*, ed. by Śri Nārayaṇa MIŚRA (with the three principal commentaries) : The *Yoga Bhāṣya* of Vyāsa, the *Tattva Vaiśāradi* of Vācaspati Miśra, the *Yoga Vārttika* of Vijñānabhikṣu, Varanasi, Sima Press, 1971 (Bhāratiya Vidyā Prakāśana). —Tr. by J.H. WOODS : *The Yoga system of Pātañjali* (...), *The Comment, called Yoga Bhāshya* (...), *The Explanation, called Tattva-Vaiçāradī* (...), Harvard University Press, Harvard Oriental Series 17. Reprint, Motilal Banarsidass, Delhi, 1914–66.

Yoga Vārttika of *Vijñānabhikṣu* (See *Yoga Sūtra*).

Yukti Dīpikā (anonymous), ed. by P. CHAKRAVARTI, Calcutta, Calcutta Sanskrit Series 23, 1938. —*An ancient Commentary on the Sāṃkhya-Kārikā of Īśvarakṛṣṇa*, revised new edn. by R. C. PANDEYA, Delhi, 1967.

Other Works and Papers Consulted

ARISTOTLE : *Physics. A revised text with Introduction and Commentary* by W.D. ROSS, Oxford, Clarendon Press, 1936.

AUGUSTINE (Saint) : *Confessions.* Translated by R.S. PINE-COFFIN, Penguin Classics, England, Penguin Books, 1961.

BALBIR N. ET CAILLAT C., *Yogīndu. Lumière de l'Absolu, trad. de l'apabhraṃśa.* Préface de B. Sergent, Rivages Poche/ Petite Bibliothéque, 1999.

BAREAU A., "*L'Absolu selon le Bouddhisme*", Entretiens 1955, Inst. Français d'Indologie, Pondichéry, 1956, pp. 37–43.

BANSAT-BOUDON L., *Pourquoi le théâtre? La réponse indienne,* Paris, Fayard, 2004.

BHATTACHARYA K., *L'ātman-brahman dans le bouddhisme ancien,* École Française d'Extrême Orient, Paris, A. Maisonneuve, 1973.

BHATTACHARYA S., "*The Concept of videha and prakṛtilaya in the Sāṃkhya-Yoga system*", ABORI 39, pp. 307–312.

BIARDEAU M., *Théorie de la connaissance et philosophie de la parole dans le brahmanisme classique,* Paris, La Haye, Mouton, 1964.

BRONKHORST J., *The two traditions of meditation in ancient India.* Stuttgart : F. Steiner, 1986.

———, "*Bhartṛhari on sphoṭa and universals*" Studies on Bhartṛhari, 3 in Asiatische Studien, Études Asiatiques, XLV, I, 1991, Bern, Peter Lang, pp. 5–18.

———, "*Quelques axioms du Vaiśeṣika*" in Les Cahiers de Philosophie, No. 14, "L'Orient de la Pensée", Philosophie en Indnomaje, Paris, Centre National des Lettres, 1992, pp. 95–110.

BUGAULT G., "*The uniqueness of the Buddhist way of thinking and its encounter with the West today*", Proceedings of the first international conference on Buddhism and national cultures, New Delhi, 1984. (See MK = *Madhyamaka-kārikās*)

BUITENEN (Van) J.A.B., *Studies in Sāṃkhya,* I. JAOS 76, 3, 1956 ; II. JAOS 77, 1, 1957 ; III. JAOS 77, 2, 1957.

BURLOUD A., *Principes d'une psychologie des tendances.* Paris, Alcan, 1938.

CAILLAT C., *Le Jinisme, Histoire des Religions.* Encycl. de la Pléiade, t. I, pp. 1105–45.

CALDERON, *La Vida es sueño* (*La Vie est un Songe*), éd. bilingue Aubier-Flammarion, Paris, 1976.

CHAKRAVARTI P., *Origin and development of the Sāṃkhya System of thought.* Calcutta, 1951. Reprint Delhi, 1975.

CHANGEUX J.P., *L'Homme neuronal,* Paris, Fayard, 1983.

CHATTERJEE H., *Studies in some aspects of hindu saṃskāras in ancient India in the light of "Saṃskāratattva" of Raghunanda.* Calcutta, Sanskrit Pustak Bhandar, undated.

CHATTOPADHYAYA D.P., *Knowledge, Freedom and Language: An interwoven Fabric of Man, Time and World.* Delhi, Motilal Banarsidass, 1989.

CHENET F., "*Vie et mort selon le Yogavāsiṣṭha*", Revue de l'Histoire des Religions, 201 (2), 1984, pp. 139–70.

———, "*De l'efficience psychagogique des mantra et des yantra*", Mantras et diagrammes rituels dans l'Hindouisme, (Table Ronde A. Padoux), Paris, Éd. du C.N.R.S., 1986.

———, "*Karma et Astrologie : un aspect méconnu de l'Anthropologie indienne*", Diogène, No. 129, janvier-mars 1985, pp. 103–29.

______, *Psychogenèse et Cosmogonie selon le Yoga-Vāsiṣṭha. "Le monde est dans l'âme"* tome I-II, Collège de France/Institut de Civilisation Indienne, fasc. 671–672, Édition-Diffusion De Boccard, Paris 1998–99.

______, "*La notion de saṃskāra*" [compte rendu sur l'ouvrage de L. Kapani], in *Revue philosophique*, n°. 2/ 1994, p. 203–216.

CONZE E., *Buddhist Scriptures:* A Bibliography ed. and revised by Lewis Lancaster, New York and London, Garland Publishing, 1982.

COSTER G., *Yoga and Western Psychology.* First Edn., London, 1934. Reprint, Delhi, Motilal Banarsidass, 1974.

DASGUPTA S., *A History of Indian Philosophy*, 5 vols., Cambridge University Press, London (First published 1922), 1932–69.

DAYA KRISHNA : "Trois idées fausses sur la philosophie indienne", *Diogène*, n°. 55, juil.-sept. 1966, pp. 94–109.

DE JONG J.W., "Emptiness", (critical review on F.J. Streng's book). *Journal of Indian Philosophy*, Vol. 2, n°. 1, 1972, pp. 7–15.

DESCARTES R. *Œuvres de Descartes*, publiées par Charles ADAM et Paul TANNERY, Paris, Léopold Cerf, 1897 á 1913.

______, *Discours de la Méthode*, texte et commentaire par E. GILSON, Paris, Vrin, 1925.

______ and L.G. BECK, *The method of Descartes.* Oxford University Press, 1952.

DROIT R.P., "Qui est mort", *Critique*, n°. 468, Mars 1987, pp. 182–84. [See Murthy A. ; Padoux A.C.].

______, *L'oubli de l'Inde. Une amnésie philosophique*, Paris, PUF, 1989.

______, "Au pays des concepts", in (Journal) *Le Monde, Le Monde des livres*, vendredi 21 août 1992, p. 12 (compte rendu sur *La notion de saṃskāra...*, tome I).

———, "Les paradoxes du *nirvâna*", in *Le Monde, Le Mondes des Livres,* vendredi 9 juillet, 1993, p. 27 (compte rendu sur *La notion de saṃskāra...*, tome II et sur les *Cahiers de l'Herne,* nº. sur *Nirvâna,* sous la direction de F. Chenet).

———, *Le culte de néant. Les philosophes et le Bouddha,* Paris, Seuil, 1997.

DUMONT L., *Homo hierarchicus,* Paris, Gallimard, 2e éd., 1979.

DURANDIN G., *Les Fondements du mensonge,* Paris, Flammarion, 1972.

DUTT N., *Early monastic Buddhism.* Calcutta, K.L. MUKHOPADHYAYA, 1960. 2nd Edn., 1971.

ECKHART (Meister), *Selected Treatises and Sermons.* Translated by James M. CLARK & John V. SKINNER, London, Fount Classics, 1994.

EDGERTON F., *Buddhist hybrid Sanskrit grammar and dictionary,* 2 vols., Newhaven, Yale University Press, 1953.

———, "The hour of death, its importance for man's future fate in Hindu and Western religions", Annals of the Bhandarkar Oriental Research Institute, 1926–27, Vol. 8, Part 3, pp. 219–249.

ELIADE M., *Le Yoga, immortalité et liberté,* Paris, Payot, 1954 ; 2e éd. revue et augmentée, 1964.

FILLIOZAT J., "Les théories psychologiques de l'Inde", *Bulletin de la société française de philosophie,* juillet-septembre, 1972, pp. 73–96.

FREUD S., *Introductory Lectures on Psycho-Analysis,* translated from the German under the General Editorship of James STRACHEY in collaboration with Anna FREUD, Vol. XV (1915–16), Parts I, II, Vol. XVI (1916–17), Part III, London, The Hogarth Press, 1963.

———, *Totem and Taboo and other Works.* Vol. XIII (1913–14), 1955. Reprint, 1957 ; 1962.

FUSSMAN G., "Pour une problématique nouvelle des religions indiennes anciennes", *Journal Asiatique*, t. 265, 1977, fasc. 1 et 2, pp. 21–70.

GABEL J., *La fausse conscience, essai sur la réification*, Paris, Éd. de minuit, 1962.

GONDA J., *Change and continuity in Indian religion*. The Hague, Mouton, 1965.

———, *Vedic Ritual, the non-solemn rites*, Paris, Masson, 1980.

HALBFASS W., "*Karma, Apūrva* and 'Natural' causes : Observations on the Growth and Limits of the Theory of *Saṃsāra*", in *Karma and Rebirth in Indian Thought*. Ed. by Wendy Doniger O'Flaherty, University of California Press, 1980, pp. 268–302.

HEIDEGGER Martin, *Basic Writings, From Being and Time* (1927) to the *Task of Teaching* (1964), Revised and expanded edition by David Ferrell KRELL, Harper Perennial Modern Thought, 2008.

HULIN M., *Le Principe de l'ego dans la pensée indienne classique. la notion d'ahaṃkāra*, ICI., fasc. 44, Paris, De Boccard, 1978.

———, *Shankara et la non-dualité*, Paris, Bayard, 2001.

JAINI Padmanabh S., *The Jaina Path of Purification*. Delhi, Motilal Banarsidass, 1979.

JOHNSTON E.H., *Early Sāṃkhya*. London, 1937 ; reprint, Delhi, 1974.

KAKAR S., *The Inner World, a psycho-analytic study of childhood and society in India*, Oxford University Press, 1982.

———, French translation, *Moksha, le monde intérieur, enfance et société en Inde*, Paris, Les Belles Lettres, 1985.

KANE P.V., *History of Dharmaśāstra : ancient and medieval religions and civil law in India*, 5 tomes in 7 vols. Poona, Bhandarkar Oriental Research Institute, (Government Oriental Series, Class B, n°. 6), 1930–62.

KANT Immanuel : *Kritik der reinen Vernuft*, Werke, t. 2, Wiesbaden, Insel-Verlag, 1956.

———, *Critique of Pure Reason*. Translated by J.M.D. MEIKLEJOHN, Mineola, New York, Dover Publications, 2003.

KAPANI L., "Remarques sur la notion de *vāsanā*" (Communication présentée le 22 novembre 1984 à l'Association Française pour les Études Sanskrites), dans *Bulletin d'Études Indiennes*, nº. 3, Paris, 1986, pp. 79-102 ; 201–202.

———, et Chenet F., "L'Inde au risque de la psychanalyse" (compte rendu sur le livre de S. KAKAR : *Moksha, le monde intérieur...*), *Diogène*, Oct. 1986, pp. 65–80.

———, *Encyclopédie Philosophique Universelle*, vingt-sept articles dans vol. II, t. 2 : *Dictionnaire des notions*, Paris, P.U.F., 1990.

———, *La notion de saṃskāra dans l'Inde brahmanique et bouddhique*, Collège de France / ICI., fasc. 591 et 592, t. I (314 pages), t. II (280 pages), Paris, Éditions-Diffusion De Boccard, 1992–93.

———, "Mourir à l'heure de sa mort" in l'Herne, No. sur *Nirvāṇa* (cahier dirigé par F. Chenet), éd. De L'HERNE, Paris, 1993, pp. 242–56.

———, "Schopenhauer et l'Inde", in *Journal Asiatique* (Paris), tome 290, nº. 1, Peeters Orientalist, Leuven, Belgique, 2002, pp. 163–292.

———, "Comment pense le sanskrit ? La dialectique du dépassement et le dépassement de la dialectique en Inde", in *Catégories de Langue et Catégories de Pensées en Inde et en Occident*, Textes réunis par F. Chenet, Préface de M. Hulin, Paris, l'Harmattan, 2005, pp. 125–70.

———, "L'usage des exemples dans le raisonnement philosophique indien", in la *Revue Rue Descartes*, No. 54 sur *Les Rationalités en Inde*, Collège International de Philosophie, Paris, P.U.F., 2006, pp. 8–34.

———, *Schopenhauer et la pensée indienne. Similitudes et différences*, Paris, Hermann, 2011, 270 pages.

KEITH A.B., *The Religion and Philosophy of the Veda and Upanishads.* First edn. 1925. Reprint, 2 vols., Delhi, Motilal Banarsidass, 1970.

———, The *Sāṃkhya System.* Calcutta and London, 1918 ; 2nd edn., Calcutta, 1949.

KENGHE C.T., "The Problem of the *pratyaya-sarga* in *Sāṃkhya* and its relation with *Yoga*". Poona, Annals of the Bhandarkar Oriental Research Institute, 48–49 (1968), pp. 365–373.

KOELMAN G.M., *Patañjala Yoga : from related ego to absolute self.* Pune, Papal Athenaeum, 1970.

KRAMRISCH S., *The Hindu Temple.* 2 vols., Calcutta, 1946. Reprint, Delhi, Motilal Banarsidass, 1976.

LACAN J., "Propos sur la causalité psychique", *Écrits,* Paris, Seuil, 1966, pp. 151–93.

LACOMBE O., *L'Absolu selon le Vedānta,* 2e éd., Paris, Geuthner, 1966.

LARSON G.J., *Classical Sāṃkhya.* Delhi, Motilal Banarsidass, 1969.

LEIBNIZ G.W. : *Die Philosophischen Shcriften,* éd., Gerhardt, t. 2, Georg Olms Verlag, Hildesheim, New York, 1878 (Berlin, 1879). *New Essays on Human Understanding,* translated and edited by Peter REMNANT & Jonathan BENNETT, Cambridge, Cambridge University Press, 1981.

———, *Œuvres Choisies,* par L. PRENANT, Paris, Garnier, s. d. : Aubier-Montaigne, 1972.

———, *The Monadology.* Translated by Robert LATTA.

———, *Principles of Nature and Grace, Based on Reason.*

MALAMOUD Ch., *Cuire le monde : rite et pensée dans l'Inde ancienne,* (quinze études réunies), éd. la découverte/textes á l'appui, 1989.

MAY J., *Introduction aux Douze chapitres de la Prasannapadā de Candrakīrti*(...), Paris A. Maisonneuve, 1959.

———, "On Mādhyamaka Philosophy", in *Journal of Indian Philosphy,* 6, 1978, pp. 233–41.

MISHRA N., "The conception of *saṃskāra* in the *Yoga-sūtra*", in *Journal of the Bihar and Orissa Research Society,* 1951, pp. 48–51.

———, "*Saṃkāras* in *Yoga* Philosophy and Western Psychology", *Philosophy East and West,* Vol. 2, n°. 4, 1951, pp. 308–16.

MOHANTY J.N., "Indian Theories of Truth : Thoughts on Their Common Framework", in *Philosophy East and West,* 30 Oct. 1980, pp. 439–451.

MONTAIGNE (Michel de) : *Essais,* Bibl. Pléiade, Paris, Gallimard, 1958.

———, *The Essays of Montaigne.* Translated by Charles COTTON.

MURTHY U.R. Anantha, *Samskara* : *A rite for a Dead Man,* 2nd edn., Oxford University Press, Epi S.A., 1983. [See Droit R.P. and Padoux A.C.]

NIETZSCHE, *Zur Genealogie der Moral,* trad fse, *La généalogie de la morale,* Collection Idées, Paris, Gallimard, 1964. Trad. Eric BLONDEL, Ole Hansen-Leve, Théo Leydenbach & Pierre Pénisson, Paris, GF-Flammron, 1996.

NYANATILOKA, *Vocabulaire bouddhique de termes et doctrines du Canon pali,* Paris, Adyar, 1961.

O'FLAHERTY DONIGER W., editor, *Karma and Rebirth in Classical Indian Tradition,* University of California Press, Berkeley, London, 1980.

———, Dreams, Illusions and other Realities, The University of Chicago Press, 1984.

PADMASIRI DE SILVA M.W., *Buddhist and Freudian Psychology,* Colombo, Lake House Investments Book Publishers, 1973, 2nd edn. 1978.

PADOUX A.C., *Samskara, Rites pour un mort*, Paris, Éd. L'Harmattan, 1985. [French translation of Anantha Murthy's *Samskara : A rite for a Dead Man*].

PAL K., "A Comparative Study of Psycho Therapeutic Techniques and Yoga", in *Vedanta Kesari*, Vol. 33, n°s. 4-5, Aug.-Sept., 1946.

———, "Yoga and Psychoanalysis", in *Prabudha-Bharata*, Vol. 52, n°s. 3-5.

PANDE G.C., *Studies in the Origins of Buddhism.* Delhi, Motilal Banarsidass, 1957; 2nd edn. 1974.

PANDEY R.B., *Hindu Saṃskāras : Socio-religious study of the Hindu Sacraments.* Delhi, Motilal Banarsidass, 2nd edn. 1969.

PARROT R. J., "The Experience called 'Reason' in classical *Sāṃkhya*". *Journal of Indian Philosophy*, Vol. 13, n°. 3, Sept. 1985, pp. 235–64.

PASCAL, *Pensées*, éd. Léon Brunschvicg, Paris, Hachette, 1945.

———, *Pascal's Pensées.* Translated by H.F. STEWART, London, Routledge and Kegan Paul, 1950.

PLATO : *The Republic, Book 10,* with translation and commentary by S. HALLIWELL. England, Art & Phillips, 1988.

———, PLATON, *Œuvres Complétes de Platon*, t. 1 et 2, trad. nouvelle et notes par Léon ROBIN avec la collaboration de M. J. MOREAU, Bibliothéque de la Pléiade, Gallimard, 1942.

PLOTINUS : *The Enneads.* Translated by Stephen MACKENNA, 4th ed. revised by B.S. PAGE (...), London, Faber and Faber Limited, 1969.

———, *Ennéades*, texte et traduction par E. BREHIER, Paris, Les Belles Lettres.

POTTER Karl H., *Encyclopedia of Indian Philosophies*, Vol. 1: *Bibliography*, Vol. 2: *Nyāya-Vaiśeṣika*, Vol. 3: *Advaita-Vedānta*, (etc.), Delhi, Motilal Banarsidass, 1970–81, sqq.

RĀHULA W., *L'enseignement du Bouddha*, Paris, Seuil, 1961.

RUEGG D.S., "Does the Mādhyamaka have a thesis and philosophical position ?", in *Buddhist Logic and Epistemology*, eds. B.K. Matilal and R.D. Evans Dordrecht, D. Reidel, 1986, pp. 229–37.

———, *Buddha-nature, Mind and the problem of Gradualism in a Comparative Perspective on the Transmission and Reception of Buddhism in India and Tibet.* School of Oriental and African Studies, University of London, 1989.

SARTRE Jean-Paul, (*L'Etre et le néant*, Gallimard, 1943).

———, *Being and Nothingness.* Translation and Introduction by E. HAZEL-BARNES, Washington Square Press, 1992.

SCHOPENHAUER A., *The World as Will and as Representation.* Translated by E.F.G. PAYNE, New York, Dover Publications, 1967.

SCHUMANN H.W., *Bedeutung und Bedeutungsentwickhung des Terminus Saṃkhāra in frühen Buddhismus*, Bonn, 1957.

SEN S.N., "The Impetus theory of the *Vaiśeṣikas*", in *Indian Association for the cultivation of science.* Vol. I, n°. 1, Calcutta, 1965, pp. 34–45.

SHAH Nagin J., *Jaina Philosophy and Religion* (translated by), [English translation of *Jaina Darsana* by Muni Shri Nyayavijayaji], Motilal Banarsidass and Bhogilal Leharchand Institute of Indology, Delhi, 2008.

SILBURN L., *Instant et cause : le discontinu dans la pensée philosophique de l'Inde*, Paris, Vrin, 1955, reprint Paris, De Boccard, 1988.

STALL F., and..., *Agni, the Vedic ritual of the Fire Altar*, Berkeley, Asian Humanities Press, Vols. I-II, 1983.

STCHERBATSKY Th., *The Buddhist Logic*, 2 vols., New York, Dover Publications, 1962.

STEVENSON M.S., *The Rites of the Twice-Born.* Oxford University Press, 1920. French translation *Les Rites des deux-fois-nés,* Paris, Soleil Noir, 1982.

VALERY (Paul), *Tel quel*, tome 1-2, Paris, Gallimard, 1943.

WAYMAN A., *Buddhist Insight.* Delhi, Motilal Banarsidass, 1984.

WIJAYARATNA M., *Sermons du Bouddha,* Paris, Cerf, 1988.

INDICES

Name Index

K

L

M

N

O

U

V

W

Y

Word Index (Sanskrit and Pāli)

A

K

L

M

Y